M000169712

# Unconscious Logic

Matte Blanco's theory about the way the unconscious mind structures itself is recognized as perhaps the most original since Freud. He broke new ground with the theory that emotions are similar to mathematically infinite sets. His difficult style has meant that his work has not received the attention and wide readership that it deserves.

Eric Rayner has written the first clear introduction to Matte Blanco's fundamental concepts and their uses. Using uncomplicated language and vivid clinical examples he demonstrates the value of Matte Blanco's theories for psychoanalytical therapy. Central psychoanalytic concepts are given a 'bi-logical' treatment and ideas are related to key thinkers in disciplines ranging from mathematics to anthropology.

This book shows how bi-logic brings fundamentally new ways of thought to psychoanalysis. It is a precise way of thinking about emotions. It illuminates the emotions behind thinking and the thoughts behind emotions.

*Unconscious Logic* is for all those concerned with advancing psycho-analytic thinking. It draws on the work of a group of people who have been inspired by Matte Blanco's thinking, heralding its significance for future research.

**Eric Rayner** is a psychoanalyst in private practice in London and training analyst at the Institute of Psycho-analysis, London.

## THE NEW LIBRARY OF PSYCHOANALYSIS

The New Library of Psychoanalysis was launched in 1987 in association with the Institute of Psycho-Analysis, London. Its purpose is to facilitate a greater and more widespread appreciation of what psychoanalysis is really about and to provide a forum for increasing mutual understanding between psychoanalysts and those working in other disciplines such as history, linguistics, literature, medicine, philosophy, psychology, and the social sciences. It is intended that the titles selected for publication in the series should deepen and develop psychoanalytic thinking and technique, contribute to psychoanalysis from outside, or contribute to other disciplines from a psychoanalytical perspective.

The Institute, together with the British Psycho-Analytical Society, runs a low-fee psychoanalytic clinic, organizes lectures and scientific events concerned with psychoanalysis, publishes the *International Journal of Psycho-Analysis* and the *International Review of Psycho-Analysis*, and runs the only training course in the UK in psychoanalysis leading to membership of the International Psychoanalytical Association – the body which preserves internationally agreed standards of training, of professional entry, and of professional ethics and practice for psychoanalysis as initiated and developed by Sigmund Freud. Distinguished members of the Institute have included Michael Balint, Wilfred Bion, Ronald Fairbairn, Anna Freud, Ernest Jones, Melanie Klein, John Rickman, and Donald Winnicott.

Volumes 1–11 in the series have been prepared under the general editorship of David Tuckett, with Ronald Britton and Eglé Laufer as associate editors. Subsequent volumes are under the general editorship of Elizabeth Bott Spillius, with, from Volume 17, Donald Campbell, Michael Parsons, Rosine Jozef Perelberg and David Taylor as associate editors.

## ALSO IN THIS SERIES

# NEW LIBRARY OF PSYCHOANALYSIS
## 21

General Editor: Elizabeth Bott Spillius

# Unconscious Logic

An Introduction to Matte Blanco's Bi-Logic and its Uses

## Eric Rayner

London and New York

First published 1995
by Routledge
11 New Fetter Lane, London EC4P 4EE

Simultaneously published in the USA and Canada
by Routledge
29 West 35th Street, New York, NY 10001

© 1995 Eric Rayner

Typeset in Times by LaserScript, Mitcham, Surrey
Printed and bound in Great Britain by
Mackays of Chatham PLC, Chatham, Kent

All rights reserved. No part of this book may be reprinted or
reproduced or utilized in any form or by any electronic,
mechanical, or other means, now known or hereafter
invented, including photocopying and recording, or in any
information storage and retrieval system, without permission in
writing from the publishers.

*British Library Cataloguing in Publication Data*
A catalogue record for this book is available from the British Library

*Library of Congress Cataloguing in Publication Data*
A catalogue record for this book has been requested

ISBN 0–415–12725–4 (hbk)
ISBN 0–415–12726–2 (pbk)

# Contents

# Acknowledgements

This book is a labour of gratitude and affection for Ignacio Matte Blanco. I wish he were able to receive it personally, but tragically he is not. I came to know of his work perhaps too late in life to ever think of myself as a disciple, but I know he gave me ideas which my mind by itself would never have conceived in a thousand years. However, even with this imbalance we and our families have been friends for a long time now. Apart from Ignacio until he died, we have been closest to Luciana, his wife, and Paula, his youngest daughter; but they are a united, generous and very enjoyable family and my wife and I are much the richer for knowing them all. The last few years have been terribly tragic and sad for them in more ways than one; their generous bravery has been an inspiration.

It was Elizabeth Spillius, in her role as Editor of the New Library of Psychoanalysis, who first suggested this introductory book to me. She has been a superb editor, but more than this, her psychoanalyst's critical and creative mind gave me new ideas which, the reader will discover, have become crucial to the whole argument of the book. My wife, Dilys Daws, has also put a great deal of time in patient and critical thoughtfulness into the book. No words of mine are printed without passing the scrutiny of her brilliant common sense.

This book would not exist without the London Bi-logic Group; this interdisciplinary forum has met regularly to exchange ideas for seven or eight years. There are about twenty members, mostly in London but also elsewhere. It began from an idea of Claudio Duràn of York University, Toronto. From across the world he prodded Gerald Wooster and me into organizing the group. I owe another special debt to Gerald for his inspiring combination of literary and poetic sensitivity with psychoanalysis. Fortunately, Carmen Fink took over the organization of the group and soon had it running smoothly. I would like to mention all the members but only a few must suffice.

I would have got nowhere without Ian Mordant's friendship and the generous availability of his clear mathematical mind. We have worked

xi

things out together for quite a few years now; the work on abstraction in the early chapters, as well as the main ideas in Chapter 10, are more his than mine.

The logical philosophy and friendship of Ross Skelton of Trinity College Dublin and the more theologically toned logic of Rodney Bomford have been great and delightful influences. Margaret Arden's spirit has given the book some of her adventurous imagination yet critical honesty. You will see that Klaus Fink has been our most illuminating and valued exponent of the clinical use of bi-logic. Paul Wohlmuth of the University of San Diego School of Law inspired much of the book's last two chapters, and much else besides.

Other friends who have not been members of the group gave me great help. Ken Wright was most generous with his dispassionate, clinical and theoretical mind. Harold Stewart gave me a lot of good advice. Laurie Ryavec from Santa Barbara helped me clinically and Jim Rose persuaded me to change some of my fixed attitudes. Mary-Sue Moore and Jim Meiss of the University of Colorado helped me especially with mathematical chaos theory.

Very important have been the personal contributions from Latin America; foremost among which have been Juan Francisco Jordan and Juan Pablo Jiménez from Chile and Jorge Ahumada from Buenos Aires. It was our good fortune to be invited to Buenos Aires and Santiago as the book was being completed. Though it was our first visit, going to Chile was for me somehow like going home at last, I was so linked with it already; my wife and I shall never forget it. It has been the Chilean psychoanalysts' astute depth of feeling for Matte Blanco's way of thought and applying it clinically that has repeatedly restored my resolve when European incomprehension of and indifference to bi-logic had begun to tempt me into surrender. We in the northern hemisphere must soon turn to learning much from South America. I have realized that the workshops of my Chilean friends – Casaula, Coloma, Colzani and Jordan – are going in the same direction clinically as I, but in many ways they have gone further. They give a certain fire to the book's completion.

Finally, I want to thank my patients whose openness gave me clear evidence that Matte Blanco was talking about something real. I hope I have done justice to the thoughts of those who generously agreed to being quoted in the pages that follow.

# 1

# The background

It is almost forty years since Ignacio Matte Blanco (1959a, b) started publishing his work using mathematical logic with psychoanalysis to investigate unconscious and emotional processes. It is about twenty since his mammoth work *The Unconscious as Infinite Sets* (1975) first appeared, yet he is still little known outside Italy and some parts of South America. This is not surprising, for although his writing is in many ways beautifully clear, it is definitely difficult. His precision often appears repetitive and abstruse; but there are a few of us, psychoanalysts and like-minded professionals, who have chanced upon some understanding of what Matte Blanco is driving at. A group of us in Britain has gathered together for some years and ended up convinced that psychoanalytic thinking and therapy is the poorer for having no grounding in, nor the fire of, his logical analysis. Other disciplines are also likely to be the weaker from their ignorance.

Having brought mathematical-logical intuition and analysis to bear upon psychoanalysis, Matte Blanco concluded that the mind can usefully be conceived as partly functioning by the combination of at least two distinct modes of knowing which are, however, often polarized. This he calls the *bi-logical* point of view, which we shall soon be investigating.

Freud's greatest contribution was probably to show the importance of unconscious processes in mental life and how they could, sometimes at least, be understood. Matte Blanco's fundamental contribution stems from this. Freud achieved, for the first time, the definition of an array of particular *characteristics of the unconscious*, but they remained a rather disparate collection. Matte Blanco saw that Freud's apparently uncoordinated array could well be understood in terms of the interaction of a very few precisely defined fundamental processes which, however, can often produce highly complex dynamic mental structures. These he calls bi-logical structures.

The advantage here is that psychoanalytic therapists who have put

1

themselves through the initial disturbances and grasped the wide applicability and depth of bi-logic need fewer concepts to coordinate. They are thus likely to be less bewildered and freer to be imaginative when faced by the manifest complexities of a patient's thoughts and actions. On the other hand, many busy psychoanalytic workers would say they have managed for years without such logical niceties. So there is a peculiar paradox: a few varied and more or less sane intellectuals, psychoanalysts and others find bi-logic illuminating and useful; but many more, even if they have heard of it, are baffled and probably bored.

This book aims both to find a bridge between these two views and to inform the reader about bi-logic in ordinary language. Matte Blanco found his way using formal logic. Some say he could have come to his conclusions without it; I do not think so. This book does not use chains of formal logical inference, but its final aim, like Matte Blanco's, is to investigate the *process of thinking*. Here it emphasizes the essential centrality of *classificatory* activity at all levels of thought, even in the unconscious.

Theoretical bridging and criticism will be scattered along the way, but there is no space to be exhaustive. The first step is a brief biography which may help to understand some of the strengths and weaknesses in Matte Blanco's presentation.

I first came across *The Unconscious as Infinite Sets* (1975) soon after it was published and found myself enthralled. A very few colleagues found the same enthusiasm; Margaret Arden (1984) describes this best when she says: 'Reading *The Unconscious as Infinite Sets* produces an indescribable feeling of discovering the truth that one has always known but been unable to express.'

I met Matte Blanco for the first time in 1981. A slim, shortish, athletic man in his early seventies, he had a sensitive, refined patrician face, was affectionate, enthusiastic, voluble yet incisive, and used his whole body to enhance his words. He was young for his years and had a delightful sexual charm. He looked just what he was, a Latin-American aristocrat.

Matte Blanco was born in 1908 in Chile; his father was a landowner and his family was well known. He told me that a forebear was a Spanish admiral, Don Matte de Luna by name, who vanquished a Moorish fleet in the fifteenth century. Among Matte Blanco's mother's ancestors was Toro Zambrano, Conde de la Conquista, Captain-General and President of the Chilean Province of the Spanish Empire. So too was Blanco Encalada, the first President of the Chilean Republic early in the nineteenth century. Matte Blanco also mentioned with sceptical amusement, yet demure pride, that a Spanish genealogist had told him that his family name indicated that he was descended from one of the sons of Mohammed.

He was warm, passionate, precise and logical all at the same time. He was in no way arrogant, but when thwarted he could go into tyrannical rages. He was enormously emotional and sentimental, many would say

2

excessively so. He once said: 'Ah, you must understand that I am a Latin and thus naturally very emotional, but I have at the same time a love of being severely logical and mathematical. When I was about five I remember my father christening me what in English would be "little hairsplitter". That really explains the whole nature of the work of my life – the bringing of logic and the emotions together.' This book hopes to carry forward this aim.

Matte Blanco was a great sentimentalist. He thus loved to honour the traditions and customs of other people – but particularly those of Spain, Chile and his family. Perhaps the tradition he followed most passionately was the psychoanalytic one of the early Freud at the beginning of the twentieth century.

At the age of 20 he graduated in medicine at the University of Chile in Santiago and became an associate professor of physiology by the time he was 25. However, he was soon intrigued by psychiatry, and psychoanalysis in particular. His father persuaded him that England was the only place to study. So in the mid-1930s he went to London and trained at the Institute of Psychiatry and at the Institute of Psycho-Analysis. His analyst was Walter Schmideberg, a Viennese of the classical school but also the husband of Melitta Schmideberg. She was Melanie Klein's daughter but later was bitterly opposed to her mother. His teachers were the remarkably creative British group of those years under Ernest Jones – Rickman, Sharpe, Isaacs, Strachey, Glover, Payne, Brierley, Riviere and Klein herself. He was lifelong friends with John Bowlby and Paula Heimann. As a Member of the British Psycho-Analytical Society, he more recently considered himself to be one of its 'Independents', but most of all he was international in spirit. In many ways most significant for him was Melanie Klein; she ranked second only to Freud in his theoretical estimation. Matte Blanco's admiration for the theories of these two together, above all other analysts, lay possibly in their clear-eyed view of the dark side of the human mind. He knew that their pessimism was essential but probably felt that his special talent did not lie in their sort of cool view.

In the 1930s he also began to study mathematical logic intensively, particularly that of Russell and Whitehead's *Principia Mathematica* (1910). In 1940 he sailed back to America where he spent the next four years; he married his first wife, whom he had met in England, and had a daughter. He devoted himself to psychoanalysis and psychiatry, first at Johns Hopkins Hospital in Baltimore then at Duke University, North Carolina, and at the Medical Center in New York. He continued his logical studies, being a member of Courant's famous weekly seminar in the mathematics department at Columbia University.

In the mid-1940s he returned to Chile and accepted the Chair of Psychiatry at the University of Chile. As Professor of Psychiatry he was administrative head of the department and an inexhaustible reformer. His planning of modern clinics for psychotic patients became a model for much of South America. He was a strict and demanding teacher, but was held in affection and respect by many.

His gift for sympathetic knowledge of people in the throes of psychosis emerges in his books, and came largely from years of clinical work in the psychiatry department of the medical school of the University of Chile in Santiago. At the same time he was a main founder of the Chilean Psycho-Analytical Society. In the 1950s he and his first wife divorced, but a few years later he remarried and had another six children, forming the large family he desired, in line with the South American tradition of the time.

This romantic and rather conservative man had become a profound and radical reformer of his profession in the Chile of the 1950s. However, he wanted to continue his own particular creativity, and in 1966 moved to Italy with his family and became a training analyst of the Italian Psycho-analytical Society. He was also invited by the Chairman of Psychiatry at the Catholic University of Rome to teach at the Postgraduate School, where he could continue his studies and psychoanalytic work without administrative burdens. Luciana Bon de Matte, his second wife, was Kleinian trained and is now a well-known training analyst in Rome. The members of the family mostly live in Italy now. Clever, serious, open-minded and strikingly multi-lingual, they are also memorable for their warm and unassuming generosity.

Many aspects of present-day professional and national political issues seemed hardly to touch Matte Blanco during his later years. His leaving Chile for Rome was felt as a desertion by some of the younger generation there who had followed him in psychiatry and psychoanalysis. He was aware of this and troubled by it, but was unswerving in devoting himself to his ideas which he felt were the most important things he had to give.

It has been noticed that when he could not achieve his aims by charm he would resort to noisy demands that can best be described as temper-tantrums. Some disliked this characteristic; others felt an affectionate tolerance and respect in spite of these foibles, for he was often in the right when in a temper.

The effect, for good or ill, of his sentimentality together with his intransigent single-mindedness also emerges in his writing. It is here, as strength and weakness, that readers will naturally be affected by Matte Blanco's particularly passionate character. For instance, when he was utterly engrossed in a conceptual argument of great originality within his own mind, each thought was diamond-clear; but when less sure he was prone to forget that he was writing for others and began to leap incomprehensibly and repetitively as if talking only to himself. The poor reader, unable to follow, unaware of the adventure of ideas and bored by the repetition, is left angry and helpless —and is then likely to throw the book aside.

4

Another example of his apparent loss of interest in the reader's capacity is especially evident in *The Unconscious as Infinite Sets*. Here he attempted the near impossible: he wanted his readership to include both psychoanalysts and mathematicians. The result was that most psychoanalysts recoiled from his punctilious formal logic, while mathematicians also rebuffed him, not only for apparent faults in logical consistency, but because his psychoanalysis was too emotional and imprecise for their taste.

His passionate loyalty, which can be conservative sentimentality, has great strengths as well as weaknesses. For instance, as this book unfolds you will find how Matte Blanco felt strongly and clearly that Freud's finest genius flowered just before the turn of the century. He thinks that *The Interpretation of Dreams* (1900), with its spelling out of the nature of unconscious processes, was his greatest contribution to humanity. Probably all psychoanalysts would agree here. Matte Blanco goes on from this to adjudge that psychoanalysis has slipped away from these insights and has somewhat lost its way since then. This challenging view contains an important truth; however, he does not properly examine this with respect to the manifold psychoanalytic ideas that have emerged in the ninety-odd years since then. These ideas, though flawed in places, make up the evolution of a marvellous living network of theory by which we all work and which has liberalized our culture in many ways. We can be proud of this achievement; Matte Blanco seems often to ignore it.

His particular criticisms of later psychoanalytic theorists are usually justified, and he never attacks beyond making useful points. He was never given to derision of another writer's theory. Personal malice and pious contempt, frequently psychoanalytic diseases, were not Matte Blanco's vices. In fact his ideas do not contradict the fundamentals of psychoanalytic theory, ancient or modern; but they do add a new dimension to it. Matte Blanco felt amazed that he had been privileged to discover a conceptual Eldorado.

The main point here is to warn readers that Matte Blanco can appear to ignore vital later aspects of psychoanalytic knowledge. There is little interest in developmental matters. Ideas about evolution through phases of oral, anal, phallic, Oedipal and genital zones, together with latency, puberty and later maturity, seldom appear in his theory, even though they are always evident in his technique. Apart from repression, projective identification and denial, concepts of defence are not examined in detail. Analysis of the individual self and of a particular character, together with clinical stories about them, seem of little interest in his theoretical writing. Nor is there much evidence of a study of specific neurotic syndromes, or of perversion and delinquency. Also, the relation of psychoanalysis to biology, and particularly to evolution, seems oddly absent for a former physiologist. Apart from Freud, the writer to whom much attention is given is Melanie Klein. Even here he seems to ignore such things as the

5

vital features of the depressive position as compared with the paranoid–schizoid.

His most serious omission in many eyes would be his portrayal of clinical material. He had a vast experience from fifty years of psychoanalysing and nearly as long supervising. If one reads between the lines of his slightly stiff (in English) clinical descriptions, there is a beautiful and imaginative use of classical technique. He often used case material to illustrate his theoretical writing, but in a way that some clinicians find unsatisfactory. This is partly because his English is rather formal and not idiomatic. But few recognize this, mostly because he is not aiming to tell fascinating clinical stories about characterological predicaments and the personal intimate pains and dramas of a single patient and analyst. He seldom introduces you to a unique patient standing centre stage with his or her problems and vices. Matte Blanco's strength lies in his reflective perception at a more microscopic level – in the tiny detail of interwoven thoughts. His theoretical vision comes rushing forward so that overall pictures of patient and analyst are irrelevant to what is being considered.

Some have dismissed his clinical sensitivity on this basis. This is understandable, but wrong; quite apart from his vital theoretical contribution, patients have attested that he was remarkably sensitive to them individually. He could also be astutely tough yet kind. Perhaps he lacked confidence in the art of storytelling, or had indulged himself too little in reading and learning from biography and novels. On the other hand, psychoanalysts might value clinical storytelling too exclusively, but it is certainly on his gift for penetrating conceptual precision and the abstract generality of his theoretical contribution that Matte Blanco must be judged.

Matte Blanco's attitude to logic was similar to that towards psychoanalytic theory. He devoted himself passionately to both and developed his original ideas out of two great conceptual breakthroughs, one from each region of thought: Freud at the turn of the century and Russell and Whitehead at about the same time. Then, just as analysts can complain that their recent theory is neglected, he also appears to have neglected the important work of more recent logicians such as the Model theory of the 1950s stemming from Alfred Tarski. It was this later development that Bion mostly used (Skelton 1989, 1990a, 1992). Though very different in character, Bion and Matte Blanco used formal logic with deep conviction; they knew and respected each other. In fact Bion's daughter has written a thesis upon their respective uses of logic (Bion-Talamo 1973).

An accident in 1990 left his brain severely damaged so that his memory was irremediably impaired. It was dreadful for him and for his family. Very occasionally, something magical happened, and for a few seconds his mind was clear and great again, with its old kindly emotionality and consistent logicality. It was soon gone, but was enough to remind his friends of a triumph of one human spirit. Matte Blanco died in 1995.

This book is no substitute for the original work. Being an elementary introduction it brushes aside many lines of thought which are investigated exhaustively by Matte Blanco's meticulous mind. The very value of the approach we are considering rests first upon a surrender to, then argument with, and finally use of *precise* thoughtfulness. The best way to achieve this facility is by tackling Matte Blanco himself. Read him when you have finished this book.

## 2

# Feeling and thinking

The underlying viewpoint of this book is that actual *sequences of thinking* are at the very core of the psychoanalytic trade. Thinking and disturbances in it are present in every clinical minute of a psychoanalytic therapist's day. However, with a few exceptions, it has not been psychoanalysts but cognitive psychologists, in the tradition of Piaget or Bruner say, who have devoted themselves to the detailed investigation of thinking processes and to informing us about them. Even so it is likely that all psychopathology entails at least some disturbance in thinking. This is obvious of course in the thought disorders of psychoses, but neurotic pathology involves at least some thought disturbance. Both neurotic symptoms and disabling character structures manifest obliterations or distortions of thinking processes. This is clear when we recognize that any defensive act affects thought, otherwise it could not be known as a defence.

The aim of this introductory chapter is to persuade the reader to think in a 'Matte Blanco mood'. There will be little direct reference to his work until the next chapter. For the moment we shall move from one subject to another and it will probably be best if the reader 'explores' rather than tries to follow each idea too closely.

## The historical division between feeling and thinking

It is probably true to say that western culture has tended to make a definite distinction between feeling and thinking. Thus the Greeks divided their study of the communication of these modes into rhetoric and logic. They tended to give them equal status; but intellectuals of the last millennium have often set one against the other and then given pride of place to reasoning and logical thought. Emotion was often seen as a mere disruption or immature form of logical reasoning, which was viewed as the supreme achievement of the human mind.

The early psychoanalysts were still prone, when theorizing, to see emotionality as a form of breakdown of, or regression from, clear logical thought. However, Freud, more than anyone, began the activity of two people feeling together, talking and seriously thinking in a systematic way about intimate emotional issues. Feeling states had at last become a proper subject of study – with an aim of emotional change. Freud naturally saw deception and truthfulness in both feeling and thinking.

## Freud and logic

Though sceptical of philosophers, Freud, a scientist at heart, naturally respected careful logical analysis. It was his point-by-point comparison of dreams with logic that enabled him to make the crucial discrimination of the specific characteristics of unconscious processes (1900, 1915). He saw that these assuredly did not obey the rules of ordinary logic. This is at the very core of the psychoanalytic contribution to human thought. It is exactly here that Matte Blanco starts his work, for, as already noted, he is concerned with the *process of thinking*; however, we shall remain with Freud for a moment to look at a succinct example. It comes in 'Notes upon a case of obsessional neurosis' (1909). It is not about the 'Rat Man' himself, but about a case he encountered years before. He continues:

> This happened in the first case of obsessional neurosis which gave me an insight into the nature of the malady. The patient, who was a government official, was troubled with innumerable scruples. . . . I was struck by the fact that the florin notes with which he paid his consultation fees were invariably clean and smooth. (This was before we had silver coinage in Austria.) I once remarked to him that one could always tell a government official by the brand new florins that he drew from the state treasury, and he then informed me that his florins were by no means new, but that he had them ironed out at home. It was a matter of conscience with him, he explained, not to hand anyone dirty paper florins; for they harboured all sorts of dangerous bacteria and might do harm to the recipient. At that time I already had a vague suspicion of the connection between neuroses and sexual life, so on another occasion I ventured to ask the patient how he stood in regard to that matter. 'Oh that's quite all right,' he answered airily, 'I'm not at all badly off in that respect. I play the part of a dear old uncle in a number of respectable families, and now and then make use of my position to invite some young girl to go out with me for a day's excursion in the country. Then I arrange that we shall miss the train home and be obliged to spend the night out of town. I always engage two rooms – I do things most handsomely; but

when the girl has gone to bed I go to her and masturbate her with my fingers. 'But aren't you afraid of doing her some harm, fiddling about with her genitals with your dirty hand?' – At this he flared up: 'Harm? Why, what harm should it do her? It hasn't done a single one of them harm yet, and they've all of them enjoyed it. Some of them are married now, and it hasn't done them any harm at all.' – He took my remonstrance in very bad part, and never appeared again. But I could only account for the contrast between his fastidiousness with the paper florins and his unscrupulousness in abusing the girls entrusted to him by supposing that the self reproach affect had become *displaced*.

(Freud 1909: 197–8)

It is interesting to see Freud's shock and remonstrance here. It shows that he was even then well aware of actual sexual abuse taking place, but this is not now our main interest. We see Freud and the government official in a very definitely *emotional* interaction. For instance, the patient has 'a matter of conscience' about infecting with paper florins; also he speaks 'airily', 'is not badly off' and 'does things handsomely' about sex. However, he 'flares up' and 'took in very bad part' Freud's remonstrance. Freud on his part has 'a vague suspicion' about the connection between neuroses and sexuality. His 'remonstrance' also shows he is shocked by the government official's airy unconcern about his behaviour and speaks about 'doing some harm . . . with your dirty hand', though he is implicitly more disturbed by the man's sexual abusiveness than by the effect of bacteria on the hands.

The next thing to be seen is that out of this emotional interaction Freud begins to think about the patient's logicality. He notes an underlying *equivalence* for the patient between florin notes and the girls' genitalia. In one way they *both belong to the same class* – that of being handleable; this is crucial to Matte Blanco's thinking. Freud then spots a logical inconsistency (at least from the point of view of everyday assumptions) between the patient's unnecessary care about the handling of florin notes and his careless unscrupulousness about sexually abusive handling of the girls. What is more, Freud appeals to our natural sense of logical consistency to get readers to agree with his assumptions about cleanliness and abuse rather than those of the patient, and of course most of us would feel that he is quite right in this. We can then go on to understand the explanatory model he provides about a displacement occurring, and this displacement model, too, aims to be logically consistent.

## Logic and psychoanalysis

In order to understand Matte Blanco's contribution it is useful to think of two aspects to logical discipline. First are its basic *concepts* which, from the psychological point of view, can be thought of as specific *mental operations*. These would be such ideas as event, object, class, set, affirmation, negation, relation, equation, converse and many others. To be usable in formal logic, precise *definition* is necessary.

In so far as a logic is *mathematical*, the concepts used will be all those mentioned above together with others of the greatest precision, such as unit, quantity, numeration (counting), addition, subtraction, zero, infinity, point, line, space, rate, rate of change and many more. From the psychological point of view these concepts are probably conceivable by most ordinarily intelligent people, but only at an *intuitive* level. Certainly the intuitive origins of logical and mathematical concepts can often be detected even very early in life. For instance, it is now known that a baby as young as six months can reliably detect the difference between two and three objects. This is naturally not the same as systematic counting, but it points to a precursor of it. Many examples of such pre-concepts are now being discovered by developmental researchers.

There is little doubt that we all have to use many precursors and intuitions of mathematical concepts every day as we go about our business. For instance we are always subliminally measuring, adding, subtracting and equating as we handle things, walk or drive a car. People can do this without ever having had a maths lesson.

The second aspect of logic of interest to us is the process of *combining* logical concepts into usable conclusions. This is *inference*, and it must be *consistent* to be usable. This is often the most specialized and difficult aspect of logic and mathematics for the layperson, and it is the ability to carry out long lines of valid inference that distinguishes the professional logician and mathematician from the rest of us.

Turning to Matte Blanco, there is no doubt that, though he was very competent at logical-mathematical inference, his really original contribution does not lie here. His great gift to us is in understanding how specific logical and mathematical conceptions – such as object, set, number, equation, infinity – are intuitively used by all of us every day, even in emotions. His insight has been in the understanding of human experience, not in validly working out complex inferences; he has been a psychologist rather than a logician or mathematician. So for our purposes in following this book we psychoanalysts and therapists need to exercise our conceptual acuity and ability to define ideas rather than handle chains of complex inference.

However, through the ages logicians (Hodges 1977) have pointed out to the rest of us that the mind can be essentially logical. Human beings and even other animals have to use at least some logical steps to survive. Inference, entailment and consistency, albeit simple and on a short-time base, are necessary. At times the human mind naturally spots and reacts with repugnance to an inconsequentiality, inconsistency or incompatibility in a sequence of ideas. Freud was reacting in just this logical way with his government official, and appealed to us to do the same.

Jean Piaget, more than any other psychologist, showed the way to study the individual's development of logical thinking and we shall refer to him again later. However, psychoanalysts, when concerned with pathology, need to dwell upon illogicality, but they often then proceed to emphasize only the illogical. Thence, with a few notable exceptions, many analysts conclude that the use of logical analysis, let alone formal symbolic logic, is of little practical use to the progress of psychoanalytic thought.

However, logic in its widest sense centrally concerns itself with *truthful* thought. This aims for ideas to be consistent with each other and correspond with at least some aspects of reality; so also does psychoanalysis. Thus the two disciplines must have much in common.

## Logic and thought

We shall be arguing that psychoanalysis centrally concerns itself with feelings, emotions or affects which contain thoughts about inexactly generalized *conceptions*. When these are made by precise thought into concepts and then combined consistently with other concepts, they become elements of thinking and of logical inference. Ian Mordant (Mordant 1990; Mordant and Rayner 1990) has suggested that the term *notion* is useful for such pre-conceptions. Notions have thought in them but are intuitions and approximate; they often include simple, even crude, impulsive value judgements. They are not fully definable but, as we shall see, can still be symbolized.

Logic addresses itself differently to the precise meanings embedded in *concepts*. These are more strictly definable using words or conventional symbols and can be analysed with precision into their constituents. The level or realm of emotional notions or intuitions does not coincide exactly with Freud's 'System Unconscious' nor with his primary process, but they have much in common. Likewise the realm of fully verbal, or *declarative*, concepts is close to secondary process.

Formal logic and psychoanalysis are both *analytic* disciplines. Any analytic procedure consists of *separating* out the *elements* or constituents of an entity, be it physical, formal or mental, and *specifying the relationships* between them. This procedure requires self-conscious, intellectual reflectiveness. It occurs in psychoanalysis and equally in other forms of analysis, be they mathematical, logical, linguistic, economic, political, social, chemical or physical. In this light psychoanalysis is entitled to take its place as a member of the great family of analytic disciplines.

12

Thinking is always *about* something other than itself; it involves *meanings*. It is, as they say, *intentional*. It uses signs and symbols to condense and refer to meanings such as objects, objectives, relations, forms, emotions, states, conceptions and concepts. The actual process of thinking does not involve single isolated ideas or concepts with their symbols. It is a *whole* pattern; a *sequential gathering* together of elements of knowing and *evaluating* them with an *aim* in view. It is a complex dynamic system. For coherent thinking to take place the evaluation must correspond with at least some aspects of reality: this is truthfulness. Of course thought does not necessarily *aim* centrally at truth. Cunning stratagems certainly do not, but they involve thinking none the less.

Thinking appears to be a *dynamic combinatorial activity* in a time sequence using a group of thought elements. Since elements of knowing are juxtaposed and compared, it is a goal-seeking *argument*. This is often solitary and internal but can frequently take the social form of debate, dialogue or discussion.

The word 'argument' will be used frequently in the book. Its meaning is often debased to imply little more than an irritable dispute. However, we are following a long-established intellectual tradition in using it to refer simply to a 'connected series of statements intended to establish a position'.

Thinking truthfully necessitates *consistency* as well as correspondence with at least some of reality; its argument must not proceed between elements that *contradict* each other. It is the compatibility of propositions, or of beliefs, that many logicians see as the main task of their discipline (Hodges 1977). Here the *Principle of Non-Contradiction* is crucial. This is that: 'If a proposition (or belief) is true, then its negation is not true.' This can be put alternatively as: 'Either A or not-A, but not both.' This is a fundamental basis of 'ordinary' or classical logic. Because of its 'either–or' basis it is often called *two-valued logic*; Matte Blanco calls it *bivalent logic*. This book will always be using this logical realm as an axis of reference while venturing to other ways of thought and feeling.

Human thinking, whether basically truth-seeking or not, most often desires or aims to discover the *consequences* of something, be it a thought or an action. At the heart of this is a dedication to the discovery of *implications or entailments*. This becomes clear when we recognize that ideas in argued thought sequences are imbued with: is, is not, will, will not, if–then, either–or, both–and, therefore, thus, hence, thence, because, and so, but, however, nevertheless and many similar terms. These must stand for different operations of thought concerned with implications of one sort or another.

Much *emotional* thinking of the simple kind is largely 'either A or B' rather than 'both A and B', which is combinatorial. When an exclusive use of 'either–or' is paramount, *splitting and polarization* usually follow. This has been noticed by several writers who used quite different approaches.

13

Melanie Klein (1946) showed it in her paranoid–schizoid position; Piaget (1950, 1953) did likewise in his studies of the binary aspects of intellectual development; and so did Lévi-Strauss (1963) when showing the dichotomous nature of myth and ritual. We shall also be emphasizing that 'either–or' binary polarization is a structural feature of unconscious thoughts. 'Both–and' or combinatorial thinking appears to be largely the realm of verbal conscious and preconscious thought. On the other hand, it must be noted that satisfying night dreams do occur which appear to settle things for the dreamer and have a combinatorial function, though obviously still unconscious at core.

Since any thinking process has an aim, there is always a grain of anticipation or *futurity* in it even when concerned with the distant past or with the purely imaginative. For instance, the following chain of thought is asking a, by no means silly, question. 'If Eve had not eaten of the fruit of the tree of knowledge of good and evil, would mankind still have been able to have justice in its thinking?' This is imaginative and about an almost certainly fictitious dim past. From the point of view of logical inference it is nonsense; it can only be understood if it is recognized as *metaphorical*. Its symbols would then stand for human character and emotions – otherwise it is mad. The implication in its 'if–then' contains futurity; like all thinking it has a sense of time at its core.

## Logical truthfulness

Naturally, much thinking aims towards deceitful ends, but it probably always has to account for some aspects of reality; and, sometimes at least, the aim is to be truthful. It has already been mentioned that the notion of truthfulness refers only to situations where something in one domain *represents* something in another; this is symbolization. For truth there must be some one-to-one correspondence, or matching, between the representation and the thing represented. If the intended matching is between an idea and a physical reality, the idea will be testable by reference to observable external data. This is the scientific method whose rules of inference are studied by *inductive logic*. If, on the other hand, we are concerned with the truth *within* a sequence of thoughts, then consistency or lack of contradictions in the sequence will be sought. This is the realm of *deductive* logic. The combination of inductive and deductive reasoning towards valid implications is essential in every walk of life, even in simple and instantaneous tasks; it is certainly essential in psychoanalysis.

At the same time we must not forget the mind's capacity for *untruthfulness*. This is intrinsic to the nature of any pathological *defence*; it can be passive and more or less unconscious or actively and consciously intended.

## Emotional truthfulness

Though logical reasoning is essential, it often seems not to engage with the core of the thinking about individual human selves and their emotions, which is the daily lot of analytic therapists. Such emotions might be like the following.

> 'John is really an ice cold swine – so look out if you open up, don't give your heart to him.'

> 'Bill was the loveliest teddy bear, with a heart of gold – I felt that even the most fragile creatures were safe in his hands.'

> 'You are such a fountain of wisdom, Doc, that I feel frightened of being drowned every time I come into the room.'

Viewed in one way it is obviously false to utter such phrases as these, for John cannot belong both to the class of humans and of pigs; neither can the human being Bill belong in the class of bears, nor can a patient actually be drowned by the words of a doctor. Nevertheless, the phrases communicate some essential truths. They are all using *metaphor*; this and other figures of speech, like simile, onomatopoeia, metonymy, synecdoche, etc., are the great tools for *communication of emotions*. This is the realm of rhetoric. It is present, of course, in any poetry or drama and also in everyday therapeutic dialogue. Freud used it in our example with the words 'airily' and (implicitly) 'your dirty hand' and so on.

Here are a few of Shakespeare's metaphors. Something like them is used in any therapy-talk:

> My salad days, when I was green in judgement, cold in blood.
>
> (*Antony and Cleopatra*)

> Oh how full of briars is his workaday world.
>
> (*As You Like It*)

> They brought one Pinch, a hungry lean faced villain.
> A mere anatomy, a mountebank.
> A threadbare juggler, and a fortune teller,
> A needy hollow-ey'd, slave looking wretch,
> A living-dead man.
>
> (*Comedy of Errors*)

This is how important truths are conveyed about affects, feelings, emotional states, character judgements, intersubjective experiences and interpersonal relations. These may be about transient feelings, more long-lasting moods, or, longer lasting still, character traits which are after all emotional structures. They are the grist of psychoanalytic therapy which are definite

15

statements and can have truth in them; so they must have some status as propositions. Yet the logician seems often at a loss to deal with such forms of symbolic communication. For instance, from the strictly logical point of view, use of metaphor is often called – following Chomsky (1965) – a logical 'selection mistake' (Hodges 1977). The intelligent logician obviously recognizes the importance of poetry and naturally also knows that the poet's choice of words is quite deliberate, yet he or she can still call it a mistake. To refer to a vehicle for the communication of a truth, even one of an emotional kind, as a mistake is surely absurd.

To conclude so far, psychoanalytic thinking is undoubtedly often slipshod in ignoring logic, and so also essentially is the logician if he fails to grasp the truth in emotional communication. It has been noted how Freud used ordinary logical thought in his discoveries. Matte Blanco shows that it is valuable to go further still with the precise use of logical–analytic thinking, as long as it remains imaginative.

### Susanne Langer, symbolization and metaphor

Fifty years ago the American philosopher and logician Susanne Langer made an important contribution towards showing the way to a possible solution of the divide between logic and psychoanalysis. She has influenced many thinkers including a few psychoanalysts, but only Matte Blanco used her formal logic. Schooled in the tradition of Russell and Whitehead, she wrote widely, not only upon formal symbolic logic (Langer 1953) but also on aesthetics (1967, 1972, 1982). Her quest starts with the investigation of different forms of symbolism and ends over twenty years later with the suggestion that *beauty* is experienced whenever deep feelings are truthfully expressed.

Her first book *Philosophy in a New Key* (1942) distinguishes between two forms of symbolization of ideas. One she terms *discursive*, in which symbols are formed essentially by *convention*, that is, by agreement between people. These may be subconscious and will have evolved culturally over long time periods. This mode is predominant in much everyday verbal language and is particularly necessary when describing the physical world. It takes its purest form in mathematical symbolism and is the language of logical argument. It is the means by which scientific ideas are communicated and argued.

On the other hand, there is what Langer calls *presentational symbolization*, also called *non-discursive*. This is a mode of presentation where the symbol has an immediate idiosyncratic sensory reference. What is more, the symbol and the thing symbolized seem to have a *similarity of form* or *isomorphism* between each other. Thus the word 'bang' is a presentational

16

symbol: it is a sound that is similar to and can stand for the noise of a pistol, say, being fired. On the other hand, the term 'fired' has no similarity of form to the actual noise of firing. Its usage is conventional and discursive. Langer makes it plain that *psychoanalytic symbols* are essentially presentational, thus an image of a pistol, say, can be a *visual* symbol for a penis; they both have the *same form*, being long and cylindrical and both eject objects – bullets or semen and sperms. Likewise a vase may be a symbol for a vagina since both are containing vessels. Other instances will easily come to mind. However, mention of a vase does not, of course, inevitably mean that it is being used primarily as a symbol for a vagina. The propensity to see only sexual or aggressive meanings in ideas is 'wild analysis', boring and disruptive of valid thought.

Metaphor particularly, but also other figures of speech, display the use of this sameness of form or isomorphism between one thing, often a sensory object, and another. For example: 'she came into the room under full sail', 'with thunderous face, he looked at me'. Here the symbolic phrases and the symbolized affect states are isomorphic.

Langer's major argument is that presentational symbolism, and metaphor in particular, is the central verbal means of communicating affects. Shakespeare's 'a living-dead man' refers to the man's emotional state, not that he is terminally ill. The same happens in 'Oh how full of briars is his workaday world'. The examples of 'an ice cold swine', 'a lovely teddy bear' or 'a fountain of wisdom' are similar metaphors. Incidentally, Langer has a convincing argument that music is a particular form of presentational symbolization of affective states.

The presentational aspect of Langer's theory has been cogently expressed for psychoanalysts by Rycroft (1968) who has shown how metaphor and other presentational symbolism is a particularly powerful communicator of feelings in the therapeutic process. He, like Langer, shows how presentational symbols are much more concise and efficient for this purpose than discursive or conventional ones; they are much used by patients to express themselves. Thus, everyday poetics and rhetoric are the basic tools of the psychoanalytic therapist's trade.

## A view of emotion

This chapter has so far compared and contrasted thinking with feeling. It is now time to bring them together by looking at feeling in order to introspect about it for a few moments as a crucial phenomenon in our lives.

John Bowlby, like others, was inspired by Langer's work. Following her, he sees (1969) that, in animals and humans, emotion is an *instantaneous appraisal* and evaluation of the state of the *external* environment at the *same time* as the *internal* physiological and psychological condition of the organism. Thus emotion contains, simultaneously, data about exteroceptions, body functions (both visceral and skeletal), memories, anticipations of the future, and the state of *self* with others. Note here that, in humans at least, the sense of self is central to any developed emotion.

A feeling is essentially an *overall* evaluation of the internal and external worlds together in one experience. Looking two ways at once, it is a 'Janus-faced' integration. Although rough and ready, often incomplete and mistaken compared to step-by-step analytic thinking, it can have a quickness and efficiency which logical thought lacks. It is a somatopsychic event, a gestalt, a *holistic experience* of multiplicity. Consider elements singly, apart from the others, and the feeling magically disappears; let them come together again and the emotion returns.

If affect is an undivided whole event of quick appraisal, then the view that emotion is simply a disruption of reason must be discarded. Rather, it appears that feeling can be both a preliminary and an end stage of a thinking process. Thus an overall appraisal of fear, curiosity or dissatisfaction, say, may initiate thinking. In this function it contains a motive or drive element within it; but it is not just a drive, for there are other aspects, for instance ones that are exteroceptive and interoceptive-physiological. We conclude that emotion can be viewed as an analysable *structure* with recognizable constituents and relations of its own. However, since an emotion has motivational aspects, it is a complex structure controlled by *feedback arcs*. Emotions are dynamic *systems* rather than static states.

With regard to the *end* of a thinking sequence, this also is marked by an emotion; there is an affect appraisal that ends the sequence, by satisfaction, triumph, ecstasy, delight, orgasm or gloomy failure. In between the beginning and end, other emotions will be evaluating where the thought sequence has got to already. Note also that *interpersonal attunements* and empathy give rise to *intersubjective* experiences; these are usually central to the development of emotions and hence of deeply engaged thinking processes.

In summary, an emotion or feeling is, by its nature, an undivided whole; it functions to appraise overall the internal and external situation together. Detailed thinking, on the other hand, in its problem-solving aspects, is analytic. It is concerned with discriminating the significant constituents of a whole circumstance and their relationships in the situation. Analytic thought of any sort starts with awareness of a whole question but is not holistic in its own nature.

Seen in this light, feeling and thinking are not best set against each other. They are stages or aspects of any adaptive, maladaptive or creative process. Matte Blanco's frame of theory about this is not like Bowlby's; it is not rooted in an evolutionary or biological systems theory. Matte Blanco is phenomenological; precise definition of mental processes by introspection and listening to others is his strength. But their views of emotion end up remarkably alike. Matte Blanco is always concerned to see feeling and thought together. More than any other analyst he faces up to and comprehends both the logical and thoughtful aspects of emotion. He illuminates the emotions that lie in thinking. This is his great achievement.

## Location and recognition

Finally, let us concentrate on Matte Blanco's bi-logic. Dwelling, for a moment, at a general level of ideas, imagine the emotion and thought of any human being living in and moving through any kind of environment.

In order to survive, every animal, including man or woman, must, whatever their emotion, each waking moment be aware of the objects, surfaces and spaces before them that are important. She or he must *locate* and *recognize* them. Recognition of some sort is basic to all living things; this involves systems of *memory*. However, the location of objects and of the self in their midst also involves registration of the *relationships between things*. Here the *discrimination* of *differences* is paramount. These could, for instance, be about the different distances between the things in the space before the eyes or about differences in sound sequences as another person speaks.

Such discriminations must involve the intuitions that lie behind the concepts that make up formal logic and mathematics. For instance, there are, however brief and approximate, ideas of sequence in time and space, quantity, counting, distance and interval. This is the realm of self in action with real objects and spaces. We now know that exercise in these discriminations starts within hours of birth; they are the preconcepts of mathematics. However, being about self and objects, they are also elements in emotions.

Next, it is most economical if these discriminated relationships can also be recognized as being the *same* as things already known and dealt with previously. This obviously saves a great deal of learning anew by trial and error. Such recognition using memory is at the core of any meaningfulness.

Capacity for discrimination and recognition or '*same again*' activity about complex and subtle events sets the higher vertebrates, and humans in particular, apart from the less widely adaptive species. It is the need for 'same again' awareness, to register what *quality* is in common between different things, that requires the mind to be crucially a *classificatory organ*. This is based on matching or one-to-one correspondence and is at the heart of all thinking. The mathematical consideration of such classification is called *Set Theory*. Set and class are defined slightly differently but for our purposes we need not distinguish them.

One of Matte Blanco's starting points was Set Theory. Notice here that the idea of something belonging to a certain set or class involves recognition that it has at least one quality that matches (has a one-to-one correspondence with) other things in the set. There is here, however dimly, an awareness of belonging to a *collection* or plurality. There must here be, however vaguely, a sense of quantity and 'counting'; thus the precursor of *number* must be present.

The interplay between difference discrimination and sameness registration is at the core of Matte Blanco's thinking. These functions may seem to be of such generality and abstractness as to be of little practical interest. They have not previously been dwelt upon at length in psychoanalysis. However, derivatives of sameness registration such as 'identification of', 'identifying with', 'similarity with', 'equation' and 'equivalence' are common enough. The very breadth of Matte Blanco's abstractions will be unfamiliar to most analysts and therapists; but it is his strength. The reader is advised to enter his mode by enjoying sweeping vistas of ideas. Later in this book we shall consider how this focus upon similarity and difference is of interest to other sciences.

Perhaps the most basic conceptual constituent in the theoretical tradition of psychoanalysis itself is a *dynamic* one; intention, drive and motive are central. Matte Blanco's focus, however, is about thinking and ways of *knowing* – cognition. His great love is really *epistemology*. Psychodynamics is not forgotten but his emphasis is upon cognitive structures. His 'model of the mind' does not pretend to be complete in itself and has differences from much of traditional psychoanalysis. However, he suggests that they need each other.

In summary: we shall be particularly concerned with the discrimination of difference relations and recognition of samenesses and the interplay, dialectic, or argument (as is most appropriate with verbal-level thinking) between them. Instantaneous awareness and integration of vast networks of such perceptible relations are vital since they enable the location and evaluation of the significance of internal and external objects and conditions. This is the function of emotionality. Let us now make a start on some details of Matte Blanco's thinking.

# 3

# Logic, symmetry, bi-logic and the unconscious

This and the two following are key chapters. They attempt to portray Matte Blanco's way of thinking as well as his basic theory. They have something in common with school lessons. The reader may pick up an idea and then quickly lose it, so that it has to be thought out all over again. Bouts of exasperation are likely.

Matte Blanco's own way of argument is stringent, precise, determined and persistent, going on and on until solutions are reached to his satisfaction. One may be annoyed by repetition but never titivated with mystification.

The dichotomous model of 'sameness' registration and difference discrimination has already been introduced, and so has Matte Blanco's concentration upon the emotions and his crucial focus upon the Freud of the early 1900s. The last chapter recalled how Freud (1909) spotted the illogicality in the mind of the government official; how it leapt from airy unscrupulousness about sexual abuse to hyper-scrupulosity about dirty banknotes. Freud defined this as a displacement, which he saw as one of the *characteristics of the unconscious* (1900, 1915).

The foremost of these characteristics spelt out by Freud (1915) were: *condensation, displacement, timelessness, absence of mutual contradiction* and *replacement of external by internal reality*. They probably represent Freud's most fundamental achievement for they form the path to understanding the coding of both dreams and symptoms. Matte Blanco contends that this is the vital area that has been much neglected by psychoanalysis, which suffers in clarity because of it.

Matte Blanco devotedly follows the early Freud meticulously and agrees with him that the unconscious does not obey the ordinary rules of formal logic. But it must conform to some rules of knowing, some logical structure, or unconscious material would be known *only as random* and thus never understood. Matte Blanco's deep drive here was to find some more abstract, more generalized underlying conceptualization, for this would make things simpler for the therapeutic worker. He discovered something he felt was momentous. We shall continue now largely in the order in which he presents it (Matte Blanco 1975).

He sets out essentially with a strict definition of some 'principles' of mental functioning which we shall discuss in a moment. It will be the second of these that concerns us most. This points to two forms of mental activity, of *similarity* and *difference*, whose interaction, dialectic or argument seems to underlie not only the peculiarities of unconscious processes but also of *emotional experiences* generally.

## The unconscious and generalization

Let us go straight to two principles of mental functioning which he detected. Matte Blanco thinks that their combination gives an economical understanding of unconscious working generally. They refer to deep, fundamental activities of mental life in health and also illness. The concept of 'principle' is possibly not optimal here. Such a term usually refers only to a law that is always true and it must still be doubtful if this can be said of his two principles. Matte Blanco called them this because he felt they were fundamental to normal life. However, of more immediate concern to the reader is that the first principle, to be described now, will hardly be referred to again in our elementary exposition. This order has been used because it is Matte Blanco's original way, and it would be confusing later if we departed from it at the beginning.

Matte Blanco starts, as we have done, by saying that unconscious processes work with *classificatory* activity; they seek out the *similarities* between things. From this the unconscious leaps to *generalization*. So here is his first discovery and proposal in his words:

> *The Principle of Generalization*
> *The system unconscious treats an individual thing (person, object, concept) as if it were a member or element of a set or class which contains other members; it treats this class as a subclass of a more general class, and this more general class as a subclass of a still more general class, and so on.*
> (Matte Blanco 1975: 38)

In other words, unconscious process leaps to seeing a particular thing in terms of belonging to wider and wider class membership; it 'runs up' class hierarchies. We need go no further than this here. In a late paper (1989) he refers to the principle of *abstraction* and generalization. This is an important addition because, as will be seen, it has become clear to us that a certain form of abstraction is basic and endemic in unconscious processes.

## Asymmetry and symmetry

Matte Blanco's second basic discovery takes the form of a complex proposition, *The Principle of Symmetry*, which is crucial. It is best approached in terms of two fundamental proposals. The first is simple and is about logical *asymmetry*; it is as follows:

(a) *Many relationships that are discriminated in the physical world are asymmetrical. An asymmetrical relationship is one whose converse is not identical to it.*

Think of these examples of asymmetrical relationships:

| | | |
|---|---|---|
| 'A *left* of B' | has the converse | 'B *right* of A'. |
| 'A is *before* B' | has the converse | 'B is *after* A'. |
| 'A is *smaller than* B' | has the converse | 'B is *larger than* A'. |
| 'A is *driving* B' | has the converse | 'B is *being driven by* A'. |
| 'A *engulfs* B' | has the converse | 'B is *engulfed by* A'. |
| 'A is *mother of* B' | has the converse | 'B is a *child of* A'. |

Here the converses are *not identical* to the relationships indicated in the original thought or statement. They are thus asymmetrical relations. Note how necessary and omnipresent is *thinking* with asymmetrical relations when dealing with the objects of the *external* world; such physical-geographical thinking is essential for survival. This is Matte Blanco's first step and it uses concepts straightforwardly from logical theory.

His second proposal is about *logic symmetry* and is as follows:

(b) *Some perceived relationships are, however, symmetrical. A symmetrical relation is one whose converse is identical to it.*

Here are some examples of this:

| | | |
|---|---|---|
| 'A is *near* B' | has the converse | 'B is *near* A'. |
| 'A is *equal* to B' | has the converse | 'B is *equal* to A'. |
| 'A is the *same* as B' | has the converse | 'B is the *same* as A'. |
| 'A is *negotiating with* B' | has the converse | 'B is *negotiating with* A'. |
| 'A is *sibling* of B' | has the converse | 'B is *sibling* of A'. |
| 'A is *harmonious* with B | has the converse | 'B is *harmonious* with A'. |

You will note that these symmetrical relations do not seem at first sight to be as common as asymmetrical ones when perceiving the external world with its geometry and geography of things, which are replete with difference relations between places, points, lines, surfaces, spaces and solid things. However, at the same time we must continuously use sameness relations when dealing with the world. Perhaps asymmetry comes to the

23

fore because a prime use of consciousness is to *locate* the self within a world of objects. This is a central function of the focus of attention. Notice also that we are concerned with *logically* asymmetrical and symmetrical relations, which are defined by the identity or not of their converses; they apply to much more than spacial relations.

The word symmetry simply refers to *sameness* between at least two things and thus to *matching* and one-to-one correspondence. We often think only of visual, lefthand, righthand or bilateral symmetry; but there are symmetries of rotation, displacement, not to mention those of colour, weight, time, electric charge and many others.

In all logical symmetries a *transformation* from one state to another brings about, when *repeated*, a *return* to the first state. This is precisely what identical converse means.

(c) *Many relationships are, however, ambiguous.*

For example, 'A is *external* to B' may or may not have the converse 'B is external to A'. Thus, 'The room I am sitting in (A) is external to me (B)' does not have the converse 'I (B) am external to the room I am sitting in (A)'. However, 'The room upstairs (A) is external to me (B)' does have the converse 'I (B) am external to the room upstairs (A)'.

(d) *Examples of symmetry, asymmetry and their ambiguity.*

Some of the following relationships are symmetrical, others are asymmetrical, while others are ambiguous, at least until they are more specifically defined. (The answers are given on page 39.)

1. Related to; 2. a relative of; 3. cousin of; 4. aunt of; 5. sister of; 6. colleague of; 7. enemy of; 8. master of; 9. laughs at; 10. laughs with; 11. collides with; 12. marries; 13. manager of; 14. adversary of; 15. hater of; 16. friend of; 17. lover of.

## The principle of symmetry and the unconscious

Using the concepts of symmetry and asymmetry, Matte Blanco now comes to the heart of his discovery and makes two fundamental hypotheses. Their linkage is most unusual yet simple. The first part has just been mentioned. It is that:

    I.   *Ordinary conscious logical reasoning, which includes scientific and everyday thought about the physical world, consistently entertains propositions about asymmetrical relations.*

Here the mind is conceiving of relations whose converses are not identical to them. This naturally involves the discrimination of difference relations. At the same time symmetrical relations will no doubt be entertained but, if thought is ordinarily logical, they will remain *consistently* interwoven with and do not obliterate the asymmetrical ones. The functioning of such thought bears similarity with Freud's *secondary process*. Here is the realm of two-valued or bivalent logic. It is this that must rule at the conscious and preconscious levels of thought if mental coherence of self and world is to continue.

However:

> II. *The System Unconscious selectively treats the converse of any relation as identical to it. It treats logically asymmetrical relations as if they were symmetrical.*

These very simple proposals are the keystones of Matte Blanco's work. It is these (Proposal I providing the setting of II) that he calls *The Principle of Symmetry*. Functioning in the mode of this principle is more or less synonymous with Freud's *primary process*.

Note that it is said that the unconscious *selectively* treats asymmetrical relations as symmetrical. Thus some aspects of unconscious process can still behave asymmetrically and with due regard to two-valued logic while, in other aspects, symmetry and sameness of converses may hold sway. Thus certain asymmetrical elements, in dreams for instance, can still retain clear logical discrimination. The process of selectively *ignoring* certain asymmetrical or difference relations is called *symmetrization* by Matte Blanco. We shall use this wording; the process could be referred to by such neologisms as 'identicalization', but this is less evocative than the more precise term symmetrization.

Note also at this point that symmetrization suggests a move into *greater simplicity*. It can thus be thought of as a *slippage* or regression into crudity which can then suggest an evasive or avoidant activity. There was no doubt in Matte Blanco's mind that symmetrization very often works in this way as a *defence*; but this is not its primary function, which is just to experience sameness. It has been suggested that symmetrization basically functions in the service of recognition, and this will be discussed later.

When there is an engulfment or *insertion* of symmetry, as Matte Blanco calls it, a relationship can only be known as symmetrical where full consciousness would have conceived of it as also having asymmetrical elements. The mind is said to be operating at that point according to symmetrized or *symmetrical logic* rather than in an ordinary logically two-valued or 'Aristotelian' way.

Returning for a moment to the basic functions of location, which needs difference discrimination, and recognition which needs sensitivity to samenesses. Matte Blanco uses the concepts of asymmetry and symmetry because of their invaluable precision. However, it may be easier to begin with to think of difference relation whenever asymmetry is used, and likewise of sameness when symmetry comes up. Both notations will be used here for some time, but symmetry and asymmetry are clearer in the long run.

In summary: unconscious process selectively treats converses as the same when in consciousness they can be perceived as being different.

### The symmetrization of thoughtful propositions into symmetrical logic

Let us start with some examples of symmetrical logic and symmetrization. Take an ordinary reasonable statement or thought, a proposition like: 'A is *giving* something good to B', 'A is daughter of B', 'A loves B', or 'A is in front of B'. Continuing with ordinary logical thinking, which uses asymmetrical relations, we would conclude conversely that: 'B is *being given* something good by A', 'B is parent of A', 'B is being loved by A' and that 'B is behind A'.

However, if *after the initial discrimination*, we symmetrize, and move into symmetrical logic, we would come to the following conclusions: 'A is giving something good to B so B is giving something good to A'; 'A is daughter of B so B is daughter of A'; ' A is loving B so B is loving A'; and 'A is in front of B so B is in front of A'. By ordinary consciously discriminated logical thinking these are *non-sequiturs*, but psychologically, particularly when *feeling* things, symmetrized experiences like this are very common. For instance, we can easily and automatically feel when someone is being nice to us that we are instantaneously being nice to them; or that when someone is charming to us we are charming to them; or when they dislike us we dislike them, and so on. We are probably most prone to this emotional symmetrization or identicalization when we are at our most intimate and emotionally involved with another person. This is intrinsic to common *sympathy* which must be an ingredient of *empathy*, however dispassionate this may be.

It is also common enough in the therapeutic situation that a patient feels something like: 'I am giving my analyst something good, he's being fine for me too.' Just as common is the feeling of mutual badness happening, such as 'I loath that analyst of mine, he obviously can't stand me either'. Similar experiences are natural in countertransference responses. Here, though one may at the conscious level be quite clear that self and other are different people (asymmetrical discrimination), there is a *level*, perhaps unconscious or sometimes preconscious, of experience when *subject and object are undifferentiated.*

When this happens there is a diffuse feeling akin to 'goodness', 'badness'

26

or 'threat is happening'. This is probably a particularly important affective experience between a mother and baby in the early days when they are intimately engrossed with each other. Winnicott (1965) referred to these events during 'primary maternal preoccupation' as the infant's 'contributing in'. More common perhaps is the occasion when, in remembering particularly eager discussions, one cannot recall whether it was oneself or the other person who was the first with a particular idea. Memories of the self and other have been symmetrized.

In these circumstances one may, at a conscious level, be quite clear that self and other are different people; but at a level where the symmetrization has occurred there could be a diffuse objectless feeling. This would be akin to 'there is goodness', or 'there is hate', 'love is between us', or 'it's nice'. Matte Blanco would say that these experiences were close to 'just being' rather than something 'happening'.

In this instance the separate subject and object of each 'proposition' have slipped into the background; they are interchangeable or undifferentiated – even disappeared. Only the *predicate* of the proposition remains clear. This has been called *predicate thinking* (Hall 1954; Skelton 1990a).

Another useful way of conceiving this has been suggested by Mordant (Mordant and Rayner 1990; Mordant 1992); this is that in less differentiated or symmetrized experiences *abstracted conceptions*, attributes or intuitions (e.g. loveliness, niceness, hatefulness, etc.) are floating *free* of specific relations. The effect of such an omnipresent idea is the same as symmetrization.

Note one further point. We have introduced the concept of *level* of mental functioning into our discussion. The conscious level appears to be the one that is most sensitive in discriminating asymmetries and differences of converses. Simultaneously at a less conscious level the mind seems much more interested in similarities and samenesses. Because it is a coordinator for dealing with the world, consciousness cannot manage too many samenesses. The unconscious, on the other hand, can manage this; in fact it seems marvellously equipped to do just this; however, it is not so bothered with differences. We shall return to the idea of levels again in Chapter 6.

It has been pointed out by Kenneth Wright that from his viewpoint the verb 'to symmetrize' points perhaps too strongly towards the idea that the asymmetrical is the more advanced and normal. Slipping into symmetry is then seen as an aberration or pathology. He says that registration of sameness and symmetry is primary and certainly *necessary for survival*. Out of both, leaning on each other as it were, arises a more refined combination which is logical thinking. This is undoubtedly what Matte Blanco intended. He saw symmetrization as vital to life. However, he was probably not very interested in Darwinian ideas about survival, so it has been placed upon Wright to emphasize this.

27

Two further points. Note that neither symmetry nor asymmetry is in itself abnormal, but they can both serve defensive and avoidant purposes. Remember, too, that symmetrized logic is endemic not only in unconscious processes but also in emotional states generally.

## Accentuation of both symmetries and asymmetries in the unconscious

We have been investigating how thought rests on classifying things, and this in turn rests on registering samenesses and differences together in networks or systems.

Visible in early infancy are physiological processes which evoke crude and instantaneous reactions like 'Yum (nice) – gulp, gulp' or 'Yuck (nasty) – spit, spit'. These are primitive, largely physiological, body-dominated emotions. They have an all-or-nothing, *either–or* polarized quality to them. These reactions are also instantaneous physiological *classificatory* actions. It would not be right to equate primitiveness with the system unconscious, but, primitive or not, the unconscious seems also to deal often with things in just these *polarized* classificatory ways. It appears to be the work of conscious levels to articulate, integrate or bring together, and hence recognize as likenesses and differences, the multitude of disparate events that the unconscious knows.

It must here be said that Matte Blanco probably pays too little attention to at least two important regions. One has already been mentioned; he is not very interested in developmental issues. The second is equally or more important. It has been noticed, especially by Elizabeth Spillius in personal communications, that Matte Blanco tends to underemphasize the process of *splitting* and its fundamental importance both in psychopathology and in the unconscious generally. Others, like Juan Francisco Jordan, disagree with this and argue that Matte Blanco does not underestimate the mind's basic propensity to dichotomize because he refers to this in less mechanistic terms. Even so Spillius's emphasis has validity because he hardly relates his ideas about dichotomy to the well-attested concept of splitting. She points out that splitting involves *greater, more crude or exaggerated differences* than does the full awareness of consciousness.

Splitting thus involves a *gross* process of asymmetrization. The unconscious then appears, as seen by logical and conscious thought, as *accentuating* both symmetrization and asymmetrization. It is not only symmetry that the unconscious slips into, as Matte Blanco tends to portray, at least in his earlier work. Rather, the unconscious both symmetrizes and dichotomizes. We shall discuss this later in Chapter 5; it is a central addition to Matte Blanco's prime vision.

## Examples of symmetry and asymmetry

Before going further, here is a selection of instances of the operation of symmetry and asymmetry in various spheres of mental life. A vivid place to start is that of definite pathology – plainly psychotic delusions. As a psychiatrist in his earlier days, Matte Blanco worked a great deal with psychotic patients, and it was from listening to them that he first learnt about symmetrized logic. Here are some examples borrowed from him. The readers can distinguish for themselves what symmetrizations have taken place and where asymmetrical bivalent logic remains intact.

(a) 'A schizophrenic, mentioned by Storch, upon seeing a door in the process of opening, felt frightened and exclaimed, "the animals are eating me"' (Matte Blanco 1988: 47). Here doors and mouths are symmetrized. People go through a door which is a mouth, so the door is a mouth of a carnivore, which is an animal, so an animal is eating him, and one animal is the same as many animals.

(b) 'Prison windows have bars. The windows of my room have bars and my pyjamas have stripes. . . . I am going to tear off my pyjamas to get out of prison' (1975: 162–3). (The symmetrization is obvious here.)

(c) 'A schizophrenic patient told me, "Your assistant is very rich". I asked her how she knew it. She answered, "He is very tall"' (1988: 45). (Here, things that have the adverb 'very', which is 'having an attribute in large measure', attached to them are seen as the same.)

(d) 'A man was bitten by a dog so he went to a dentist' (1988: 51). (The symmetrizations here are interesting and complicated; readers can perhaps work them out for themselves.)

Here are some other statements, by patients and others. They are not psychotic delusions, nor are they all even pathological. Readers can discriminate for themselves the essential asymmetrical relations mentioned and then look for the symmetrizations, if any.

(e) 'My wife and I had a quiet weekend, we had a late breakfast, we read the papers and went to church. We spent an hour talking to the Braithwaites about the summer fair then we went home to a quiet cold lunch. It was getting well into the afternoon so we went out and did some gardening till it was time for supper. One of our children then rang and we had a long time on the phone. We read for a little while, watched some TV and then decided it was time for our bed.' (Here there is no evident symmetrization. It is perhaps a sign of a pathological inhibition of affective expression.)

(f) 'Mother was in one of her moods, father came home and said straight away "what's the weather like?".'

(g) 'I can't bear the thought of this coming holiday, I just can't get death out of my mind, your death, my death, I don't know which – it is to be the end, of the analysis, the term, of you, of me – it's just an ultimate end.'

(h) 'Yesterday evening I at last finished writing the book, what a relief, I went to bed very late, then in the middle of the night I woke up with a dreadful feeling that I was the pages of the book.'

(i) A patient said 'I can't remember whether it was you or I who said it'. (This is a symmetrization of selves, a common occurrence and at the heart of all empathy.)

(j) Now one from Freud. 'July 12 (1938) . . . "Having" and "being" in children. Children like expressing an object relation by an identification: " I am the object". Having is the later of the two; after the loss of the object it relapses into "being". Example: the breast. "The breast is part of me, I am the breast." Only later; "I have it" – that is, "I am not it" ' (Freud (1938), SE 23: 299, quoted in Matte Blanco 1988: 44).

(k) Here is another from Matte Blanco. 'A young man . . . was working for his Sc.D. in geology and geography. He fervently desired to know the region where he was born very well and wanted to write a detailed monograph about it. . . . He had studied his region with the help of maps, economic surveys, geological researches. . . . At this point it is to be noted that he was the eldest child of a large family . . .' (Matte Blanco 1975: 168).

(l) An interesting exercise is to think in erotic imagery and observe the symmetries and asymmetries involved; it is particularly so when doing this in perverse ways. Here there will be *equating* parts of the body for pleasure, both one's own and another person's. A penis can be imagined being sucked as a breast; or that a sucking mouth is a vagina; that a clitoris is a penis being sucked as a breast; and that an anus can be a vagina being a mouth sucking a breast. Likewise imagine being someone of the opposite sex having pleasure from someone who is claiming to be of the opposite sex to what they actually are. All involve symmetrization.

(m) Here is an example from the Bible: 'And he took bread, and gave thanks, and brake it, and gave unto them, saying, Take, eat; this is my body which is given for you: do this in remembrance of me. Likewise also after supper he took the cup, saying, Drink this, all of you; this is my blood of the new covenant, which is shed for you' (Luke: 22).

(n) Another one from the Bible shows asymmetries emerging from symmetries: 'In the beginning God created the heaven and the earth. And the earth was without form, a void, and darkness was upon the face of the deep. And the Spirit of God moved on the face of the waters. And God said, Let there be light: and there was light. And God saw the light, that it was good: and God divided the light from the darkness. And God called the light Day, and the darkness he called Night. And the evening and the morning were the first day. And God said, Let there be a firmament in the midst of the waters, and let it divide the waters from the waters. And God made the firmament, and divided the waters which were under the firmament from the waters which were above the firmament: and it was so . . .' (Genesis: 1).

## Some modalities in which symmetrization can ordinarily occur

### Time

Consider the conception of a *time relation*. Ordinarily we discriminate, say, 'event B *follows* event A', then, recognizing an asymmetrical relation, we would easily step to a conclusion that 'A is *followed* by B'. However, if a symmetrization intervenes we would go 'B follows A – A follows B'. When this happens succession is not distinguished; there is then no awareness of time sequence – our knowing of *time has disappeared*. This happens most obviously in dreams, and through these Freud made his historic leap to understanding the timelessness of the unconscious. From another point of view there is also a timelessness about well-established long-term memories at levels where 'time labels' are not attached – as manifestly happens in dreams.

### Space

The conception of *space*, like time, involves relations which are essentially asymmetrical. Take points in a line: they must stand to the viewer in an asymmetrical relation to each other. Thus, if B is to the left of A then A must be (in the opposite direction) to the right of B. But if there is an insertion of symmetry, then the thought would be, 'B is to the left of A – A is to the left of B'. With this, points along the line become interchangeable and this cannot be distinguished; there is no awareness of extension and the conception of *space disappears*.

Note that in this example a single symmetrization of space is occurring which is strictly limited to points on a line; other zones of a space may well remain unaffected. This partial symmetrization is very common. It is difficult to imagine intentionally and consciously a symmetrized part of a space. However, it certainly happens without trouble at unconscious levels every night in the condensation of ideas into dream imagery.

Although Freud described the unconscious as being timeless, he omitted to refer explicitly to the spacelessness of the unconscious. However, it is definitely implicit in displacement and condensation which he clearly theorized about. These processes happened, for instance, in the case of the government official's act of equating paper florins with female genitalia. In actuality these two sorts of object can hardly reside together in exactly the same space but it is this that is implicit in the official's symptom.

The omission of spacelessness as a characteristic of the unconscious by Freud may have given later analysts the licence to use notions of psychic space rather indiscriminately. We shall see later that Matte Blanco insists that mental space is a useful concept but it is necessary to be clear about its use, for psychic spacelessness is omnipresent and confusions easily arise. Finally it is important to note that the phenomenon of *merging of selves* rests upon a spacial symmetrization.

### The equation between a whole and its parts

A thought about a whole object 'B' and a part of it 'b' involves a space or time relation between them such that B *includes* b, while b *is included in* B. Such thoughts or propositions naturally use asymmetrical logic. But when symmetrized, thinking will be in the form 'B includes b – b includes B'. Space within the object 'B' will have disappeared. Thus, where symmetry rules, *whole objects are experienced as identical to their parts*.

On first glance this must seem a dotty and pointless exercise, but our everyday emotional thought is riddled with such part = whole equations. This is of central psychological importance. The equation is most obvious in psychosis when, say, someone may feel that the whole spirit of evil is emerging through a boil on the nose. Here is another such equation: it is usual for a man to be able to recognize that his penis is part of his body in a certain location. But in normal dreams, as well as consciously in psychosis, it is commonplace for penis, whole body and self to be un-differentiated, identical or interchangeable.

In more muted form it probably occurs in any neurosis such as when the feeling of impotence refers equally to the experience of a particular disfunction of the penis, to weakness of the whole body and to the incompetence of the overall self. In normal circumstances the part = whole equation is easily seen with failing an exam: an ordinary person might simply say 'I have failed this time'; a neurotically depressive person might say 'I am an utter failure'; while a psychotic person may say 'I am failure'. Note the different degrees of conscious and preconscious level of sym-metrization. Another example would be when a parent says 'You are a bad boy' when an otherwise nice child has done some small thing wrong.

Crude polarized, all-or-nothing states emerge very frequently. Only later, when other experiences have been related with asymmetrically, can one say to oneself, 'I was weak, bad or a failure on that occasion but it has not always been so with me'. It is an important phenomenon in any emotionality, both healthy and pathological.


### Classification

We know that a class or set is a collection of any sort of things that have at least one characteristic, quality or attribute in common.

First, being a collection, thus having an extensive, quantitative, numerable, 'counting' or 'population' aspect, it deals not only with attributes but also in 'more than oneness'. This does not necessarily involve precise counting. Second, members having a defining attribute or quality in common means a set has a *qualitative* aspect as well.

One of the functions of symmetrization is to dwell *only* upon the common quality, the defining attribute, of the members or things in a set. This ignores the individuality of its members and entails the *obliteration of the quantitative aspects* of the class or set. Matte Blanco (1975) discusses this as we shall see; but it has been Mordant (1990) who has clearly shown that when a class attribute is separated from its members it becomes an *abstract notion*. Skelton (1990a, 1992) has addressed the same question equally cogently using the conception of predicate thinking.

Let us look further into this question. The specific idea of a class usually refers to a set whose members need bear no consistent relation to each other except that they have some attribute in common. An individual becomes a member of the class if he, she or it is seen to bear the common attribute. Thus members of the class English can be scattered anywhere over the globe but they still remain English as long as they carry the attributes of Englishness. Dwelling only upon the attribute of a class, say Englishness, is an act of abstraction, and the characteristic quality of a class without its members can be seen as an abstracted attribute, conception or notion.

Now, being fully a member of, or being in the relation of belonging to, a class, necessitates asymmetrical thinking on at least two counts. First, members must be *located* in space or time to be individuals; second, the relation of 'belonging to a collection' is obviously also asymmetrical. However, if a symmetrization rules *within the whole class* then the locatable individuality of the members has been obliterated or ignored; further, the belongingness of its members to the class disappears. The class and its members are then only known or experienced as the same. *The whole class and its parts become identical.* Note that this is also exactly what can happen

33

to a *whole object* and its parts under the effect of symmetrization.

This again may seem an absurd exercise but every day we engross ourselves in such logic both pathologically and in normal emotionality. De Gaulle, for instance, did this in his well-known phrase, 'La France c'est moi'. This may not be good logic but it is definitely not meaningless – it even carried an important truth at the time of the Second World War which probably could not have been conveyed by means of a chain of logically consistent phrases. Likewise, Marley's ghost in Dickens's *Christmas Carol* announces that 'I am the spirit of Christmas past' – he is a specific individual ghost and at the same time the attribute of a whole class. It is emotionally unforgettable.

More commonplace was the patient who said of her husband with dismissive abandon: 'He's the same as all you men, of course, an exploiting capitalist.' In equating her husband with the whole class 'male' which was equated in turn with the class 'exploiting capitalist' she was probably using symmetrization in the service of plain malice or perhaps even friendly humour rather than more gross paranoid pathology. She certainly appears to avoid the use of such asymmetrical means as would have located individual attributes in her husband that were not necessarily shared by all males. Thinking about his individuality might well have made her realize that in many ways he was not totally an exploiter; as a matter of fact, he often slaved for her. Perhaps thought about her own dismissiveness was likely to be embarrassing, so she conveniently obliterated it. Or, as far as we can tell, she might have just been amusingly provocative. At all events, we see here a symmetrization in the service of untruthful defence and the pleasure principle; it appears to have quite naked primary process in it.

Simplistic exaggeration like this is a common hysterical characteristic. Note again that this can involve accentuation of asymmetrical, and not only symmetrical, relations. So, though Matte Blanco hardly mentions it, 'asymmetrization' in splitting is as pronounced in pathology, and in the unconscious generally, as is symmetrization.

The whole realm of emotional communication, useful or not, is imbued with symmetrizations or identicalizations. This could be in intimate love, anger or pain; in gossip, politics, poetry or literature – in any rhetorical expressions.

Such emotional activity uses both ordinary logic, which scrupulously adheres to asymmetrical relations, together with symmetrical logic at the same time. Matte Blanco calls this a *bi-logical mode*, be it in unconscious or emotional thought. Following Spillius's observation mentioned earlier, a bi-logical mode can perhaps best be viewed as thought where there is an *accentuation* of either symmetrical or asymmetrical inferences, or both, as compared to fully logical consciousness.

Patterns of feeling-thought, where symmetrizations occur enmeshed with asymmetrical relations, are called bi-logical structures by Matte Blanco. Thus the thought system employed by the woman who called her husband 'just an exploiting capitalist' was a bi-logical structure.

Pathological thought with its tricky, avoidant defensive systems involves exaggeration, or slippage in certain regions away from consistent use of both asymmetrical discriminations and symmetrical recognitions. When symmetrizations (and accentuated asymmetrizations) serve to obliterate painful affects we can say they serve defences; they are then 'economical with the truth'. For instance, the woman with the 'capitalist' husband probably avoided recognition of how dependent she was upon him. For more usefully creative purposes, bi-logic and symmetrizations can function by consciously controlled intentional 'dipping' into symmetries; this will not be in the service of avoidance, but for rich and meaningful emotional communication. There will be more about this in Chapter 5.

## Bi-logical dialectic and bi-modality

Matte Blanco naturally defines separately the operation of symmetry and asymmetry but shows that their *interaction* or *dialectic* (Durst 1988) is psychologically very important. Incidentally, Matte Blanco at one time put forward the terms *homogeneity* and *heterogeneity* in interplay but finally settled for symmetry and asymmetry since they describe very well the logical functions involved, so we shall keep to this usage.

It will now be plain that registration of sameness or symmetry is a necessary function in even the most logical and rational of thought. But it must function together consistently with asymmetry. For instance, any class or set, including a mathematically rigorous one, is defined by its members being the same in some way – symmetry. However, if it is ordinarily logical and not a bi-logical structure, its standing with regard to its frame of asymmetrical relations is still strictly definable and consistent – thus gross symmetrization will not have occurred. Neither symmetry nor asymmetry will have been 'on the loose' as it were. This looseness only occurs with bi-logical structures.

Summarizing: A symmetrization is seen to emerge or 'insert' itself only when a difference relation, an asymmetrical converse, *detectable to the consciously logical mind*, is *ignored* in favour of a simple registration of sameness which is a symmetrical relation. The same can occur where symmetries are ignored and some asymmetries exaggerated. In other words it can be said that bi-logic as a discipline concerns itself with the systematic investigation of complex combinations between identical and non-identical relationships.

Of course, purely logical thought is also never devoid of both asymmetrical and symmetrical relations. There can be no thought without recognition and this entails classification with its symmetry or sameness registration. But when thought is ordinarily logical, symmetries are bound or contained by definite asymmetrical relations so that consistency of inference is maintained. Matte Blanco calls the structure of such consistent thought *bi-modal* as opposed to bi-logical.

As an example, by its nature any external *physical object* can, on the one hand, be perceived as a whole which is distinct from (asymmetrically related to) other things. On the other hand, all the parts of the object must also have at least one symmetry or sameness in common – that they are all together members of that one whole object. Thus, for instance, it is vital for survival to perceive that one's motor car is distinct from and asymmetrically related in a multitude of ways to other cars. But the parts of the car – wheels, engine, seats, etc. – must also have a symmetry in common: they all belong together as members of that unique car. Wholeness and uniqueness of an object depend upon both asymmetrical and symmetrical relations. For survival in the physical world these must be consistently related to each other. The concept of the car is then bi-modally structured. However, at the same time cars can have all sorts of other more emotional meanings; for instance, they can be symbols of potency or of maternal care. Where this happens the notion of the car has become a bi-logical structure.

## Hierarchical levels of classification

To illustrate bi-logic so far, here is a commonplace example of hierarchical classification using both bivalent and symmetrized logics. It is also an example of Matte Blanco's *The Principle of Generalization*. We discriminate, say, a baby. Doing this we can readily leap to a *hierarchy*: 'this is a baby in some ways the same as and in some ways different from all other babies, who are in some ways the same as all human beings, who are in some ways the same as all living things, who are in some ways the same as all touchable things'. This is using symmetry, but the logic is consistently bivalent; no symmetrization is yet evident. For instance, we can recognize that babies and stones are the same in that they are both touchable. But both symmetry and asymmetrical relations are being consistently used; we still know that babies and stones are also different, they are simply *equivalent* with regard to the class attribute of touchability.

However, if *one or more asymmetrical relation is ignored or obliterated* symmetrization emerges. Then when it comes to the most general level of this hierarchy, symmetry could rule. When that happens, a baby is known *only as the same* as anything touchable, and so too is a stone. So, in this case, a baby, all babies, all human beings, all living things and all stones are only known as *identical*. All that is known about them is their common attribute – something like '*there is touchability*' or '*touching is*'. For Matte Blanco this happens at the deepest levels of the system unconscious.

This can seem a pedantic intellectual exercise but it can highlight serious matters. For instance, some mothers, even in moments of apparent intimacy, refer to their babies as nothing but 'it' and this can send a shudder down the listener's spine. Such a mother seems to be revealing a level where ordinary feeling has disappeared and she is automatically equating her baby with a 'thing' – anything alive or dead.

Likewise a psychotic person may experience no incompatibility between being alive and dead at the same time. Here live and inanimate or dead things are all touchable, so it appears that a symmetrization of psychotic proportions has obliterated all discrimination of the manifold differences that can occur between the members of the class of touchable things. At this level of thought all touchable things are nothing but the same. Again, feeling will have disappeared when symmetrization is very gross.

Even so the two logics can normally operate together in ordinary rich and emotionally evocative imagination. A child may lie on the beach lapped by the waves and declaim 'I am a stone'. If he is playing he will know very well that he *is not* a stone but the point of the game is that he *is* a stone. This is a *paradox* inherent in any make-believe play. Without symmetry there is no metaphor and with no metaphor there is no make-believe play. But without the self having a containing framework of awareness of asymmetrical relations play breaks down into delusion. The child *believes* he is a stone. This occurs in psychosis of course and also normally in dreams. It is muted in affective states and in neurotic anxiety when a person may *feel* he has turned to stone but knows very well consciously that he has not.

What is more, the simple dramatic play of 'I am a stone' can perhaps be the beginning of a poetic drama. For instance: 'A stone I was, washed by the waves of life, battered by storms, rubbing against my fellow men, my self remained the same.' We are back to metaphor. It reminds us of Langer's (1942) presentational symbolism which is naturally evocative and used for quick communication of emotional states. Symmetrization plays a vital part in the *simplification* necessary for this form of communication.

Freud was, of course, aware of the similarity or isomorphism between symbol and symbolized involved in dream imagery. In fact he realized it was quite crucial. For instance he said:

Aristotle (De divinatione per somnum) remarked in this connection that the best interpreter of dreams was the man who could best grasp similarities; for dream pictures, like pictures on water, are pulled out of shape by movement, and the most successful interpreter is the man who can detect the truth from the misshapen picture. Similarity, consonance, the possession of common attributes – all these are represented in dreams by unification.

(Freud 1900, SE 4: 319–20)

Jones (1916) was also quite explicit about the central importance of similarity as a characteristic of 'psychoanalytic' symbolism. Sharpe (1937) likewise described both metaphor and dream imagery as being alike in both having a crucial similarity between the form of the symbol and symbolized. Other authors have done the same. However, they usually refer loosely to 'similarity' – and this concept combines sameness with a certain amount of difference. It has been Matte Blanco's inspiration and task to link systematically a host of apparently disparate mental functions by seeing that they have the fundamental function of symmetry with its pure sameness registration in common, to which varying degrees of asymmetry may be added.

The bi-logical point of view provides, for instance, one disciplined way of investigating the symbolization which is a keystone of psychoanalysis. Here it is possible to see that psychotic symbolic equations involve gross symmetrizations which *distort the extent of the self* in relation to external and internal reality. Quite different is metaphor which, though still symmetrizing, is a valuable means of communication and can be self-enhancing. Conventional symbols, though involving symmetries, need use no unbounded symmetrization and would thus not be based on bi-logical structures.

Symmetrized and bi-logical structures also predominate in *pre-object* states. Perhaps, in order to avoid unwarranted developmental assumptions, it would be better to call these *non-object states*. These would be found most commonly in mood states but also in oceanic feelings, self–object fusions and symbiosis, not to mention more sophisticated mystic experiences.

### Intersubjective symmetrization

As most readers will know, there is now much evidence of sensitivity to other people from the earliest days of life and even the first hours after birth (Sandler 1993; Stern 1985). Infants and mothers are seen to resonate, mimic, tune-in or *attune* and take turns with each other in their movements and gestures at feeding and other times. Intersubjectivity is fundamental to the human and starts very early. This becomes most apparent where emotional expressions are concerned. Such early resonant matching appears to be at the heart of sympathy, empathy and mutuality. These act as the very keystones of psychoanalytic therapy (Kohut 1971; Wolf 1988; Rayner 1992), not to mention ordinary friendship and affection generally. Matte Blanco has been aware (1975: 439–48) that such mutuality does in fact involve *interpersonal symmetrization*, but he did not make it a central aspect of his theory. This was a pity for there is now a great body of research and thought that is seeing how important inter- personal mutual experiences are in the development of even the most intellectual of activities. One has only to glance at the infant research and attachment literature to see how strong is this line of thought. Matte Blanco's apparent lack of central interest in developmental matters has tended to leave his ideas isolated and unheeded in this region.

It quickly becomes obvious that experiences of such symmetrical awareness is an essence not only in intersubjective mutuality, attunement and empathy but also in the structuring of any consistent adaptive identification. It must remain for us in the future to make good his omission.

[*Answers to Example (d) on page 24*: 1. sy; 2. sy; 3. sy; 4. asy; 5. amb; 6. sy; 7. amb; 8. asy; 9. amb; 10. sy; 11. amb; 12. sy; 13. asy; 14. sy; 15. amb; 16. sy; 17. sy.]

# Bi-logic and Freud's characteristics
## of the unconscious

The outcome of the first theme of *The Unconscious as Infinite Sets* (Matte Blanco 1975) follows Freud (1900, 1915) closely and argues how the main characteristics of unconscious functioning can be seen as arising out of symmetrized thought taking over where full consciousness would see asymmetrical relations as well. You will remember that Freud essentially distinguished five of these characteristics: timelessness, displacement, condensation, replacement of external by internal reality and absence of mutual contradiction.

At this point note first that when, as now, we are arguing and reading theoretically, our own minds' basic frame of reference must be that of *conscious* level ordinary logical thought which consistently uses asymmetrically structured relations. Seen from this level it is appropriate to speak (to another person also thinking at a conscious level) of the symmetrization of thought at an unconscious level; for that is how the unconscious will appear to two consciously structured minds. However, at the unconscious level, in our dreaming selves for instance, we would be in no position to discriminate that such a process was occurring.

Here is an introductory idea of Matte Blanco's fundamental argument about the characteristics of the unconscious. He distinguished (1988) many more from Freud's texts, but we shall confine ourselves to his original five.

## Characteristics of the unconscious

### Timelessness

This has already been mentioned. When the converse of a time relation is experienced as identical to it, as happens when a symmetrization emerges, then sequentiality cannot be known and time as we know it is not discriminated as existing. 'After' is then felt as no different from 'before' or 'at the same moment'.

A selective emergence or insertion of timelessness occurred, for instance, with a child who believed for a time that cats were cats, adults were adults, and all children would always remain children. He had not, of course, lost all sense of time, but only that children did not transform with time into grown-ups – it was a selective symmetrization.

Timelessness is also obvious in sleep. We often wake up in the night and have no idea how long we have slept. However, this time-symmetrization is *only partial*, for many unconscious biological clocks still operate. For instance, the timing of REM and non-REM periods of brain activity proceed consistently throughout sleep. On the other hand, a prime example of timelessness occurs in the way dreams readily manifest events; the distant past and the previous day may come together as if at the same time. Such sleep examples are quite normal, but we often have waking instances where serious blocking of thought is associated with a sudden loss in the time sense.

What makes the dividing line between a *normal* and *pathological* symmetrization? It appears to do with whether a symmetry is 'held' – contained or integrated by the central organizing self or ego at its appropriate level so that it does not invade the conscious use of logical inference in the service of an adaptive judgement. Exactly the same applies to the holding of relevant asymmetries in consciousness, and keeping these too in bounds so that maladaptive splitting and disintegration do not occur. We also noted earlier how awareness of *space* disappears with symmetry. Freud did not mention spacelessness, but the next three of his characteristics imply it.

### Replacement of external by internal reality

The idea of *external* reality necessitates the asymmetrical conception of *space*, of inside and outside or 'psychic' and 'material' reality. With a symmetrization of it, space ceases to be known there. Thus to the experiencer, *inside and outside become the same* in that region. However, to an outside observer the difference may still be evident, so to that person the experiencer appears to be replacing external by internal reality. Perhaps it would be better to say that external and internal are replaced by non-discrimination.

Such non-differentiation is apparent in any person when self-absorbed; it is also most obvious and well documented in the appearance of any projection or projective identification.

## Condensation

Here ideas derived from different times and object relations, differently placed in space, are experienced as belonging to a singly located object in time and space. The separation of places in space and time have disappeared; individualities have gone. This can occur naturally with a symmetrization in one or more spacial or temporal aspect or dimension. Remember that a pure state of symmetry or total sameness is unknowable to consciousness. The condensed images we remember from dreams are mixtures of symmetrical and asymmetrical and are bi-logical structures.

Examples of condensation come every day in analytic practice. Freud's *Interpretation of Dreams* (1900) and early case studies are full of them. Here are two present-day dreams.

EXAMPLE 4.1

Before a holiday a patient dreamt that 'she was going down a ski slope with her instructor. Part of the way down he stopped but she continued the rest of the way easily by herself.' The session then showed how she had experienced parting from 'givers of instruction' at different times of her life. The ski-instructor could be recognized as a condensed timeless image of her mother, father, elder brother and her analyst, as well as the knowledgeable side of herself (Rayner 1981).

EXAMPLE 4.2

A patient's parents came to stay in her flat for the weekend and she gave them her bedroom. She then had the following dream. 'Mice were in the bedroom, her mother was phobic of mice, so she had to kill them for her, but they then turned into rabbits, so she would have to kill them too, but they had long ears – which turned into fierce long teeth.' Her associations led to the theme of disturbers of the peace, modes of disposing of them, and their possible retaliation. She herself was phobic, not of mice, but of spiders and was terrified of trying to kill and dispose of them. Her mother was prone to be scathing of her father and readily disposed of his character by squashing him with verbal criticism. The patient was said to have often been bossily dismissive, disposing of her brother when she was small so that he was sometimes a bit overawed by her, but as he was much bigger than she, he was easily able to knock her about. As a grown-up she could not openly boss men about or verbally dismiss them, though she could not help doing that to herself. It was fairly easy to detect that she was readily afraid of what her male analyst would hear with his long ears, and of what he might then say or do to her. His long ears would, as it were, turn into fierce long teeth. But she knew in her heart that her own scathing dismissiveness was not far away. We can see that the mice and fierce rabbits condensed several contradictory or conflicting aspects not only of herself but also of her mother, father, brother, analyst, men in general, and perhaps her mother's imagined babies. The dream images condensed not only many parts of the self and objects but also various forms of sexual or aggressive impulse and emotional state. The dream contains many quiet and hidden equations through symmetrization.

### Displacement

This is perhaps the most crucial characteristic of the unconscious since it lies at the basis of *symbolization, transference, projection, introjection* and *sublimation.* Matte Blanco points out that in displacement a person is seen by an *outside* observer to be shifting feelings and ideas from one primary object-relation to another. But, from the point of view of the unconscious of the person, both objects are only known as identical. To the conscious-level self, objects may well be registered as having a *similarity*, as belonging to the same class, which is having a quality in common but also with differences. Then, with symmetrization endemic in the unconscious, the objects are conceived as identical, as being nothing but the same. When this occurs, one object can be felt as having any of the qualities of the other.

For example, in the case of the patient (in Example 4.2 above) who was afraid of spiders, it was fairly easy to discover that her mother and the class of spiders had several qualities in common, such as activity akin or identical to weaving webs that entrap. Spiders in themselves were known to be harmless, but, as they had something in common with her mother, they took on other maternal attributes, and then being afraid. A defence of *denial* may then come into play so that the idea or feeling is *not consciously* recognized as belonging to the primary object but only to the secondary one – the patient was thus not afraid of her mother but of spiders instead.

Here is another example (Rayner 1981).

EXAMPLE 4.3

An hour or so before a session a patient was relaxing, looking forward to a bite to eat and then pottering down to her session. Her husband came in and said gallantly, 'I'm going that way, let me give you a lift.' He then remembered something and said, 'Oh damn, I must get that letter off; be a darling and type it for me would you?' Without a second thought she dashed upstairs and hurriedly typed it out. They swept out in the car and arrived near her analyst's consulting room ten minutes early. Grateful as she was to her husband for the lift, she none the less stood on the pavement feeling jangled and then suddenly very hungry. 'Damn the blasted analysis,' she thought. 'I need a pizza and a coffee.' She thus arrived at the session ten minutes late, fed up with herself and irritated with her husband.

On the couch in the session she began to think about this and said, 'It's not you I am angry with at all, it's that husband of mine; how I do split the two of you switching about turning the one bad and the other good.' Here she was accurately using asymmetrical means to understand and make an interpretation about herself. The analyst affirmed this and also pointed out the symmetry behind her displacement by saying: 'Yes and as well as that, this switching must mean that your husband and I are easily interchange-able and thus *the same* in some way in the first place.' To which she replied: 'Yes, I see what you mean; if I punish you by being angry and late for what he has done then you and he must be the same in some odd way.'

### Absence of mutual contradiction

Here Freud refers to wishes which, to the ordinary logic of consciousness, are contradictory and would thus be expected to nullify each other, but neither gets diminished in the unconscious. Matte Blanco says that Freud rightly seems to be saying that conflict is *not* experienced at this level in the unconscious. Others, such as Klein, would perhaps differ for they see conflict always at the very heart of the system unconscious. In fact, as will appear in Chapter 6, Matte Blanco sees the deepest unconscious level as conflict free whereas levels nearer consciousness are likely to be full of conflict. If we consider the simple case of two wishes, then the functioning of a symmetrization may be seen in the following way. To be experienced as contradictory the two wishes must be felt to *oppose* each other. This is the same as each wish being the non-identical *converse* of the other, which is essentially asymmetrical. When a symmetrization occurs within this idea, only that which is the same between the wishes will be known – and this largely unconsciously; they will be experienced as identical and not differ-ent and contradictory.

For instance, some time ago, long after my mother had died, I had a dream of a common enough sort. 'My mother was dead and also alive, she was quite tangibly present and it was quite natural that she should be that way.' There is no need to analyse this dream in detail. In the ordinary conscious logic of real life, to be alive is in contradiction to being dead. To be not-dead is to be alive. But the dream can be seen as the expression of a wish for a mother to be again present and alive, and thus no doubt giving and loving, etc. But why also dead? Well, that which is dead is much more manipulable to the whim than if alive; an alive mother can be controlling and an awful nuisance. So it seems I wanted something that is both giving and manipulable, alive and dead. Thus the dream seems very cleverly to find, via the notion of tangibility, something which is the same for both alive and dead things. It is clear that dead and alive are identical at the level of being touchable. Unconscious symmetrization seems to have found this commonality, or level of sameness, to satisfy both of my otherwise contradictory desires. There was no experience of contradiction in the dream which was expressed by the feeling *it was quite natural to be that way.* Asymmetrical elements, however, can still be seen in the dream, for the states of being dead and alive are, albeit half-heartedly, distinguished.

That completes this consideration of Freud's characteristics of the unconscious in the light of the working of logical symmetry and asymmetry in a combinatorial dialectical way. It is this that is the primary key in Matte Blanco's work. We now reconsider some of these concepts by looking at them from a few alternative angles.


## Negation

Absence of the mutual contradiction of impulses is probably a particular case of absence of negation. This, too, can be seen as a function of a logic that has symmetrized elements in it. The very act of a negation is to assert that there is a difference in a relationship, a 'this is *not* that'. This is an essential awareness in asymmetricality, which is the noting that a converse is *not* the same as the original relation. Myriads of instantaneous acts of negation seem to permeate every moment of waking mental life; they occur in every asymmetrical discrimination. Are these experiences perhaps the outcome of some patterning of the 'on–off', or the 'yes–no' of neural functioning?

The same phenomenon of negation can be seen at more complex levels as follows. Without negation there is no sense of external reality. For instance, Freud's (1925) paper on 'Negation' pointed out the importance of negative judgements in the development of the sense of external reality. Matte Blanco comes to a similar conclusion but starts from different premises. For him the sense of external reality depends on the ideas of space and time. The location of external real objects is obviously important to any animal. All these – space, time and their offspring location – have been seen to be dependent upon a logical functioning of the mind which includes asymmetrical relations. These depend upon negation functions where a conceived relationship and its converse are *not* the same. In particular, when these are symmetrized, awareness of the 'externalness' of reality can disappear.

Negation and its absence are both at the very core of any bi-logical thought. A serious difficulty appears to arise here. It is obvious that valid inference depends upon the logical consistency inherent in ordinary conscious level, traditional two-valued logic. It has already been said that the essence of two-valuedness is that things which 'are so' are not 'not so' at the same time. Here the non-contradiction 'If A, then not not-A' is crucial. However, if Matte Blanco is proposing a system where this principle of contradiction can be absent, then surely everything and nothing can be explained by it and the theory is useless. This has been skilfully argued by Skelton (1984). Matte Blanco (1984) argued back that he was sorry; he did not invent the way the unconscious levels of the mind work. Nor is he precisely proposing a mind that *never* knows negation or contradiction anywhere – very definitely not. His view is that *selective*, localized symmetrizations occur in the unconscious, and thence in emotionally charged thinking of any kind.

Furthermore, though minds at unconscious levels may grossly symmetrize, it is the job of the theorist to remain firmly on a level where two-valued logic still consistently applies. The theorist's task is to specify when, where and how the symmetrization occurs within the object of study.

A similar challenge faces the analytic therapist who must symmetrize between personal self and the patient's self. This arises in the very act of empathetic instantaneous identification with a patient. The first step in psychotherapeutic understanding is by the therapist symmetrically matching or *attuning* his or her mind with the patient's *mood*, which will lie behind or between the overt words spoken. This is vital to the necessary emotionality of the analytic dialogue. However, a psychoanalytic therapist must not rest there, but always at the same time maintain a combination with the asymmetrical two-valued logical functioning necessary for objectivity. It has been argued that the facility for free, *unbiased movement* (using asymmetricality) of often highly emotional identifications (using symmetrization) seems to define analytic *neutrality* (Rayner 1991, 1992).

We have noted already that Matte Blanco paid little attention to symmetrization both intersubjectively and between internal objects. His failure to engage with these issues tends to make him appear rather on one side of, and away from, a strong flow in modern analytic thinking.

## The unconscious, abstraction, propositional functions and predicate thinking

It will be recalled how symmetry plays a part in classification. When classification works with two-valued logicality, different members of a class remain distinct individuals but are seen as similar though different; they have some class-defining quality or attribute in common. But the result of a symmetrization *within a class* can be that not only do the differences between the members themselves disappear but also between them and the idea of the whole class. When this happens all that is known about the class will be that which is in *common* between the members. This will be the *defining attribute* of the class itself.

Take, for instance, ideas of several whole collections such as, say, eagles, drains, left shoes or lice; now symmetrize away all the differences between the members of each of these classes. When this happens, all that is left to conceive of are the essential attributes which distinguish eagles, drains, left shoes and lice from other beings. We could call these attributes 'eagleness', 'drainness' and the like. It has been noted, following Mordant (Mordant and Rayner 1990; Mordant 1992; see also Chapter 3), that these are really *abstracted* conceptions or attributes. If they are abstractions of a sort then we are driven to a remarkable conclusion: if the unconscious is characterized by symmetrization, and if the outcome of much symmetrization is to dwell exclusively on abstracted attributes, then *the unconscious deals in something close to abstractions*. It must be recognized here that the abstracted ideas *within* themselves contain asymmetrical relations. For instance, the notion of 'drain', say, involves spacial and distinct part–whole relations – liquid in a conduit, distinct movement in one direction and so on. But the whole gestalt or form of the abstract idea of 'drainness' itself floats free, as it were, of other relations; it can be anywhere at any time. Abstractions 'float in a sea of symmetrization'.

Mordant thinks that the phrase 'unconscious notion' is useful for such imprecisely abstracted ideas, but the terms 'conception' or 'intuition' will do as well. The unconscious appears to be most extraordinarily abstract! This seems to go against the model produced by our ordinary thinking, which is that abstraction is the preserve and fruit of the highest conscious thought processes. The argument here would be: it is the unconscious that is full of primitive urges and their particular symbols, and surely primitive urges cannot be abstractions?

The answer would appear to be as follows. Abstract thinking usually refers to consistent combinatorial activity using logically definable abstract concepts. The instances of such usable concepts, like 'the square root of two' or 'justice', *cannot be directly presented to the senses*. In other words, they cannot be seen, heard, touched or smelled. It is well known from such researchers as Piaget (1950) that such thinking with abstract concepts is not normally possible until later in childhood, and no one would say that the unconscious only starts functioning then.

However, Piaget (1950, 1951), Stern (1985) and many others directly studying mental functions in early infancy, have noted that there is considerable evidence for a more simple level of abstraction occurring. This can be called *sensory abstraction* which is a form of *selection*. For instance, the very understanding of the *general meaning of a word*, such as a noun or verb, depends upon distinguishing a class attribute. This is usually observed by about a year old, as long as actual instances of the objects of the words are easily visible and tangible. Incidentally, Piaget (1951) used the term 'abstraction' for an aspect of this naming function which can be involved in any early classificatory activity.

What is more, it has already been noted that very early abstraction has recently been discovered in another aspect of development (Meltzoff 1981; Stern 1985). Infants of only a few days old can pick up a *pattern* in *one sense modality* (touch, say) and use their knowledge of this to *generalize* to something of the same pattern in *another modality* (sight, say). Or again, a rhythmic pattern, picked up first by sound, will be recognized as the same pattern if presented later visually. This is called *cross-sensory* or *amodal* perception, and the scientific evidence for its early importance is now well established. It is abstraction of a primitive kind. There is thus little reason to doubt that simple abstractions must easily form part of early life. It does not necessarily mean that they then must join the great array of the unconscious, but it makes it possible.

Others (Etchegoyen and Ahumada 1990; Ahumada 1994; Emde *et al.* 1991; Stern 1985) observe that patterns of emotional activity are, in health, automatically selected or abstracted from their context and reacted to from the earliest infancy onwards. Ahumada, for instance, notes that Bateson (1973) saw that imitation of *emotional* patterns was the basis of animal communication. Bateson called this *analogic* communication. When such an emotional pattern is selected out from its context, it must at least partially be 'floating freely' of the context; it is then acting as one of Mordant's abstracted attributes. Langs (1979) seems to have been thinking along similar lines when he spoke of the abstracting and particularizing aspects of mental activity.

Less specifically than Mordant, but much before him in time, Matte Blanco too indicated that many of the prime inhabitants of unconscious imagination are sensory abstractions. He says (1975: 121), for instance, that we do not talk of a particular locatable 'left or right breast', it is '*the* breast', '*the* good breast', '*the* bad breast', '*the* nipple', '*the* penis', 'faeces'. These are notions, conceptions or imaginary objects; they are *generalized ideas*; they are not representations of particular locatable objects of actually perceived reality.

48

These ideas must have qualities that are fantastical but cannot be said to be just fantasies, for they refer to aspects of real things but in a generalized or abstracted way. Thus, when described by Freud, Klein or any other analyst, unconscious objects are certainly abstractions of a sort. They appear to be simple abstractions both in the infant's mind, and also in anyone else's at unconscious levels. However, 'the good breast' or 'the penis' are now traditionally called *part objects* by psychoanalysts. So *part objects are primitive abstractions* and they are also based on symmetrizations. They are not simple fragments, three-dimensional things, but are of an abstract nature and the product of symmetrization. Such notions can be 'pure' and dissociated, split off that is, at unconscious levels. Perhaps splitting must play an essential part in their formation. When this invades conscious structuring then, of course, mental disturbance is manifest.

In the next chapter we shall emphasize that symmetrization mixed with asymmetrical discrimination is not only a characteristic of unconscious activity but also of emotionality, even at more conscious levels. We shall see that such emotional activity is crude and liable to prejudice. It may have been initiated by splitting for pathological reasons, but it can also enable *quick evaluations* to be made, communicated and carried out.

Matte Blanco did not pursue the question of the *primitiveness* of abstraction. He was neither particularly interested in developmental dating, nor did he have recent infant research findings available (Stern 1985). He approached the question with great imagination from introspective and logico-deductive points of view. Following Russell and Whitehead (1910), he pointed to what they called a *propositional function*. This is a thought which is only very general indeed because it contains as yet neither a *defined subject* nor a *specified object*. It is thus *so general* that it is not yet a definite proposition about anything. Thus a statement such as '*x* is hurt' is a propositional function. In this case *x*, called a *variable* in logic, is so general that the statement is saying nothing specific as yet. It is pointing nowhere in particular. *x* could be a mouse, a cat, a human or any being, even an imaginary one. It only becomes a definite proposition when *x* is specified – say, to 'my friend John Jones is hurt'. This specification of a particular person or thing involves clear asymmetrical discriminations. On the other hand, phrases like 'hurtness is happening', 'rage is occurring', 'adoration is' and 'there is threat' are all more or less propositional functions. These refer to endogenous *moods*, and it appears that something close to them populate the unconscious.

In summary, Matte Blanco considers that through symmetrization the *unconscious deals largely with propositional functions* and not with fully specific logical propositions. Similarly, as just mentioned, the unconscious does not deal with fully defined classes, which are definite collections of different members. Rather it deals with abstract class attributes, notions or conceptions (hatefulness, loneliness, lovingness, mousiness, cattiness or humanness and so on) which are the equivalent of the propositional functions of the class. The same phenomenon repeatedly impresses itself. The unconscious largely deals not with particular logically asymmetrically locatable subjects and objects, but with abstract attributes, qualities or notions. Put in another way, these propositional functions are adjectival and adverbial; they lie behind verbal nouns: lovingness, frighteningness and so on.

So propositional functions or abstract attributes are fundamental constituents of the unconscious. It is perhaps the most revolutionary contribution of bi-logic.

Matte Blanco points out that we are in good company. Freud in 'The Unconscious' (1915: 204) wrote: 'We may, on the other hand, attempt a characterisation of the schizophrenic's mode of thought by saying he treats concrete things as though they were abstract.' Though not a quote directly about the unconscious as such, this can be inferred since, for Freud, both schizophrenic thought and the unconscious operate largely with primary process.

Skelton (1990a, 1992), as seen in Chapter 3, refers to this sort of 'promiscuous' unconscious use of abstractions as *predicate thinking*. Here the specificity of the subject and object of a proposition are of such little interest that they are interchangeable; all that matters is the predicate of the thought. Skelton also drew attention to the fact that this was first noted as a characteristic of schizophrenic thinking by Von Domarus (1944), and then used by Calvin Hall (1954), before Matte Blanco's ideas crystallized. Segal (1957) also began thinking along these lines many years ago, when she differentiated *symbolic equations* from truly differentiated symbols. However, it is Matte Blanco who has systematically developed this question.

It is of interest that logicians appear to have focused on a similar area of functioning when discussing *equivalence relations* (indicated by an equals sign '='). They note, 'every equivalence is expressed by some sameness predicate' (Hodges 1977: 187). What is more, when such predicates are drawn together, the result is called the 'abstraction' of the predicates. The words chosen are remarkably similar to ours. Perhaps this is not surprising since we are finding out that the unconscious is remarkably adept at handling great numbers of equations, samenesses, equivalences, or = s at the same time. But it does this by selectively ignoring many asymmetries and difference relations which would be recognizable to consciousness. What is gained on the roundabouts is lost on the swings.

Concluding: the remarkable unconscious facility for the intuitive detection of similarities is of constant use in *rapid* evaluations; it is also a central characteristic of emotional thought. There are drawbacks; its very quickness is prone to promote *prejudices* which readily remain untamed, and become antisocial. When such instantaneous evaluations abound and then go out of the central ego's control, mental breakdown is likely.

Kenneth Wright, in a personal note, adds this important conclusion:

> The notion of 'rapid evaluation' links symmetrization clearly to the processes of actually living and responding in immediate ways in the world, rather than to the relative luxury of thinking and reflecting. In the primitive world, what is important initially is to know what sort of thing is looming up – not the kind of thing that it is not! In the wild, life would depend upon this; and it would be better to kill an innocent intruder than to miss a dangerous one. It's often struck me quite forcefully that life in the raw has to be built on paranoid premises. It seems that the 'fight/flight' response of the organism fits well with symmetrical or predicate thinking.
>
> (Wright 1993: personal communication)

## Some clinical illustrations using bi-logic

In what ways do the highly generalized concepts of symmetry and asymmetry contribute to the therapeutic process? The clinician usually has to face a welter of patients' particular patterns each day with the help of a rather disparate array of bits of theory. Bi-logic's very generality helps make quicker sense of what the clinician hears and he or she is thus less prone to get tired. A highly generalized framework, like Matte Blanco's, can be useful as long as it truly corresponds with the forms of the patient's unconscious, and bi-logic does this very well. Here are some possible lines of thought in this direction.

### *The ordinary person's natural logicality*

Psychoanalytic therapists, trained to deal with irrationality, may underestimate the importance of a person's sensitivity to the inconsistencies in chains of thoughts. However, logical thought of a simple sort is vital to the individual's attainment of any desires, even the most libidinous. Preoccupation with formal logic alone has a cold and narrow scope, but logic at an intuitive level is at the core of any social–verbal living, including therapy.

51

## *The precise spelling out of symmetrizations*

Patients naturally cannot use complex argument during a session, but the simple spelling out of logical steps is rarely felt as wasteful by them.

One major use of bi-logic by the analyst is the careful pointing out of the *identities* or equivalences that are experienced by the patient at different levels of feeling. This is the region of *transference* interpretation, and consists of the systematic pointing to specific *symmetrizations*. The conscious mind appears able to encompass up to half a dozen people or things being brought together at any one time and experiences them as the *same*. It is probably essential for experiences to be *combined* like this for establishment in *future memory*. What is helpful is the clarification that, at one level, a thing is known to be just *similar* (the same but also different) to another, while at the same moment, at another level of the feeling, it is experienced as absolutely the *same*. The words I use to indicate this experience of identity tend to be in the form: 'X *is* Y', 'X *just is* Y', or '*is the same as*', or '*equals*'. Laurie Ryavec, an American colleague, uses '*is equivalent to*'. She adds that some patients are most keen to spell out these equivalences for themselves. She thinks it is the more fragile borderline patients who find this detailed spelling out most useful.

We are here in the region of Segal's (1957) *symbolic equations*. She was concerned with the gross equations in psychotic conscious processes. Our equivalences are often unconscious but not necessarily repressed and can easily be unfolded.

Here are two examples of spelling out the symmetrizations, not from borderline-psychotic patients, but from people being slightly 'ordinarily mad' at the time.

EXAMPLE 4.4

A man was particularly bothered about expressing aggressive thoughts and this had come up on many occasions in several years of analysis. He recalled in one session that he had gone to bed at 10.30 the previous evening instead of his usual 12.30 a.m. and had fallen fast asleep. His wife, forgetting he had done this, came in and carried on her usual routine, switching on the light to go to bed at 11.30. He was suddenly woken and utterly furious: 'I could have killed her, it was terribly intense' he said most seriously to his analyst. Then he must have heard himself going on too earnestly about aggression for he broke out chuckling at himself. This self-observant mood made it easy for the analyst to say that he must have felt like killing her because sleep being interrupted at that moment would be the same as his very life being interrupted. He thought this was right and said that perhaps his murderousness had a bit of justification at times, but it could be ridiculously excessive if loss of sleep were the same as loss of life. Incidentally, common parlance supports this equation, for we say 'I am dead tired' and so on.

EXAMPLE 4.5

Another patient said that she felt absolutely dreadful; but she thought that other people would be unlikely to understand why.

Her youngest child, Jim, aged 11, had just gone off to boarding-school for the first time. After ups and downs in the first weeks he now seemed very happy with the place. 'But I feel awful – there's me feeling awful, while he rang yesterday and was singing. I am convinced this school is the right place for him, and can't blame anyone for I organized it all myself.' She then hazarded an explanation: 'The fact is, I feel I am losing my body – a part of myself has disappeared.'

The analyst and patient together then worked out the following samenesses or equivalences. First: Jim was once inside her (during her pregnancy) = Jim is inside her = Jim is part of her = Jim is her. Second: Jim has gone to board at school = Jim has left her house = Jim has left her = Jim has left her body = (since Jim is her) she has left her body = her body has left her.

At first sight this is pedantic but the patient by no means thought so. It made perfect sense and probably helped break her painfully depressed mood. Her conscious, asymmetrically articulated level of thinking, which recognized differences, was *combined in one thought* with a symmetrized emotional level of mental activity. Previously this confluence of levels must have been felt as clashing contradictions. The patient's conscious sanity then held itself together only by a very tight and sterile mental grip which came with depression. When the analyst verbally addressed the confluence of levels, the patient tuned-in to his words and then could move in ideas again, coalescing several views at once and the depression lifted – for the time being at least.

Of course, this process of stating the identity, sameness, equivalence or symmetry between apparently disparate ideas is old, for this is just what psychoanalytic transference interpretation itself is about. Matte Blanco has simply added a precise way of bringing together difference discriminating functions of the mind with those of sameness experience – asymmetry and symmetry.

53

## *Anti-logicality*

Let us turn from logic-seeking to how a child's logical functioning can be most vulnerable to another person's conscious intention to destroy it. We have been familiar for years with brain-washing by the use of repeated threats by secret-police interrogators. Similar understanding has recently been gathered of what can happen between ordinary sexual abusers and their child victims.

Many consistent abusers, especially if they ritualize it, go to lengths to *excite* themselves and their child victims by systematic *perversion of* normal *logical forms*. For example, the abuser will often initiate the child into a sort of secret language or code, full of innuendo, which is exciting just because it flouts everyday verbal–logical usage. Thus the child may be taught that when the abusing adult uses the word 'nasty' it means 'nice', and vice versa; 'good' equals 'bad'; 'bum' equals 'mouth'; 'willy' (penis) means 'tongue'; 'fanny' (vagina) equals 'bum' and so on. The child is being tempted into symmetrizations which are remarkably exciting.

It is strange for most of us when we hear that this simple flouting of logicolinguistic rules has such potential for excitement. However, it is an extreme and malignant variant of the ordinary delight of being naughty; when erotic zones are introduced into the game, the pleasure is multiplied tenfold so that its orgasms can become just as perversely compulsive for the child as for the adult. Thus, abuse of logic can play an arousing foreplay part in a perversely sexualized orgasmic sequence. At the same time threats may be used to terrify the child into submission. With this admixture of threat and excitation the child is hooked.

The long-term effect on the abused child can be chronic erotization of thought. The ritual flouting of logical contradiction can also lead to chronic thought confusion and thence to long-term intellectual impairment. The abused are often prone to become compulsive abusers themselves when adults. Here is a use of symmetrization for perverse ends.

Naturally other psychopathologies use quite different mechanisms. For instance, splitting is often endemic and this uses gross asymmetricalization. But here, too, bi-logic might be a useful investigative mode. There will be more clinical examples as the book continues, especially in Chapter 8 which is devoted to them.

# 5

# Bi-logic, affects and infinite sets

Let us now discuss some of Matte Blanco's deductions, which introduce *infinity* as a working concept into psychoanalysis for the first time. This brings us to what might be an important watershed – the individual's *experience of infinity*.

## The concept of infinity

Matte Blanco begins by being intrigued by two phenomena he spotted when engaged with emotional as well as unconscious matters. The first is the frequency with which a *whole and part* of something can be *felt as the same* (see Chapter 3). For instance, Matte Blanco mentions a schizophrenic woman who, after a blood test, developed a delusion. At times she complained that her blood had been taken away from her, at others that her whole arm had been removed. You will recall how other body parts, the penis for instance, can be equated even in non-psychotic people with the whole body and the self. The same part = whole equation can happen more widely with ideas about classes and sets of things, as when we equated a baby with all touchable things.

The second thing that Matte Blanco saw was that not only does the mind tend to generalize at emotional all-or-nothing levels but it is also prone to *maximalize*. This happens, for instance, in dramatization when we say 'everyone was desolated' meaning that quite a lot of people were upset, or 'this country is mad' when a government minister has made a silly pronouncement, and so on.

Could these two related phenomena, part = whole equation and maximalization, somehow be comprehensively understood? Convinced as he was that some of the basic concepts of mathematics reflect essential func-

55

tions in mental life, Matte Blanco naturally turned to the concepts of mathematical logic. He then made the deductions described in this chapter, which are remarkable and could hardly have been arrived at except through a mathematically tuned psychoanalytic mind.

Searching for a mathematical equivalent in set theory for the 'part being the same as the whole', Matte Blanco asked the question: 'In mathematics, *when is a sub-set equivalent to the whole set?*' (i.e. when does a part or sub-set have as many members as the whole set?). This sounds bizarre but a mathematical answer was discovered by Georg Cantor in the last century. It is: '*only when the set is infinite*'. This is Matte Blanco's first fundamental step.

A rough explanation is quite simple. One way in which an infinite set can loosely be defined is that it is a collection where *the counting of its elements or members does not, conceptually, come to an end*. In other words, there is *no limit to the counting*. The parallel *psychological experience* arising from confrontation with an infinite set is naturally that of 'non-finiteness' or *limitlessness*, of there being no end, no boundary, no constriction, no control, a *lack of negative feedback* and so on. These *infinite experiences* are commonplace and easily recognized by introspection.

An example using a series of numbers will make the peculiar mathematical paradox, of a part being equivalent to the whole, more comprehensible. Take the set of all *whole* numbers 1, 2, 3, 4, . . ., etc. There is no limit here, it is an infinite set. Now take a part of this set, say the sub-set consisting of all *even* numbers. This sub-set (2, 4, 6, 8, . . .) is also infinite. If so, then the sets are of equivalent size, in which case every member of the set of whole numbers must have a *corresponding partner* in the set of even numbers. In other words, for every whole number there corresponds one and only one even number. For instance, to 1 corresponds 2, to 2 corresponds 4, to 3 corresponds 6, and so on *ad infinitum*. There are thus *as many even numbers as whole numbers*. This is true in spite of the fact that even numbers comprise only a sub-set of whole numbers. This is made plain by the fact that the set of whole numbers is also comprised of *odd numbers*. This part = whole equivalence is a most peculiar paradox which characterizes infinite sets but not finite ones.

Questions of infinity, infinities, and their types and levels are naturally by now a large body of theory in pure mathematics. There are in fact many conceivable forms of infinite sets. Note that we are talking about *conceivability*, not whether such infinities can actually occur in external reality; that would be a question for physics. Conceptually, a straight line can be an infinite number of kilometres long. A line a millionth of a millimetre long can, conceptually, be divided into an infinite number of lines. A point can take up an infinite number of positions inside a sphere a millionth of a millimetre across, and there can be an infinite number of such spheres.

There can thus conceivably be an infinite number of any infinity. These can conceptually go on up to an infinite number to the power of infinity, to the power of infinity and so on to the power of infinity. There can be infinities of smallness and infinities of largeness, intensive and extensive infinities, and so on *ad infinitum*. Incidentally, all the infinities described here arise out of sequential ordering, but there are, I believe, others; for instance, those derived from division by zero. This, however, is beyond our scope.

An infinity can still be *bounded* or *contained* by a finite boundary. This is evident in our case of the millionth of a millimetre sphere and the infinity of conceivable points inside it. In the psychotherapeutic realm there is a very real parallel question. This lies in the task of finding boundaries and of limiting or containing infinite experiences – a task of serious importance to the therapist when dealing with a *manic process*, for instance. We shall mention this again.

As it is, the study of self-perpetuating complex organizations, Systems Theory, may be beginning to be of prime importance to present-day psychoanalysis. It seems worth while to try to see if the concept of infinity has a place in such a framework. It then soon becomes apparent that an experience of infinity can arise when a *negative feedback* or control function does *not* occur. This must happen when a limit-setting function, a 'super-ego' control element perhaps, is loosened or lost for whatever reason. Likewise, an infinity can arise in circumstances of a *positive* feedback 'running away with itself'. Perhaps in this region lie two of humankind's most powerful emotions: the joy of *freedom* and the dread of *chaos*. Specifically, emotional infinitization gives rise to *mania*, which will be discussed later.

These findings suggest that there is a use for a phenomenological approach, a mathematical-introspective thinking, in the psychoanalysis and psychology of the future. Matte Blanco thinks that the mathematician's very refined conception of infinity rests on a similar experiential basis to that of emotional and unconscious intuitions. For him they are, including mathematical infinity, all bi-logical structures – the product of symmetrization in interactive combination with asymmetrical processes.

Some mathematicians have been interested in Matte Blanco's ideas; many others are more sceptical. This is not surprising because he and they are working with rather different orders of phenomena. As already mentioned, Matte Blanco's great gift has been to discriminate mathematical intuitions or preconcepts that we all experience and use every day. Professional mathematicians begin with the same basic intuitions but then develop them and their complex combinations in making inferences that are necessarily rigorously consistent in a logical way. Thus, mathematicians and Matte Blanco start with similar intuitions but part company and develop their use in quite different fields: the mathematician's aim is consistent inference, Matte Blanco's is psychological insight.

In the psychological realm Matte Blanco is on more certain ground. Having introduced the concept of infinity, he has been able to show how omnipresent is its experience in our everyday lives – not only in the unconscious but also in waking emotionality. It is a quiet discovery that contains genius: from symmetry to part = whole, to mathematical infinity, thence to its omnipresence in experience. What specific light does it throw on psychoanalytic thought and therapy?

## Infinite experiences

Once alerted, it is surprising how frequently an experience with some feeling of infinity or unlimitedness emerges in what a patient, or anyone, says when speaking emotionally and with emphasis.

Here are a few common *mood* phenomena first pointed out by Matte Blanco. However, the elaborations here are the present author's. *Omniscience* clearly has an infinite basis. An omniscient idea contains the notion, 'I can know everything that it is possible to know' or 'there is no limit to my knowing'. If a limit is acknowledged, a *negation* occurs and the conception becomes a *bounded* sweep or grandness of thought; it is a contained infinite experience. A moment of introspection tells one that the difference of affective tone between a bounded and unbounded omniscience is obvious; the one has steady self-confidence in it, the other excited overconfidence. *Omnipotence* likewise involves an infinite set: 'I can do all conceivable things, there is no limit to my power.' Shakespeare was aware of this when he wrote:

> *Glendower.* I can call spirits from the vasty deep.
> *Hotspur.* Why so can I, or so can any man; But will they come when you do call for them?
>
> (Henry IV, Part 1)

Such self-expansion must often have wishful and defensive roots. Probably any *dramatic exaggeration* uses an infinity, whether it be manic-hysterical at root or a valuable evocative gesture to bring out an emotional truth.

Rodney Bomford (1992) has shown how often metaphor and other figures of speech can be used subtly to imply an infinity. For instance, repetitions like 'again, and again, and again' or 'into the far, far distance' evoke an instantaneous sense of infinity. In music, too, there are many ways that indicate infinity, such as the soaring sound of many violins in a symphony orchestra or the flights of a church organ. The electric guitar or keyboards in pop music often do the same.

*Impotence* can at root be seen as 'I cannot do all conceivable things' which is the same as 'I can do nothing'. Here the start is with a negation but it is infinitely extended. It is a negative infinity. In *idealization* the self is not conceived as omnipotent or omniscient, but another object is endowed with infinity while the self remains safely impotent or infinitely small. The guilt-reducing and defensive value of this is obvious.

All these can be lasting emotional states, or *moods*. Notice their importance; a mood is a state *without as yet a specific or particular object*. It is not a particular object relation, but seems to be a state of *self-readiness* for a certain sort of happening. Different moods have different 'postures' of the self in relation to the world – a looking down on things in omniscience or cowed looking up in impotence, and so on. These are often pathological but many are valuably adaptive. The non-specificity or objectlessness of a mood often allows it to be a state of readiness to make quick responses to many different objects which have some simple feature in common. Thus when in a 'car driving mood' one is in a state of alertness for other things on the road but not particularly for spotting butterflies or what is on the back seat. Moods deal in generalities, they are more symmetrized than specific object states. Being relatively objectless they tend to infinities. And if a mood is crudely applied to a specific object then *prejudice* is very likely to emerge. Note here the biological *survival* value of the general infinities that occur in moods.

Matte Blanco suggests that many emotions can be examined in their cognitive aspects under a similar light. Consider a few extreme or intense states. Take *being in love*. It would be absurd and emotionally untruthful for a lover to express his feelings by saying 'I am in love with you for a finite time and only in specific locations'. Rather the true lover feels that it is timeless, no matter where the lover might be. At its height the loved one's beauty is all beauty and their love is all love. Infinities are ruling, parts can be equal to wholes, time and space stand still. It could be said that armies of symmetrization are on the move. From another point of view idealization, with its infinities, pervades the lover.

In extreme *fear*, say of the dark, one is not afraid of a specific robber or murderer but of the essence of an unknown and unlocatable threat. In fact when something is located in reality, the particular extreme fear or *panic* is transformed at least into no more than useful fear. It appears that panic is the result of an unbounded, infinite, imagining or fantasy. The asymmetrical function of locating its source brings the panic within limits. This will be seen in Chapter 8 as one of the functions of a therapeutic process. It may be that much cognitive-behavioural therapy works in this region.

Take *grief*. This is the result of a locatable experience in real time, of loss, of the end of a relationship. Its root is thus finite and involves asymmetrical bivalently logical processes. But at its height grief irradiates, everything good is lost for all eternity. The valuable therapeutic function of *generalization*, a product of symmetrization, can be seen in the mourning process. Grief over one person lost often recalls many other losses, so that the mourning of one encompasses the mourning of others. By this means an *overall maturation* of character may be achieved as we go through a deep life experience. This recalls Klein (1940) as well as many other authors on mourning.

Perhaps most important of all for psychopathology is the infinity in *mania* and any manic mechanism. By its nature *mania obliterates control* and containment, it inevitably seeks limitlessness. It is this escape from control and limits that is the joy of elation – and the triumph, terror and social destructiveness of mania.

Note that the enemy of mania is *control* whose policemen and soldiers, as it were, limit the grandiose-self by fighting with the weapons of negation. Such wars can appear not only in depression but in obsessional states as well. Mania can be as violently destructive of ideas as it is of people and things. Incidentally, being overcome by limitlessness probably occurs in many thought-blocks.

However, breaking free from a specific limit is essential in any originality, so that some *nearly* manic element must operate in any creativity. It is most obviously present in the ability to 'think big'. The key to the difference between the useful sub-manic state and pathological mania probably lies in the safe functioning of thinking coherently within the wide limits needed to contain some free infinities; this is intrinsic to *elation*.

These descriptions have been of extreme and all-embracing emotional states. They display qualities of irradiation and *maximalization*; they are endemic in dramatization whether it be for truthful or false purposes. Time can stand still, and space is enormous or nothing. If other extreme emotional states and moods are examined it is likely that an infinity will be found to rule there also.

What of the quieter, ordinary and muted emotions of the steady times of life? Matte Blanco contends that extreme emotions can be contained, perhaps pre- or unconsciously, as *nuclei* in any feeling. Then perhaps different emotions are combined preconsciously together in muted affects. They do not run wild like untamed animals; they are perhaps contained or delimited by cognitive networks of asymmetrical awarenesses combined with symmetries such as are typical of many specific object relations. If this view is correct, it can be concluded that in *their cognitive aspects* all *affects* contain elements of *symmetrical logic* which take the form of *experiences of infinite sets*. Hence *affects are bi-logical structures*.

One of Matte Blanco's great contributions has been to emphasize the cognitive structuring that occurs in emotion. We saw in Chapter 2 how there is a 'Janus-faced' awareness in emotion so that external and internal worlds can be comprehended together. Emotions are essential evaluative processes and Matte Blanco has provided a means for their psychoanalytic investigation.

EXAMPLE 5.1

Here are some instances of infinity and emotion. It is possible to make a (very) rough 'rank-order' of the affects in each of the following groups of emotions, in terms of the 'proportion of infinity' in the emotion; it makes an amusing exercise. Thus, in the group 'adulation, admiration, respect' it would probably be largely agreed that 'adulation' contains more infinity than 'respect'. Now put the following in a similar order:

(a) Liking, adoration, love
(b) Loathing, annoyance, dislike, hate
(c) Amazing, interesting, inspiring
(d) Striking, impressive, noticeable.

## Unrepressed unconscious as infinite sets

We now turn to the words of Matte Blanco himself. You will need to attune yourself to his thought, which is in a different rhythm or idiom from this book so far. Some of this chapter will now consist of his quotes (with much condensation, marked by . . .). Clarifications by the present author linking the quotations are in square brackets, '[ ]'. Much of what is said here by Matte Blanco has been mentioned already, but it adds something of a flavour of his thought.

For those unacquainted with Matte Blanco, the present author's prose may at first sight be easier to follow, but it has none of his astringent, evocative imagination, leaps of curiosity and sudden illuminations. For all his repetitiousness he has a capacity to dance and fly with ideas in order to light upon strangenesses in thought, upon unexpected paradoxes and painful antinomies. His capacity to inspire honest, searching thoughtfulness is probably as important to the reader as his specific theoretical contributions. This book offers no such enthralling journeys; Matte Blanco himself must be read.

After affirming that there is a distinction between the *unrepressed* and the *repressed* unconscious, as Freud did, Matte Blanco suggests that much of our mental life is unconscious, simply because *consciousness cannot manage symmetries except in small doses*. This is a core reason for the existence of the unrepressed unconscious. Much of unconscious content is, for Matte Blanco, still dynamically repressed for defensive purposes just as Freud specified, but a new picture emerges of why other content is not conscious.

In Matte Blanco's view there is a *structural* or organizational reason for much mental content being unconscious, and this is quite different from repressing into the unconscious. His reasoning is as follows: because symmetries and infinities can only be managed by consciousness in small doses they only emerge in glimmers. The reflective person watches out for these slight signs from his feelings; others may be blind to them. This is described further in Chapter 8 which returns to discussion of the idea of 'unfolding' in the therapeutic process.

We shall now turn to the concept of infinite sets. To give a direct idea of Matte Blanco's words on these we begin by quoting him just after he has quoted Freud on Schreber about God and Flechsig (Schreber's psychiatrist) who is often called 'God Flechsig'. Matte Blanco says:

> Schreber treats two elements of this class of fathers (God and Flechsig) as identical in so far as they belong to the same class. . . . The unconscious substitution of the identity between the elements of a class for the equivalence between them, *within the class*, results in a blurring of the limits between the individuals. . . . *The unconscious does not know individuals but only classes or propositional functions which define the class*.
>
> (1975: 138–9)

From this discussion of the blurring of part and whole within classes, Matte Blanco goes on to consider another instance of part = whole, that of part and whole objects.

> We may say that an individual mother . . . is an element of . . . the set of all mothers. The propositional function [attribute, conception or notion] which defines this class of mothers . . . would contain . . . pregnancy, which implies the womb, and that of breast feeding, which implies the breast. . . . [However, with the operation of] symmetry . . . the breast is identified with the class of all mammal mothers. But this . . . is a sub-class of a more general class of mothers in which any action of (loving) giving is considered as breast feeding . . . . This is very visible when the patient feels that the analyst withdraws the breast: he feels he is being deprived of a supreme treasure.
>
> (1975: 143)

You will notice that with the idea of the breast as a 'supreme treasure' we are entering the realm of infinity. This leads us to a new step.

## The unconscious dealing in extremes

Matte Blanco continues:

> In the early days psychoanalysis . . . always referred to whole persons
> [more recently part objects have been added]. . . . We always assume
> these to have the maximum of the potentialities connected with the
> concept. . . . The unconscious cannot conceive of a given quality in
> a small degree: the good breast, for instance, is not mildly good;
> maximum goodness is attributed to it. This is just the expression of
> the replacement of the individual by the class, of the identity between
> the part and the whole. . . . So, at deeper levels . . . the individual
> either has the good breast or the good mother . . . or it does not have
> it, or her, at all. In this latter case . . . mother (or breast, etc.) is
> bad. . . . Then it becomes supremely bad. . . . Zero does not seem to
> exist for the unconscious, and this corresponds to Freud's absence of
> negation.
>
> (1975: 143–4)

Matte Blanco here bears comparison with Klein's (1946) description of
polarization in the paranoid–schizoid position.

At this point it is important to stop and dwell for a time upon the
question of infinity and the paranoid–schizoid position. The question of
splitting and what part it plays in Matte Blanco's bi-logical model was
raised first in Chapter 3 and has been referred to several times since. He
would probably have done more justice to many aspects of psychopathology if he had investigated splitting and polarization in his bi-logical
models more centrally and insistently.

As already mentioned, Elizabeth Spillius with her Kleinian expertise has
privately raised this systematically and cogently. Her main point is that
asymmetries are not the only things that are ignored or obliterated in the
unconscious. In gross splitting or dichotomization into extreme *good* or
*bad*, it is *similarities*, that is symmetries, which are clearly *obliterated*. For
instance, this is clearly evident in any severe prejudice. Thus a bigoted
Christian may be prone to feel that all Muslims are totally bad religiously,
and of course the sentiment can be reciprocated by a bigoted Muslim. The
same is just as evident in racism, sexism and probably an 'ism' of any kind.
In these cases an asymmetry, the difference between Christian and Muslim
say, is accentuated while human qualities common to both are obliterated.
Thus, in splitting, asymmetries are accentuated while symmetries are
expunged. Gross asymmetrization occurs in splitting.

There is an important corollary to this, which Spillius also notes. It
seems that in gross splitting, not only is there accentuation, but *asymmetrization tends to infinity*. Infinities certainly abound in the unconscious.

However, they are not just those of symmetry, but, because splitting is endemic, there are also *infinities of asymmetry* which abound in the unconscious.

If this is so, Matte Blanco's particular model (especially the 'stratified structure' to be discussed in Chapter 6) needs to be amended by including unconscious splitting with its attendant infinitized asymmetries. This must be a natural feature of a paranoid–schizoid organization.

What would Matte Blanco say in reply? He might say that this book has done him an injustice. There is no doubt that Matte Blanco said little or nothing about actual splitting in his first great book (1975). By the time of writing *Thinking, Feeling and Being* (1988) he fully gripped the importance of projective identification and other facets of paranoid–schizoid structures, including splitting, and goes to great lengths to investigate them using the tools of bi-logic. It can be said that he fully understood the process of splitting and took it for granted without writing about it very much. He well understood paranoid–schizoid mechanisms and saw them to be of prime importance.

Juan-Francisco Jordan has drawn attention in a personal communication to the fundamental importance Matte Blanco attaches to a mental function that amounts to splitting. This lies in his conception of the 'fundamental antinomy of being and world' (Matte Blanco 1988: 77–99). The concepts Matte Blanco uses here are undoubtedly of a phenomenological and philosophical nature and alien to the more mechanistic thinking of ordinary psychoanalysis; but they are also undoubtedly addressing a question of dichotomization in a similar manner to splitting.

However Spillius's observation, that the part played by the infinitization of asymmetries has been neglected by Matte Blanco, still appears to stand. The necessary revision of theory does not appear difficult and would enhance the general usefulness of bi-logic.

Spillius's point, that gross splitting involves the infinitization of an asymmetry, particularly deserves close investigation. For instance, we have seen earlier in this chapter that infinity itself can be generated by a 'whole = part equation'. We have already seen that this is the product of symmetrization. So it appears that symmetrization plays a part in the infinite accentuation of an asymmetrical relation that occurs in splitting. This is an interesting paradox. It could be argued that, since symmetry plays a part in splitting, Matte Blanco has been right all along to give pride of place to symmetrization. It would then be necessary to ask what takes prior place. Does splitting with accentuation of asymmetry come first, to be followed by symmetrizations; or can splitting come as a mere corollary to symmetrization? There is no answer yet.

In summary: it appears that a more central inclusion of splitting and paranoid–schizoid processes enhances the bi-logical point of view. At the same time the bi-logical approach seems to contribute towards greater coherence in Kleinian theory.

## Emotion, infinity and thought

Matte Blanco thinks it curious that many of the same concepts which have been employed with regard to the unconscious as infinite sets apply equally to emotion. This poses the question of the relation between emotion and the unrepressed symmetrical unconscious. Psychoanalysis has been vague on this. He starts with a quotation about intense emotion from Plato, which begins with being in love and then discusses the wider aspects of love.

> Plato suggested . . . 'Because the right road of love . . . is to begin by the inferior beauties and to raise itself to the supreme beauty, passing, so to speak, through all degrees of the scale from one beautiful body to two, from two to all others, from the beautiful occupation to the beautiful sciences until from science to science one arrives at the science par excellence, which is no other than the science of the beautiful itself, and one concludes by knowing it as it is in itself.'
>
> (Plato 1946, vol. 2, *Symposium* C–D)

[Matte Blanco then takes over]:

> It is interesting to note that . . . Plato arrives at the love of the science of the beautiful. This would be the love not of one individual, but of an abstract thing: the beautiful. These remarks are reminiscent of the replacement of the individual by the propositional function which defines the class. . . .
>
> If the propositional function that defines the class entails infinite love [or any other emotion], the intensity . . . may be felt in the unconscious to be infinite. . . . The action of psycho-analytic therapy consists of divesting persons [and] things . . . from their symbolic meaning (which itself leads to the confusion of the individual with the whole class) and transforming them [by] conscious thinking, into what they really should be, that is, circumscribed entities in which the halo of the class does not interfere with their . . . meaning, by making them appear more than what they actually are.
>
> (1975: 184–5)

## A phenomenological-psychoanalytical-logical approach

Matte Blanco, now well into the exploration of emotion by introspection, moves into it as simply a personal experience at the level of consciousness. It is a good sample of his meticulousness. He links emotion with physiology and finally, after many pages of thought, reaches an important conclusion about the relation of emotion to thinking. It is close to Bowlby's view given in Chapter 2. Here is a short version of this thought-chain and its ending; it is included here particularly because it is typical of Matte Blanco's way of arguing.

> We [have] known since . . . the Greeks [of] the distinction between three basic expressions or varieties of psychical phenomena: *thinking, feeling, and willing or striving. . . .* [However, emotion] *in its very nature must be viewed as a psycho-physical phenomenon. . . .* If I am afraid, my heart may beat faster than usual and I may become pale. Faster pulse and paleness . . . are *integral aspects of that phenomenon called fear.* Similarly, tense muscles may be considered integral aspects of the emotion which is called expectation. . . .
>
> Each emotional state conforms to a quite specific *pattern* of physical events, even if the elements of the pattern . . . are the same for all emotions.
>
> *We may conclude that, seen from the point of view of introspection, emotion is experienced, not as a mental but as a psycho-physical event.*
>
> (1975: 217–18)

## The first component of emotion

### *The passage of sensation-feeling to image and perception*

[Matte Blanco's argument, gathering steam, goes like this:]

*The initial 'pure' experience of the senses always blossoms into an image. From this it proceeds until it develops into a perceptual experience.*

This perceptual experience may be of two kinds: it may consist of an actual evaluation or estimation of the sensation in terms of the nature of the [alien] stimulus. . . . Alternatively, in a second type one re- mains within the limits of the sensory experience . . . without turning to the actual external world. A *comparison* is then made in terms of past experiences; that is in terms of former perceptions without giving a judgement as to the actual nature of the stimulus. . . . [In both cases] *propositional activity* takes place, . . . which naturally entails . . . propositional functions. . . . [Thus,] the initial experience of the senses is submitted to a process of propositional activity . . . [this is] a process of thinking, or establishment of relations. [In the circumstances] when an actual perception cannot occur . . . then we resort [even more] to a utilisation and at times an elaboration of past perceptual experiences. This is the work of . . . imagination.

(1975: 224–5)

### Sensation, consciousness and attention

Matte Blanco now turns from looking outwards, as it were, to largely interoceptive sensations. Having recognized the unconscious sensations arising from physiological processes, he sees that a *conscious* psychological process comes into play when the sensations go above a certain threshold. Consciousness always comes into play through the activity of *attention* (this, incidentally, is probably the very central act of *localization*, which is essentially asymmetrical). He comes to this conclusion:

*Objectless attention does not exist in consciousness.* . . . However . . . if we have a *perception* . . . we have sensation inextricably mixed . . . with establishment of relations, that is, with thinking. . . . So sensation seems to be born in consciousness in a naked state . . . [but] in order not to disappear immediately from *existence*, [it] needs to be clothed in thoughts [and meaning], that is establishment of relationships. . . .

The dentist's chair is a good laboratory [for examining these experiences] . . . if one tries to escape . . . pain, one will feel it all the more. If one does not shrink from it, but tries instead to define exactly what it consists of, several interesting facts soon become evident. . . . Defining these images consists of making the relations existing between the parts more precise . . . towards a more precise perception . . . one which is more permeated with establishment of (asymmetrical) relations. . . . We are trying to bring the establishment of relations into the focus of attention, correspondingly the proportion of pure sensation . . . must necessarily diminish. . . . It is in this way that we are able to bear pains that otherwise would be quite intolerable.

(1975: 230–1)

### The progress from sensation to awareness of relations and then to thinking

[Matte Blanco observes:]
By its very nature sensation is not at ease in the macular [central]

region of consciousness whereas it belongs naturally in the periphery
. . . . The macular region, the fullness of consciousness, in contrast, is
the natural territory of the establishment of [asymmetrical] relations
. . . . When we [introspectively] wish to become fully conscious of
our being conscious, then our consciousness of being conscious
becomes blurred. . . . We can [only do this] in a tangential, fleeting
way. . . . In order to grasp it, our attention must move from one
point to another.

Compare these remarks with the observations by neurophysi-
ologists. When we look our eyes are never still but . . . move quickly
from one point to another of the object looked at. This rapid
movement can be recorded. . . . If we try to look at one point . . .
our vision becomes blurred: in order to look we must move our eyes.
Exactly the same seems to be the case with the 'mental vision' of
consciousness.

(1975: 231–2)

### The timeness of thinking and 'timelessness' of feeling

Having started with emotion and proceeded to sensation-feeling, Matte
Blanco slowly works his way back towards *thinking in the setting of emotion.*

Consciousness . . . soon becomes exhausted and attention must be
shifted to another point which is still 'unused'. This peculiarity of
consciousness is appropriate for thinking but not for sensation-
feeling. Thinking, establishment of relations, is essentially an analytic
process which subdivides its object into its elements . . . [not so
sensation-feeling]. . . . [Pain, for instance] is *felt* as simple, as one
unity . . . while thinking is *experienced as a complex unity*, a structure
made of many aspects or *parts*. Thinking . . . *develops in time*, whereas
sensation-feeling is simply *there*. . . . Feeling, having neither previous
nor present or subsequent elements, may be said to be *felt outside time*
. . . *it is experienced as something that does not happen but is, simply is.*

(1975: 231–4)

### The second component of emotion: thinking

Matte Blanco now turns to examine in more detail the propositional
activity that occurs in emotions. He goes through various strong emotions,
as we did in the last chapter: a man in love with a beautiful girl, fear of the
dark, discouragement, sadness, anger and so on. He finally summarizes his

reflections about emotions and propositional activity as follows:

> The thinking implicit in emotions entails generalisation, maximis-
> ation and irradiation.
>
> Emotion in so far as it is emotion, does not know individuals but
> only classes or propositional functions and, therefore, when
> confronted with an individual, tends to identify these individuals
> with the class to which it belongs (or the propositional function
> applied to it).
>
> Once we arrive at this simple formulation, the mysteries of emo-
> tion begin to become understandable. . . . If propositional activity is
> a constituent aspect of emotion then we are immediately freed from
> the tremendous confusion that pervades the psychological literature,
> including the psychoanalytical, about the relationship existing
> between thinking and emotion. Everybody accepts the enormous
> influence that emotions have on thinking, but nobody, as far as I
> know, has been able to present a comprehensible account of how a
> link can be established between both. . . . Whenever we view an
> individual from the vantage point of our own emotions, the 'thinking
> aspect' of our emotion does not see an individual but a class, and this
> entails all the potentialities implicit in the corresponding propo-
> sitional function. But from the point of view of adult logical thinking
> what is seen is only an individual, *a member of a class* . . . not all the
> potentialities of this propositional function.
>
> (1975: 242–4)

## Discussion

One of the aims of the second part of this chapter has been to give an
opportunity to exercise with Matte Blanco's way of thinking at first hand.
It will have been noticed how densely packed are his thoughts and how
stringently precise he can be. The full text is many times longer than the
selections presented here. He moves here and there, seeing new ideas,
antinomies, ambiguities, contradictions, paradoxes or *non sequiturs* along
the way and wanders off to examine them. He is also repetitive. However,
each new reading seems to bring another discovery, for his ideas are
packed, even hidden, by their closeness. He is definitely difficult; but he
brings a new sort of searching, intellectual zest into psychoanalytic thought.

The pages summarized here are powerful. He says that in intellectual
history the notions of emotion and thought have found themselves
divided. This is not new. We have, for instance, mentioned Susanne
Langer's great contribution (1942) in bridging this division. However,

Matte Blanco, in his particular way, also shows how wrong it has been to contrast emotion and thought. Elements of the one are in the other. He has done this by teasing out phenomenologically the sensation-feeling and the thinking aspects of emotion. Then he concentrates upon what sort of thought can occur in emotion. Based upon his original logic of the symmetry–asymmetry dialectic, he shows how emotion is imbued with infinitized thought. What is more, this comes about because emotional thought intuitively dwells upon the propositional functions (abstract intuitions or notions in the language of this book) applying to the classes of things being emoted about. It is obvious when thought about, but it is new.

By showing how emotionality generally seems to have some central characteristics in common with those of the unconscious, Matte Blanco has posed a great question for us: should analysts talk simply of 'emotionality' instead of the time-honoured phrase 'the unconscious'? Rightly, Matte Blanco definitely does not agree to this substitution. He stresses that there are two important reasons why consciousness cannot embrace unconscious ideas. One is the act of *repression* (more generally, *defence*) which is needed to keep the conscious experience of intolerable anxiety at bay and away from consciousness. This stands just as strongly for him as for Freud. The second reason is, as we have seen, quite different: it concerns *structural* considerations. This is, that *consciousness cannot cope with much symmetry emerging* at any one time. Hence it cannot cope with the infinities present at the deeper more generalizing levels of feeling-thinking. This he sees as the *unrepressed* unconscious. So the particular systematic or structural nature of the unconscious with its differences from consciousness remains of central importance to psychoanalysis, even though many of its attributes can also be detected in emotions which have conscious aspects. As we know, conscious emotions are glimmering signs of what lies hidden. It might even be said that much of the unrepressed unconscious could be preconscious if it can be partially conscious in glimpses. However, this is not a question we can discuss here.

It was at this point that our discussion brought in Spillius's view that Matte Blanco's theory tends to emphasize symmetrization in the unconscious too exclusively. This means that he neglects the importance of splitting in the unconscious and the infinitizations of asymmetry that are part of this mechanism. We have leant towards agreeing with this, and see it as a useful critique by which the bi-logical approach can be enlarged.

Matte Blanco uses much introspective and phenomenological thinking, as the previous pages show. Out of this comes the idea that symmetry is a manifestation of the mind's mode of just *being*, while asymmetry comes from the mode of active *happening*. He also refers to 'just being' as the *indivisible* mode ('undivided', 'gestalt' or 'holistic' would be equally

70

appropriate). In contrast to this is the *divisible* mode (here 'divided', 'differentiating' or 'analytic' might be just as appropriate). His reasoning is that at symmetrized levels time and space stand still. There is no movement; here is a state of just being which is phenomenologically quite different from happening.

Matte Blanco has moved now into ontology. The present writer is frankly now on unsure ground; he is neither well acquainted nor exercised in this mode of thought, and is thus perhaps pedestrian by comparison. Matte Blanco's explanations here appear metaphysical and must not be objected to on that account; but to an empirical mind, proper explanation must bear a correspondence to the things explained. They must also be consistent with other explanations in an author's argument. The bi-logic of the combination of symmetry and asymmetry that we have been describing is on the whole specifically and logically defined and can be happily grasped by the empirically minded. 'Just being', on the other hand, seems to be in a different category and is less easy to grasp. Matte Blanco seems even to be mixing categories without warning. On the other hand, it must be admitted that good scientific empiricists (especially British ones) have not been very enthusiastic helpers of psychoanalysis. Perhaps it is the very phenomenological and idealistic clarity with enthusiasm of Matte Blanco that is the fresh air needed among the too-exclusively empirically minded British and North Americans.

It is useful at this point to bring in a valuable recent contribution by Carlo Strenger (1989). He uses Schafer's (1976) examination of underlying psychoanalytic attitudes under four contrasting philosophical visions: romantic, tragic, comic and ironic. Strenger modifies this and views the psychoanalytic movement in the light of two great contrasting philosophical visions or interpretations of reality. These are the classical and the romantic, both of which reached their finest crystallization in the eighteenth century: the classical vision was epitomized by Kant and the romantic by Rousseau. The classical attitude has a sceptical suspicion of human nature; it values most the striving for autonomy from base animal drives by using the fine discriminations of reason. It has an ironic and tragic view of existence. The romantic vision, on the other hand, sees supreme value in the development of individuality and in the rich spontaneity of subjective experience.

Freud himself, Strenger says, was certainly profoundly classical in his vision; he was pessimistic about humanity, ironic and tragic in outlook. It was his dislike of utopianism that pressed him to advise psychoanalysts to be 'cold like a surgeon'. However, there has also been a strong romantic impulse among some analysts. This can be seen in Ferenczi and later especially with Winnicott who emphasized the need for the 'true self' to find realization through spontaneity. A similar view also emerges in

Fairbairn, though in less romantic language. Strenger sees the quintessence of the romantic psychoanalytic vision as being expressed by Kohut (1971).

Strenger thinks that analysis inevitably engages at the axis of a tense emotional dialectic between the two philosophical visions; and he concludes that neither the classical nor the romantic is right in isolation. The dialectic must be comprehended, lived through and reconciled by every analytic thinker.

How does Matte Blanco fare in this light? He is certainly highly discriminating, asymmetric and intellectually rationalist, and thus a deeply rooted classical visionary. However, he is not by nature pessimistic, suspicious and ironic like Freud. His emphasis upon 'just being' and of the basic homogeny or oneness of mental life is romantic in nature. So in one dimension at least he is definitely romantic. Insofar as he sees the necessity of the dialectic between asymmetry and symmetry he shows some features of the need to find and reconcile the classical and romantic visions just as Strenger recommended.

Furthermore, Matte Blanco's emphasis upon the *dialectic* between asymmetry and symmetry, and between 'happening' and 'just being', does act as a fine antidote to *omniscience*. Pleasure in such grandiosity, with its infinite roots, is surely a crucial force for the maintenance of intolerant and arrogant certainties. The emphasis upon balancing symmetrical infinities with the other side of the dialectic, which is asymmetrical discrimination, perhaps ensures bi-logic's remarkable open-mindedness.

Summarizing the last few pages still further, we are helped to see that emotion is an aspect or stage in a thinking or problem-solving process. It is essentially a Janus-faced, holistic, gestalt or overall appraisal of outside and inside, of world and body, at the same time. It is a psychosomatic event. Problem-solving thinking now emerges out of the *frustration* experience of the problems which arise from emotional appraisals. Thinking now becomes less holistic; symmetry largely gives way to asymmetry; analysis has started. There is now an attempt to differentiate the essential elements in a situation and discover relations between those that will lead to a resolution of a problem.

This appears to be a process of *argument in thought*, a form of dialectic between holistic experience and appraisal on the one hand and analytic discrimination on the other. As the asymmetrical discriminations become more precise and definable, the dialectic becomes verbal-level argument.

Matte Blanco gives the opinion that symmetrical and asymmetrical modes interact, but they never quite meet to affect each other at their cores. Whether this be so or not, the interplay can certainly be wholly internal to a single individual, or it can be interpersonal or social. Whichever it is, at the near-conscious level it is best called argument. The dialectic shows itself as a process of proposing alternatives and comparing them with the aim of finding a resolution.

Though Matte Blanco says remarkably little about the physical life sciences, a reader can come away with two strong visions about biological processes. The first, mentioned earlier, is that symmetry involves sameness registration, so that it must be concerned with recognition and hence with the use of memory in the evolution of adaptation. The second is that dream research has recently pointed definitively to dreams having a central role in establishing long-term memory structures (Palombo 1978; Hartmann 1984). Thus both symmetry and dreams, which are of course full of symmetries, concern recognition and memory, and both are functions of the un-conscious. Hence it can be concluded that the unconscious is about memory and its vicissitudes.

Another vision has been spelt out already in the quotation from Kenneth Wright at the end of Chapter 4. This highlights another biological function of symmetrization. As the Janus image emphasizes, emotions are concerned with preliminary *appraisals* of external and internal at the same time. Such overall impressions of inwards and outwards can quickly grasp important issues with their dangers and values. Wright pointed to the primitive basic need to be paranoid to survive. Quick discrimination of friend or foe, prey or predator, is needed, at least in a predatory world. Here the mind must not get lost in unnecessary details. *Sweeping judgements are needed*, and the thought necessary for these is quick classification; crudeness does not matter, it is even an advantage. This is the essential outcome of symmetrization and infinitization. This is the fruit of emotion dwelling nigh exclusively with loose abstract notions or pro-positional functions rather than fully articulated and developed logical propositions. The same process was seen with regard to the emotionality of *moods*, which can be *states of readiness* with which to deal in broad categories and not with particular objects. Such emotionality may generate wild hysteria in the highly complex social living of today which demands much intensely articulated asymmetrical discrimination. But emotions are vital for survival.

# 6

# Psychic structure, space and dimensionality

Let us turn to some overall structural aspects of the mind that can be explored by the bi-logical method. Matte Blanco never attempts to construct an overall model of the mind but confines himself to various separate visions of mental functioning seen in a bi-logical light.

## The stratified bi-logical structure

This is an important conception (Matte Blanco 1988: 43–69): the mind has some sense of the 'proportion' of symmetrization in any experience. Some of the assertions here can be investigated and tested by the reader's own straightforward introspection.

The proposal is roughly this: those experiences that are entirely bounded or delimited by *asymmetrical* discriminations, as with an immediate and unemotional perception of the physical world, are consciously felt as having *no emotional depth*. However, when some measure of 'unbounded' or 'free' symmetrization occurs, there is an experience of an infinity, of course, but also of some emotional or psychic depth. What is more, the greater the proportion of symmetrization, the greater is the sense of depth as viewed from the level of consciousness. What is developed is a hierarchy of levels of experience from the most asymmetrically structured consciousness to the deepest unconscious which is virtually structureless. Here is a summary more or less in Matte Blanco's own words (1988: 52–4).

### First stratum: conscious and well-delimited objects

This stratum is that of the conception or perception of a well-delimited person or material object, or a well-defined thought referring to a particular

74

fact ('the temperature is rising'). This is the level of delimited and quite *asymmetrical* thinking or perception.

A second, also conscious, level of the same stratum would be that in which one becomes aware of or explores the relations between actual objects – their similarities and differences; and the classes to which such objects belong and do not belong.

### Second stratum: more or less conscious emotions

Here emotion makes its first appearance: 'I like it', 'I hate him', 'I fear him' and so on. These are bi-logical structures where symmetrizations begin to show, but they are well delimited and largely at the conscious level. For instance, one may feel, 'this person is like a tiger'; but a normal person will not feel he *is* a tiger. Incidentally, this is perhaps the level of thought and affect at which the cognitive-behavioural therapist predominantly addresses a patient.

### A third, deeper stratum: symmetrization of the class

Much of this level is normally unconscious. Things belonging to the same class become identical not only with regard to the property which defines the class in question, but also to all properties within it, so that each member becomes identical to all others in the class in all respects. Thus all the members of the class 'same race' or 'tall people' will only be known as identical to each other and the class attribute (this is the region of notions and propositional functions). Here is profound symmetrization. Each individual becomes the class. If the set is that of angry mothers, then she or any part of her, say the breast, will be felt as immensely dangerous or marvellously good. *Intensity* tends to infinite values. Aggressions are at their most intense. Matte Blanco says that Klein has masterfully explored this stratum and has found a rich harvest of strange, almost incredible, yet true and stimulating facts. It is to this stratum that moods may largely belong, though, like icebergs, they may show a small aspect of themselves above the level of consciousness. This, together with the second and fourth strata, will predominantly be the level at which the psychoanalytic therapist addresses a patient.

### Fourth stratum: formation of wider classes which are symmetrized

Here different classes or sets are known only as joined to become wider and more comprehensive sets. Thus the class of humans comprises that of men, women and children, so that, when symmetrized, to be a man is identical to being a woman or a child. Matte Blanco believes this is the stratum where some schizophrenics feel at ease. Here, with more symmetry, the great aggressions of the previous stratum are no longer found. Intense aggression requires a good proportion of asymmetry. This, Matte Blanco suggests, is important in understanding schizophrenia. Some tend to think that the emotions of schizophrenics are extremely intense. This is only partially true. Those who display extensive symmetrizations are frequently quiet 'serene' people.

### The deepest strata: the mathematical limit

From this point 'downwards' the amount of symmetrization is so vast that thinking, which requires asymmetrical relations, is greatly impaired.

The conceptual end is pure indivisibility, where every thing is everything else. The endless number of things tend to become, mysteriously, everything else.

### Discussion of the four strata

Matte Blanco's relating of the experience of depth to the *degree of symmetrization* is completely new. But, of course, there are other more usual ways to think of depth. For instance, an element of anything upon which *other things* rest, thus being *dependent* upon it, can be thought of as *deeper* than the dependent things. Hence the foundations of a house are thought of as deeper than the roof-tiles because the tiles depend for their place upon the foundations, and not conversely. Perhaps it is the same with mental depth; those structures upon which many other structures depend are felt to be deeper. These are different from Matte Blanco's idea, but perhaps they are not far apart, for are not our *deepest* feelings concerned with the *widest* generalizations? We know that wide generalization is related to degree of symmetrization, and we depend much upon this breadth to bring experience of depth.

Yet another meaning in the conception of depth comes from the integration of different points of view, as in binocular vision. This can produce a sense of dimensionality. Perceptually the greater the number of dimensions that are integrated together in one experience, the greater the feeling of depth. Thus three dimensionality has depth while one or two dimensions do not. We shall explore this more fully below.

It has been noticed several times that the model of the stratified structure rests centrally upon the idea of a correlation between degree of sym-metrization and the depth of the unconscious. In this model, as asymmetry comes to play less and less part, the deeper becomes the unconscious. We have also said previously that there is insufficient place for splitting and the infinitized asymmetrizations in Matte Blanco's models as they are at pre-sent. Unconscious splitting mechanisms appear to be of central importance to the unconscious mind, so their absence in the stratified structure seems to be an omission and the stratified model will have to be reshaped. However, this is not fatal to Matte Blanco's basic bi-logical approach.

The stratified structure is Matte Blanco's major essay into creating a model of the whole mind at work rather than the functioning of aspects of it. It does not pretend to be complete, nor the only one possible; it is simply one way of looking at the mind overall. It is different from both Freud's id, ego, super-ego model and, for instance, from Fairbairn's endo-psychic structure; but it is not intended to be a replacement for either.

It must be said again that a central limitation is that it contains no evolutionary or developmental aspect. Being only about the form of ideas and thus basically static, perhaps it is too exclusively Platonist for many tastes.

## The fundamental antinomy of being and world

The next step is to something new, but again it brings out Matte Blanco's emphasis upon a phenomenological inquiry which uses intensive and meticulous introspection with psychoanalytic intuitions and observation. Perhaps it is akin to French existential thinking; British and American psychoanalysis uses less meticulous introspection and often mixes it with empirical and biological evidence. Phenomenologists and empiricists often find themselves puzzled by each other. The author of this book is no exception and the reader must be warned that what follows is the work of a phenomenological amateur.

Upon the question of a 'fundamental antinomy', as he calls it, we have Matte Blanco at his least empiricist and most stirring, so it is best to proceed by following him closely.

An antinomy is *the incompatibility between two assertions which can claim equal rights to be true*. Matte Blanco thinks that in the very nature of human beings there is a co-presence of two modes – of asymmetry or 'happening' and symmetry or 'just being' – which are incompatible with one another. This is the antinomy. However, in spite of this they exist and appear together in the same subject. They appear together yet remain incompat-ible and never fuse to form a wider unitary concept which comprises both.

This antinomy is fundamental because it seems not only to be present in human beings but also elsewhere in the physical and living world. Matte Blanco speculates that when you see patients with their emotions you find that they present examples illustrating some fundamental philosophical questions that psychoanalysis is only now bringing to the fore. He says (1988: 73):

> Every time we stand before a bi-logical structure we are in front of the fact that the same reality is simultaneously treated as . . . divisible or heterogeneous, formed of parts and, . . . as if it were one and indivisible. This is probably the most important insight which follows from Freud's discovery of the laws which rule the unconscious, especially the non-respect of the principle of contradiction.

Matte Blanco goes on in this mode to emphasize that when abstraction occurs in *logical* thought, an identity (symmetry) is discovered; but it is immediately circumscribed by awareness that there are a great many properties that *distinguish* from each other the collection of items under scrutiny. There is, as it were, a coexistence of the two modes, both of which are fully operational. As there is no evident symmetrization it must remain consistent with two-valued logic. Matte Blanco calls this a *bi-modal* as distinct from a bi-logical structure. It looks like a form of cooperation between both modes. In fact he thinks they 'ignore' each other; 'they are so to speak solitary, yet always together. Only ourselves, as fully bi-modal beings, are able to see the advantage of this mutual setting of barriers' (1988: 79).

This insistence upon the mutual solitude, or independence, of the two sides of the bi-modality will not be entirely clear to many of us. Matte Blanco maintains that what appears to be a 'cooperation' is really only an appearance, but it is difficult to see how he can be sure of the completeness of this separation when, for instance, his whole thesis shows that our very lives are the fruit of their interaction. Interdependence seems more than a mere appearance. It might be that at great depth there can be a total independence between the two modalities, whereas at more superficial levels coalescence between their derivatives could take place. But it would be difficult to verify when and how this does or does not occur.

On the other hand, Jim Rose, in Matte Blanco's defence, has pointed out in a personal communication that any profound psychic conflict is essentially experienced as an antinomy. In like manner, Juan-Francisco Jordan has said that splitting is likewise an antinomy. In both these instances there are urgently important assumptions or beliefs which are experienced as vital, yet can only be known as utterly contradictory and incompatible. It is then the task of analysis to investigate whether this is true or not. Perhaps British empiricists should take more phenomeno-logical wings in the future.

It is of note that Matte Blanco's mode of thought in this puzzling region bears striking resemblances to Zen and perhaps other mystic disciplines; and he was in fact quite aware of this. For instance, the 'sartori' or state of enlightenment examined by Zen Buddhist masters (Suzuki 1949) is attained by a long and stringent discipline aimed at breaking up encrusted structures of category, verbal and objective thinking – asymmetrical discriminations in other words. The long and arduous master–pupil relation needed to attain sartori bears a resemblance to some aspects of the analytic relation. Sartori or enlightenment is the achievement of close to a oneness with infinity. 'In the state of enlightenment there are no categories, no words, no time, no things' is a crude approximation to a teaching of Zen masters. One master, when asked what enlightenment was, replied by saying nothing but 'no thing'.

## Space and mind

Though Freud did not develop theoretical concepts about *psychic space* explicitly, it has recently been much used (e.g. Bion 1963; Meltzer 1967; Winnicott 1971; Khan 1974; Bollas 1989; Stewart 1992). However, the underlying meanings embedded in the general concept of space itself have not been seriously investigated by psychoanalytic writers, and Matte Blanco begins to make up for this lack.

He notices that Descartes was a prime mover in turning the philosophy of mind away from notions of space by saying that mind or spirit was *intensive* while physical matter was *extensive*. Matte Blanco thinks this was mistaken, adding that in physics the Newtonian notion of absolute space has now been replaced by the concept, originating with Leibnitz and now expressed by Einstein, of space as a *system of relations*. He looks into this as follows.

### The varieties of space

Both as child and adult we basically relate external physical objects to our own body, using it as a prime reference point. We speak of: in front of, behind, above, below, to the left-hand side or right of, and so on. Piaget (1950, 1956) spelt this out from a developmental point of view, suggesting that the sense of physical space emerges through an integration of ideas or mental operations of *muscle movements* and their timing with touch, sight and sound. Thus, sense of space depends on *timing*. It also depends upon potential *freedom* of movement: the greater the degree of freedom the more the space.

Matte Blanco has, in fact, a thoroughgoing structuralist approach. He says that the perception of space is a notion that is *above* the experience of *one* sense organ alone, it is *intersensory*. Aristotle would include it as a 'common sense'; Bion likewise defined common sense as a 'multi-sense'. Modern infant researchers would say it is an amodal or cross-sensory perception (Meltzoff 1981; Stern 1985).

Matte Blanco thinks that intuitive notions about external space could together be called *psychological space*. On the other hand, internal or inner space can be used to refer to the idea of the place where our experiences happen. Next, we conceive of *physical* space when we use *non-anthropocentric* thinking in order to give places to external objects and events.

Second, there is *mathematical space*. This is an 'ideal' space which may be employed for scientific conceptions of the physical world. Mathematicians are quite clear that they often deal in 'fictions'. These are 'hypotheses' which can correspond to physical reality but start as fictions none the less.

In mathematical space the everyday, own-body oriented conceptions of 'in front of', 'behind', 'to the side of' and so on are replaced less anthropocentrically by length, width, height, etc. Here are three basic *dimensions*. These, too, must have originally been derived from everyday anthropocentric psychological–spatial intuitions. The dimensionality of mathematical space, however, achieves a *generality* and clarity vital for logically analytic, deductive thinking.

Matte Blanco now goes in the well-known direction that physical phenomena can be expressed in a four-dimensional continuum, including time. Mathematical space, however, being ideal or conceptual, need not rest here but can go on to conceive of 5, 6, 7 . . . on to *n*-dimensional space, and thence to an infinite number of dimensions. Our achievement of scientific knowledge about the external world owes its marvellous progress to the development of mathematical conceptions of space, for it is only by these means that vital calculations can be carried out.

In contrast to this view, Matte Blanco observes that spacial conceptions about mental phenomena lag behind. This is possibly due, he thinks, to the rejection by Descartes, followed by others, of concepts of space in their model of the mind. At all events Matte Blanco thinks that any notion of a form, pattern or *structure*, be it about outside things or the mind, entails conceptions of *space* and/or *time*. Furthermore, our ideas of the mind are completely permeated with spatial comparisons. We must take the concept of space seriously in the study of mental phenomena.

However, mental phenomena involve spatial conceptions which are very different from those habitually employed with material phenomena. We can describe physical phenomena with a four-dimensional continuum (three of space plus time), but Matte Blanco thinks that there is overwhelming evidence to show that three-dimensional space plus time is insufficient to put an order in the understanding of mental phenomena (1975: 407–8).

This is the first crucial step in his contribution to the conception of psychic space, and thus one of his approaches to psychic structure. *Notions based solely on three or four dimensions just will not do.* What is more, psychoanalysis has naively accepted the use of these crude models. Because of this, many vital issues have eluded us. He says decisively that we can be certain of one thing, *the mind is not a bag.* We shall now discuss Matte Blanco's reasoning about this. It will be brief. Serious study can only come by referring to his own work (1975: 409–24; 1988: 273–318).

### Concepts of multi-dimensional space

We have just observed with Matte Blanco that there is no reason to assume that mental events must conform to the same spatial laws as does external physical reality. For instance, we can easily see that the idea of mental space may actually refer to the degree of *freedom* or 'room' to *think* and to *store* in *memory.* Thus mental space concerns the ability of mental operations to *manoeuvre representations* of the external world, internal objects, notions and concepts. All of these can, of course, be heavily biased affectively.

With this in mind it is next necessary to consider the idea of a *space of more than three dimensions.* This is used very widely in mathematics – why not in psychoanalysis?

### A geometric view of n-dimensional space

Matte Blanco's main purpose here is to look at what happens when a figure in a space of a given number of dimensions is *represented* by a figure in a space of a *smaller or larger number* of dimensions. To the unmathematical eye very odd things then seem to happen.

Take a simple example, a *triangle*, which obviously is a space in *two dimensions.* This is a *surface* ABC, as shown in Figure 6.1. It is possible to represent this triangular group of relationships in various ways. One is by points on a single line. This is a representation in a space of *one dimension*, which is less than that of the two-dimensional triangle. All that needs to be done is to rotate sides AC and BC until they are in line with AB. Now the triangle is represented by the straight line CABC. This representation misses certain aspects of a two-dimensional triangle, like angles and area, but it is otherwise satisfactory. However, it will be noticed that in the *two-dimensional triangle* the *point* C (of *zero dimension*) occurs only *once*, whereas when in *one dimension* it occurs *twice*. It is also possible to separate all three lines AB, AC and BC, in which case each point, A, B and C (zero dimension), appears *twice*.

In summary: when representing a *two-dimensional* figure in *one dimension* a *repetition* of points occurs. It will become too complicated to demonstrate in this book cases of more than two dimensions, so we shall simply state Matte Blanco's conclusions.

If a cube (three dimensions) is represented on a surface (two dimensions), each *area* (two dimensions) appears *once*, every *line* (one dimension) appears *twice* and every *point* (zero dimension) appears *three times*.

When the converse occurs, if a form is represented in a *higher* number of dimensions, then a coincidence (the opposite of repetition) of forms does not always occur. However, there are some transformations between dimensions which can create such *coincidences* or *condensation* between points, lines, volumes, etc., which had been separate before the transformation. Thus, in a three-dimensional world it is impossible for two people to sit in the same space on a chair, but transformations into higher dimensions can be specified where this can conceivably happen.

Returning to dimensional reduction from the psychological point of view, introspection will remind you that spaces of more than three dimensions cannot be visually imagined. However, it is possible to think and make deductions about such a space. Hence its dimensions can be represented mathematically and calculated. It is then found that when

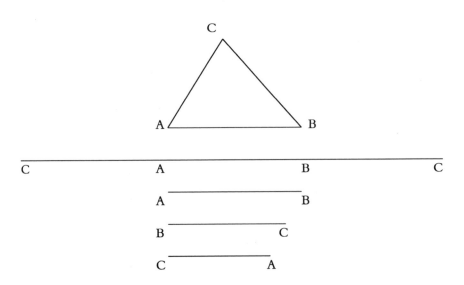

*Figure 6.1* (Taken from Courant and Robbins 1941: 231)

spaces of *higher than three* dimensions are represented in terms of only three dimensions, they will have *volumes*, as well as areas, lines and points *repeated*.
Summarizing:

(a) Dimensional reduction is necessary if many dimensions are to be consciously and visually imagined, for conscious imagination can only manage three dimensions plus time. The result of this reduction entails repetition of images.
(b) Some other mathematical dimensional transformations can entail coincidence or condensation of images.
(c) Matte Blanco's main suggestion is that these features of 'inter-dimensional' representation occur in the human mind when moving from one level of awareness to another, such as from unconscious to conscious and vice versa. Clearly, repetition and condensation are natural features of dreams, so here is a vital and normal example with which to investigate multi-dimensionality.

### Multi-dimensional space, dreams and the unconscious

Here Matte Blanco reiterates his most fundamental argument that the unconscious, as shown by dreams, moves from representing particular things (three dimensions + time) to abstractions (possibly in many dimensions) and back again. The principal thing to remember for the dream interpreter is that the abstract expression of dream thoughts is replaced by a particular visual or pictorial expression which is *capable of being represented* in conscious imagination. In this way images may serve as symbolic (metaphoric) representations of thoughts, particularly of an emotional kind. Matte Blanco quotes Freud (1900: 312):

> When the whole mass of the dream thoughts is brought under the pressure of the dream work, and its elements are turned about, broken into fragments and jammed together – almost like pack-ice – the question arises, what happens to the logical connections which have hitherto formed its framework?

[Matte Blanco (1975: 415) continues:]

> If we assume that we are following the natural human tendency . . . [and] apply the concept of space to thought-processes, then one is struck by the fact that the . . . well ordered succession of wakeful life [gives way] to an interpenetration of the various elements of the dream, [it becomes] a sort of mutual getting inside one another. In terms of three-dimensional space this appears chaotic, but if we consider the question in terms of dimensions higher than three, it is

no longer so. We must suppose that various dream thoughts [actually] happen *simultaneously* in the unconscious. . . .

If we represent these thoughts or feelings in terms of [visual] images, these must show that each thought or feeling occupies the whole of the ego while at the same time being only part of the ego. This is what the dream thought does in the work of condensation. . . . Exactly the same image may serve in its totality to express various thoughts. These two requisites of 'partness' and 'wholeness' coexist if three-dimensional material images are employed for a representation. Hence the peculiar impression that dreams produce when they behave as if this were possible. . . . This representation is no problem if we are dealing with a space of more than three dimensions which is being represented in terms of three dimensions. . . . [Hence] a volume may appear several times. . . . In this way that which appeared chaotic becomes perfectly well ordered. . . . *The dreamer 'sees' a multi-dimensional world with eyes which are made to see only three dimensions.*

### The means of representation in dreams

We continue quoting Matte Blanco. He says:

Freud says dreams 'reproduce *logical connections by simultaneity in time.* Here they are acting like the painter who, in a picture of the school of Athens or of Parnassus, represents in one group all the philosophers or all the poets. It is true that they were never in fact assembled in a single hall or on a single mountain-top; but they certainly form a group in the conceptual sense'.

(Freud 1900: 314)

Matte Blanco continues:

We see that the same thing happens with time as with space: an abolition of succession, which is replaced by one moment 'getting inside another'. . . . Contiguity and succession are held in contempt by dreams. . . . [And] when Freud speaks of logical connection being expressed in terms of simultaneity, . . . he is calling attention to the fact that continuity is abolished in the dream, all of which shows the *contempt the dream has for the limitations of three-dimensional space.* . . .

If I sit on a chair nobody else can; this is an 'either–or' proposition: my volume displaces any other volume. *But in a space of dimensions higher than three the problem does not exist.* Freud points out that it is the narrator who generally interprets in terms of 'either–or', and this seems natural, for he is thinking only in terms of a three-dimensional space, he cannot do otherwise.

When [as described by Freud (1900: 317)] . . . a dream refers to something which is at the same time a garden and a sitting-room it demands from the imagination something which [it] may meet only with difficulty. . . . [One method of dealing with this is by] what Freud calls the screen and which is also employed with regard to persons . . . [simultaneity, consonance, the possession of common attributes, are all represented by a unification.] . . . On certain occasions the ego is hidden behind various persons which appear in the dream; in this way the dreamer may play several roles at the same time. *This constitutes a splendid way for escaping from the limitations imposed by three-dimensional space.* . . .

[Furthermore] the dreamer ignores the category of contraries and contradictories. As Freud writes: ' "no" seems not to exist so far as dreams are concerned. They show a particular preference for combining contraries into a unity or for representing them as one and the same thing' (loc. cit.: 318).

(Matte Blanco 1975: 421)

## Conclusions so far

Matte Blanco (1975: 423) sums up his argument:

We may say that numerous facts which at first sight appear completely chaotic become perfectly well ordered if we apply the concept of space of more than three dimensions. The dreamer (and the unconscious) behave like a geometrician who handles a number of variables superior to three and who is forced to use in his representation a space of dimensions not higher than three.

This might be one of Matte Blanco's most important insights. However, we cannot help but ask the question, what do all these dimensions consist of? If they exist, the unconscious must handle them and then represent them in the three-dimensional images of consciousness. If Matte Blanco is right, the unconscious is a geometrician of a very peculiar sort, but a geometrician none the less.

## Possible emotional dimensions of the unconscious

When it comes to the actual details of what makes up each of the many dimensions in the unconscious that Matte Blanco is proposing, he is frankly

85

rather vague. So a rough model devised by the present author, as to how things might be, will be attempted.

First, it is plain that much of what must be represented in the unconscious are conceptions about *emotions*.

Dimensions are, by their definition, means of *measuring* – that is, they concern *quantities*. How can emotions be linked with quantities in the unconscious of all places?

Quantification usually implies the meticulous operation of counting sets of entities. For instance, a simple graph is a spatial representation in two dimensions. This is prepared by showing two straight lines, ordinate and abscissa, crossing at right angles to each other. These are used to represent two variables ($x$, $y$, say). The lines are then usually marked off in equal intervals so that a point twice as far from the centre of the graph indicates twice as much of the quantity represented on that dimension, and so on. A curve showing the relation between the two variables ($x$, $y$) may then be constructed in the space between the two straight lines.

Note that the graph is spatial but the things being represented are not necessarily so in themselves. For instance, a graph can be drawn to represent atmospheric temperature on one dimension against time of day on the other, but temperature and time of day are not in themselves spatial qualities.

It will be objected that it is all very well for characteristics of the physical world to be measured like this, but emotions are *experiences*. No doubt there are physically measurable correlates, like sweat secretion and blood pressure, but, psychologically, an emotion is known by *introspection* of conscious content – it is experienced. This can only be available directly to one person, the introspector. Conscious content just cannot be measured reliably. For instance, there is no way of being clear that someone is feeling, say, twice as angry at any one moment as at another, and so on. Therefore, since measuring the experience of emotions is full of error, so too must be the use of psychic dimensionality. As an example of this sort of error, mathematically minded psychologists began many years ago to attempt to measure, among other things, the quantities of certain emotional attitudes in groups of subjects by means of the technique of factor analysis. Mathematically this is highly sophisticated, but many difficulties arose about the reliability and validity of the findings when it came to introspective reports. How could it be known whether one reported emotion was, say, really twice as big as another, or whether reporters were telling the precise truth about their feelings, and so on?

However, neither Matte Blanco nor the present author is talking about *somebody else* measuring *your emotion*, but about *you* 'quantifying' it *intuitively* for *yourself*. When you distinguish your own emotions about things, you often have some idea, however imprecise, of their *intensity*. This refers to their strength, clarity, degree, etc. These are *experiences of quantity* and must thus be *intuitively* measurable by the mind. For instance, you can roughly distinguish your happiness on Tuesday morning and compare it to that on Friday evening. Similarly, you can know such things as the intensity of your disappointment when you failed your driving test compared to when you missed the last post of the day; your resentment of something your boss is doing which threatens your job compared to that when a friend happens to forget to ring you, and so on.

Such emotions as these have distinguishable intensities, however vague. And intensities do *not* have to be measurable with the precision of a scale having *equal intervals* on it in order to 'calculate' *intuitively* – at least approximately and instantaneously. Even in formal mathematics, scales of statistical measurement are well established that are 'non-parametric', that is, they only require 'bigger than' or 'less than' judgements. These are *intensity* judgements.

Introspection tells us that all the mind needs is to distinguish emotional qualities, however imprecise, that have some sense of 'size' about them. When one thinks of it, the ordinary mind makes calculations about many factors together instantaneously when going about everyday business. Crossing a busy road, for instance, is a highly complex calculation, a weighing up of risks, often involving distinct emotions, such as exasperation, fear, challenge and relief. Mental registration in an intuitive dimensional way appears in this light to be present all the time.

The contents of these *dimensions do not have to be spatial.* Physics can think of all sorts of non-spatial things, like humidity, electrical charges, tension in springs, weights and so on, and represent them in a dimensional way. So why should not the individual mind also be a rudimentary intuitive mathematician and think dimensionally even about emotions? Full measurement using equal intervals, etc., naturally seems to occur only very sporadically and in a most limited way in the system unconscious (though the present author once dreamt of the answer to a physics problem done in an exam the previous day – and woke up to discover that the dream answer was correct and the actual answer given in the exam was wrong!). But for the experience of multi-dimensionality only a loose sense of greater or less is needed.

## Three clinical examples of dimensionality

### Case A

Here is a more or less verbatim sample of ordinary human rumination. It is a patient talking to his analyst, but it could be almost anyone.

Well, I'm frankly really quite glad to be back after the holiday. There is a lot to talk about. One thing I've noticed – I still get into those muddles, and I am sure I will get into a muddle today, but I am aware that I don't panic like I used to. I realize that, because I panicked so much, I never saw how very depressed Sally can get. My panics were so dramatic and exaggerated that I did not bother somehow to see clearly that she was depressed quite apart from me. . . . We had some time in a hotel in Florence this holiday, just the two of us, Sally and I. It was quiet and not hectic. She was very fraught though, she bought some tickets to a concert, not much money, and couldn't find them and she got into a state of deep depression about it. We got back home and Jane's (a daughter) diploma results came through, they were much worse than predicted, she was devastated, and Sally got very depressed – so was I, very upset. I was expected to handle it as usual and was utterly exhausted with both Sally and Jane's depression. However, Sally and I and Jane talked it all over at length and began to get ourselves sorted out; Jane felt better and thought about how to go about swotting, resitting and getting better grades. Then a day or so later Jane came home from her job and said she'd got into a mess again. She was being slow, the manager asked what the trouble was; she said she was bored, the silly girl, and the manager said she'd better speed up or look for another job. Sally as usual got into a state about this and then worried herself helpless over weeding the garden. I was talking to John (eldest son) about his mother's depressions and he said, 'But mum has always been depressed, didn't you notice?' I really had not. All this used to be my fault. It was me being omnipotent, I can see now – this taking all these things over so they become my responsibility – is just that – omnipotence – then I resent the burden. I can see Sally's moods as more out-there now. Weeding the garden, and Jane, and all those things, are both our responsibilities, not just mine. It was very much the same with my mother, she used to make us kids all responsible for her, now I can see that she too, like Sally, was depressed herself all the time.

Here the patient is doing a lot of reflective self-analysis. The emotional states that he mentions are portrayed as having a greater or less degree of intensity; they have some feeling of *quantity* in them. He is carrying out a series of crude, intuitive emotional calculations. Naturally they are manifestly conscious or preconscious, not unconscious, but they point to the possibility of an 'emotional calculus', however rough.

Here is a list of the emotions: quite glad; still in a muddle; not panic like I used to; panicked so much; very depressed; dramatic and exaggerated; not bothered to; not hectic; deep depression; devastated; very depressed; very upset; utterly exhausted; began to sort ourselves out; a mess again; was bored; worried helpless; always depressed; all my fault; omnipotence; resenting; responsibility. At least eighteen different emotions of differing intensity or quantity are referred to. Thus, in this not very long sequence of conscious thought, we have the possibility of at least eighteen different experiential dimensions being conceived of. This could at times be, perhaps, a sort of eighteen-dimensional psychic 'space'.

There is no contention being made here that the mind unconsciously operates in a logically consistent way and never contradicts itself upon so many precisely measurable factors at one time. All that is being suggested is that this number of emotional patterns of different intensities might be intuited together. That must suffice as a general indicator of the feasibility of dimensionality occurring unconsciously.

Here are two more clinical studies. They both come from South America and show two experienced psychoanalysts using multi-dimensionality theory in a sophisticated and useful way.

### Case B

In 'Inner space and the interior of the maternal body', Juan Francisco Jordan (1990) sees an equation occurring between mother's body, own body and own mind. He describes his analysis with a schizoid young man who felt intensely isolated. A key feature was that a sister was born when he was 13 months old and a brother when he was just 2. These seem to have been fundamental traumata. Jordan soon notes interpretations being received by the patient as if bombs had exploded in him. Separations also appeared to be cruel cuts in the relationship. This sense of cruelty seemed to arise from an experience that patient and analyst *occupied the same space*. So when the analyst was absent from him, he also lost an essence of himself. Self and object were equated, *symmetrized*.

After some time Jordan begins to see that the analyst is conceived of essentially *only* in spatial terms – as a *place* not a person. After two years' analysis the patient had the following dream just before an examination:

> *I dreamt I was in the exam and that I looked at my answer book and I didn't find any blank pages for my answers. Then something more confused happened. I dreamt of geometric shapes and how they turned into other shapes with fewer faces, cubes into pyramids, for instance. In the dream I asked myself if it was a linear reduction, and it seems to me I do the same with people.* I remember a real case when I found only one blank page during the test. While I looked through the answer-book I thought the assistant professor would think that I was cheating. Linear reduction is a branch of algebra that, in

abstract terms, describes the functions or operations which must be executed to pass from one aggregate or space to another.

(Jordan 1990: 436)

Here the patient, clearly a student of mathematics, is explicitly pointing to the experience of dimensional transformation. Jordan then says that he, the analyst, too seems often to be reduced point by point to fit the patient's fantasy. He shows how the patient feels that it is absolutely essential for him to intrude upon another person's space; he needs to occupy the same space as another human being in order to exist. But he is then left in fear of being invaded in retaliation. There is never enough space to go round. *Voracity*, either by himself or his objects, marks his internal world.

The patient responded:

> The other day at the University I had to make great efforts to talk, I felt I had to destroy myself in order to tell somebody something, it is like a pot that is empty, but the leftovers sticking to the side must be scraped with strength . . . with strength . . . scraping the leftovers with desperation.

(*ibid.*: 437)

Jordan describes how the patient feels filled with babies – or ideas – who are engaged in a desperate fight for survival, with no unoccupied maternal space to receive his projections. It is a fighting for nourishment but also to develop himself. There are dreams of carnivores, of invading armies eliminating inhabitants and thus generating their own rejection. Jordan related these to thoughts battling for space within the patient's mind. However, slowly, the patient is seen just beginning to allow such thoughts to coexist, to be given space in his mind, and with it there is obviously a profound relief and the beginning of structural change in the patient.

## Case C

This clinical example is from 'Some technical consequences of Matte Blanco's theory of dreaming'. Juan Pablo Jiménez (1990: 455–69) shows how the technique of dream interpretation has recently assigned increasing importance to the patterns of *manifest* dream. This is contrary to Freud's warning not to fall into the temptation of regarding the manifest content as a genuine psychic product. In Freud's model dream work is a function of censorship against forbidden wishes, distorting latent contents until they appear disconnected and meaningless. According to Jiménez, dream work in this model is essentially defensive and regressive.

But it increasingly appears, thinks Jiménez, that distortion theory, though still necessary, is not now sufficient as an explanation of every aspect of dream work. He argues how *primary process* and dreams serve an *organizing* function. Censorship disguise need not be ubiquitous. Thomä and Kächele (1987) think the *manifest dream* can be a gestalt or *comprehensive self-representation* of unconscious wishes and other problems of the dreamer. With this in mind Jiménez examines several dreams. One (Jiménez 1990: 461) is recounted in a paper by Joseph. He quotes her:

> The dream: there was a kind of war going on. My patient was attending a meeting in a room at the seaside. People were sitting round a table when they heard a helicopter outside and knew from the sound that there was something wrong with it. My patient and a major left the table where the meeting was going on and went to the window to look out. The helicopter was in trouble and the pilot had baled out in a parachute. There were two planes, as if watching over the helicopter, but so high up that they looked extremely small and unable to do anything to help. The pilot fell into the water, my patient was wondering whether he would have time to inflate his suit, was he already dead, and so on.
>
> (Joseph 1985: 69)

Joseph then gives the essence of her interpretation to the patient about the dream, which we shall not dwell upon here.

Jiménez points out several salient features. First, the war *atmosphere* which is the predominant effect. Next, that the patient's self is represented at least twice, first as an observer and then as the pilot. Both are pervaded by masochistic fascination and excitement (as Joseph clearly points out in her interpretation). However, it is not only the patient's representation of self which is split, the analyst-object is also split – into both the enemy and the two planes unable to help.

Jiménez considers the dream as a bi-logical structure. It is not then seen as simply a distortion for he also uses views provided by cognitive science and psychobiology. Along this line he finds Freud saying, 'at bottom, dreams are nothing more than a particular *form* of *thinking* made possible by the conditions of the state of sleep' (Freud 1900: 507).

In the dream the patient's 'internal' world is not distinguished from the analyst's consulting room. The analyst is represented within the patient's mind not once but probably three times (observer, enemy and planes). There is no difference between the space of the consulting room, represented by the meeting-room in the dream, and the total space of the dream in which the war scene takes place. Jiménez says that when a mathematician represents an $n$-dimensional space by means of a space of fewer dimensions, there is repetition in the representation. This is seen in the repeated images for both patient and analyst. In this case, the patient, the analyst and the relationships between them are experienced affectively and cognitively in a *hyperspace* of more than three dimensions. But for psycho- physiological reasons we are unable to perceive a space of more than three dimensions, so it is collapsed into a three-dimensional one.

Jiménez concludes, agreeing with Matte Blanco, that the conception of a *structural unconscious* conforms better to the present-day discoveries of the cognitive sciences about the processes of sleeping and dreaming (REM, stages of sleep, etc.) than does a simple classical *distortion* model all alone standing by itself as a complete explanation of dreams and the unconscious. Jiménez ends: 'Matte Blanco points out that the conception of mental life as a defence, the core of Freud's dynamic conception, may be subordinated to two general functions *psychical regulation* and *psychical growth*' (1990: 468).

## Dimensionality of objects and the internal world

### *Summary so far*

We have been seeing a peculiar mathematical phenomenon. When forms or patterns in a number of dimensions are represented in a reduced number of dimensions, a repetition occurs. Furthermore, the greater the dimensional reduction the greater the repetition. In the opposite direction, other mathematical transformations can take place; here dimensional increase may produce a coincidence or condensation of forms.

Matte Blanco contends that this happens in the interchanges between psychic levels, such as between unconscious and conscious thinking and vice versa. Repetition and condensation in dreams, where there can have been a change in dimensionality, appear to do this. It also happens with the processes of introjection and identification, where representation of the *self* and *another self* can actually *occupy the same psychic space*. Conversely, in projection the self can occupy several different spaces at the same time. In addition to projective defences, the ability of the self to move into other selves, and to separate from them, is essential for both patient and analyst in the process of therapy and in maturation generally. Facility in this particular spatial transformational model may be quite directly useful to the clinician.

A conclusion to be drawn is that conscious thought, operating only in three dimensions, has to sacrifice registration of many symmetries. The unconscious seems able to process data in more than three dimensions but cannot integrate these into a *coherent* network of *asymmetrical* relations. Thus, for the mind to go from conscious to unconscious thinking and to operate within its many psychic dimensions, it must sacrifice much of its acuity of asymmetrical discrimination.

The unconscious, since it can simultaneously contain great numbers of generalized ideas, notions, propositional functions or emotional conceptions, is, as it were, a capacious dimensional 'mathematician'. But it is worse than consciousness as a geometrician of location in space and time. Also, transformation from *fewer* to *more* dimensions has the *same effect as symmetrization*. Two things can become one; that which is not the same can become the same. Negation can disappear. Whole and part can be equated and so on, with all the sequelae already seen in symmetrization. It is all very strange. Matte Blanco is possibly mistaken (and we psychoanalysts are poorly equipped to decide upon this question) but, as far as mental phenomena are concerned, his model seems to fit many psychic facts and must be worthy of serious consideration.

We conclude so far that symmetrization, infinitization and 'interdimensional transformation' are three ways of representing the same sort of phenomenon. It could be said that Matte Blanco has generated two distinct models of the mind: first, that of asymmetry–symmetry–infinity and, second, dimension-transformation. They are not contradictory; they are in fact complementary and can be combined. The stratified structure is yet another model, derived from asymmetry–symmetry, which is also complementary to them both.

### The internal world

Matte Blanco (1988: 314) goes on from here to think of various meanings that have been attached to that spatial notion – the internal world.

> The first meaning would be the *set of internal objects*. These may be thought of as being 'isomorphic to . . . the regions of the space corresponding to the self. . . . My suspicion is that all [internal] objects are "sub-spaces of the self".'

Another meaning of internal world refers to the self as a *structure*, seen as a multi-dimensional space. Yet another meaning is derived from seeing a certain mode of functioning, that of the *distortions* of physical spaces created by the mind in dreams, etc. Matte Blanco takes this opportunity to make clear how his examination of the various meanings of psychic space reveals oversimplifications and confusions in most psychoanalytical models.

He thinks that certain notions are frequently bound to concepts of either the external or internal world where both are thought of as three dimensional. Some people then make the assumption that when they reach an understanding of the relationship between the individual and his or her internal objects, they must have reached something final. So they can speak of the relation to the internal breast, internal mother, and so on, as the *summum* of understanding. This is an illusion. There are essential facts about the mind and the relations with other individuals which cannot be grasped in terms of the antithesis external–internal. These facts refer to the mind's non-three-dimensional aspects.

Conscious thinking tries to conceive of such aspects in terms of space, but when it does, the best it can achieve is to use infinity or infinite-dimensional space. The concept of infinity, Matte Blanco (1988: 316) says, underlies but is not explicit in, for instance, many Kleinian formulations. The attempt to translate the non-spatial and timeless aspects of human nature into space–time is necessary to thinking but is insufficient for further progress in understanding mental functioning.

Matte Blanco's introduction of symmetry, infinity, the stratified bi-logical structures, and now dimensional transformation, must be puzzling but they have exposed some of the limitations of present-day psycho-analytic theories. Probably no other self-respecting science would tolerate the simplistic theoretical crudities that psychoanalysts harbour. Matte Blanco has exposed some of these and has begun to provide alternatives for psychoanalysis to use. No self-respecting theorist can now talk about mental space in simple three-dimensional terms without thinking twice. A mind can no longer be talked about adequately as a bag.

We are now at the end of our direct presentation of Matte Blanco's work. The chapters that follow are devoted to its relation to other regions of knowledge. Chapter 7 is about bi-logic in relation to some core aspects of traditional psychoanalytic theory; Chapter 8 is about Matte Blanco's con-tribution to therapeutic technique; and Chapter 9 considers similarities with some major theories in fields outside psychoanalysis. Chapter 10 considers mathematical chaos theory and bi-logic; and a few conclusions are collected together in Chapter 11.

# 7

# Bi-logic and central psychoanalytic concepts

To start our brief examination of the relation of bi-logic to other aspects of psychoanalysis, here are a few quotations, more or less at random, from some well-known psychoanalytic authors. Symmetry, asymmetry and infinity seem to infuse them all. If you have understood the gist of the previous chapters the quotations will explain themselves. We shall make very few explanatory comments.

Freud has been quoted previously, so we shall lay him aside for the moment. Here is one from Klein which appears to illustrate the part = whole equation.

> Excrements and bad parts of the self are meant not only to injure but also to control and take possession of the object. Insofar as the mother comes to contain the bad parts of the self she is not felt to be a separate individual but is felt to be *the* bad self.
>
> (Klein 1946 [in Klein 1952: 300])

Here is a dream from Fairbairn which he used to illustrate key aspects of his view of endopsychic structure. It was designed by Fairbairn to illustrate the resultants of splitting. From the bi-logical point of view it is possible to detect many inter-object symmetrizations. Also, in terms of the object repetitions manifest in multi-dimensionality given in the previous chapter, one can detect one object, the self, being in several locations at once.

> The (manifest) dream to which I refer consisted of a brief scene in which the dreamer saw the figure of herself being viciously attacked by a well known actress in a well known building which had belonged to her family for generations. Her husband was looking on but he seemed quite helpless and quite incapable of protecting her. After delivering the attack the actress turned away and resumed playing a stage part which, as seemed to be implied, she had moment-arily set aside to deliver the attack by way of an interlude. The figure

then found herself gazing at the figure of herself lying bleeding on the floor; but, as she gazed, she noticed that for an instant this figure turned into that of a man. Thereafter the figure alternated between herself and this man until eventually she awoke in a state of acute anxiety.

(Fairbairn 1952: 95)

Next, here is Greenson giving an example explaining transference resistance. It gives a clear picture of the symmetrizations in transference experiences.

A young man seems to be hesitant to tell me anything derogatory about his wife. Whenever he finds fault with her he is quick to excuse her. . . . When I point out this defensive attitude to him, the patient first denies it then tearfully admits that I am right. He acknowledges that he tries to cover up his wife's deficiencies because he is sure I would expect him to get a divorce if I "really" knew how inadequate she is. When I pursue this . . . the patient recalls that in his childhood his father repeatedly threatened to divorce his mother whenever he found fault with her. Thus, it seemed clear that the patient's hesitancy indicated that he was afraid that I would act like his father. He tried to protect his wife from me as he wanted to protect his mother from his father. . . . Only after the patient recognized this source of resistance could he go on to realize that it was he, not I, who had such a strong 'fatherly' resentment against his wife.

(Greenson 1967: 27)

Here is Ernest Wolf writing about selfobject needs. Incidentally, this term, introduced by Kohut (1971), itself suggests a self–object symmetrization by eliding two words into one. Wolf gives a schematized outline of an individual's possible selfobject needs. Here are the descriptions of three of the five he lists.

*Idealizing needs*: a need to experience oneself as being part of an admired and respected selfobject; needing the opportunity to be accepted by and merge into a stable, calm, nonanxious, powerful, wise, protective selfobject that possesses the qualities the subject lacks.

*Alterego needs*: a need to experience an essential alikeness with the selfobject. . . .

*Merger needs*: a. extension of self: a primitive form of mirroring need that finds confirmation of self only in the experience of being totally one with the mirroring selfobject.

b. with idealized selfobject: an intensification of the idealizing need that requires being totally one with the idealized selfobject.

(Wolf 1988: 55)

Lastly, here are several short quotes from Winnicott on *transitional phenomena* and creativity. We shall dwell on Matte Blanco and Winnicott a little longer than the others.

> It comes from without from our point of view, but not from the point of view of the baby. Neither does it come from within; it is not a hallucination. . . .
>
> For instance, if we consider the wafer of the Blessed Sacrament, which is symbolic of the body of Christ, I think I am right in saying that for the Roman Catholic community it *is* the body, and for the Protestant community it is a *substitute*, a reminder, and is essentially not, in fact, the body itself. Yet in both cases it is a symbol.
>
> (Winnicott 1971: 5–6)

> The mother at the beginning . . . affords the infant the *illusion* that her breast is part of the infant. . . . Omnipotence is nearly a fact of experience. The mother's eventual task is gradually to disillusion the infant.
>
> (*ibid.*: 11)

> Two separate persons can feel at one, but here at the place I am examining the baby and object *are* one. . . . Psychoanalysts have perhaps given special attention to the male element or drive aspect of object-relating, and yet have neglected the subject–object identity to which I am drawing attention here, which is the basis of the capacity to be. The male element *does* while the female element (in males and females) *is*.
>
> (*ibid.*: 80–1)

The symmetrizations alluded to here by Winnicott are obvious. It is worth looking for other bi-logical functions appearing in these quotations. It is perhaps apposite here to make a more general comparison between Winnicott and Matte Blanco.

My Chilean colleagues have pointed out that these men have much in common and complement each other usefully; they stress that this is especially so when thinking of the psychoanalytic process. At first sight this seems a strange idea, for Winnicott never showed the slightest theoretical interest in logic, while Matte Blanco was noticeable by ignoring both development and the environment. So what did they have in common?

The similarities quickly emerge. Both men had genius in them, they both had a basis that was strictly 'classical' (Strenger 1989) and rational. But they both certainly refused either to be enslaved by or become a pious pillar of the psychoanalytic establishment, while they searched idiosyncratically and courageously to clarify what they thought was important. They present a similar moral model for us, happy to leave us free to emulate them or not as we choose. More than this, they had a certain other style in common in the way they danced unpredictably with ideas from one flash of illumination to another. Neither was interested in the pedestrian spelling out of systematic theory; thus both are hard to follow in an orderly way.

This brings out their most important similarity. They, like all good analysts, were good introspectors, they had a strong phenomenological bent, especially Matte Blanco; but more than this, they were also both romantic in vision, especially Winnicott. They both revelled in, and illuminated, the multitude of paradoxes in mental life. It is the zest for paradox that is rare among analysts and which makes both Matte Blanco and Winnicott open-minded and most remarkably unpedantic and also sensitive to subtleties. It is this zest for paradox that beckons to us as a model of open-mindedness.

Not only did they have a certain temperament in common but there is one region of common theoretical ground. Perhaps the most important of Winnicott's contributions was his introduction of the concept of *transitionality*. Of course, not only is this imbued with paradox but it is essentially about the identities with and differences between self and objects at the same time – about symmetry and asymmetry.

Returning now to the quotations of psychoanalysts, the statements by the different authorities are in everyday English, and it could be said that bi-logic adds nothing new to them. Does it do more than put old ideas into a different language? It certainly does, because it evokes a different way of thinking about mental processes. Its way has a microscopic and meticulous rigour of method and a generality in its conceptual comprehensiveness that makes for a new simplicity. We have emphasized already that bi-logic introduces the essential importance of mathematical intuitions (concepts or preconcepts) into psychoanalysis. Bion was doing the same at about the same time or even earlier in a rather different way (see Chapter 9).

Let us briefly list some of the basic concepts of ordinary psychoanalysis to see how they might look when informed by bi-logical analysis. Recalling the dynamic, topographic, structural, developmental and economic points of view, Matte Blanco's ideas are like these in that they are *metapsychological* structures. They do not primarily fall into any of Freud's metapsychological categories but centre upon knowing. His ultimate intellectual love was epistemology.

Matte Blanco's basic elements are the dynamics of cognitive structures, their interrelationships and the contradictions between them. As we have seen, he always took classical and Kleinian theories for granted, but he thought psychoanalysis had strayed after Freud's great early discoveries. He must in part be faulted here. Though never fully ignoring theory since 1900, he does not often fully engage with it in his theory. Apart from

Freud and Klein, other authors are little mentioned. Matte Blanco's deep understanding and use of psychoanalysis is always in evidence, but there is a lack of detailed theoretical interest in the workaday guts of such concepts as the *self* at the centre of drives, defences, symptom formations. After all, a sense of self appears to lie in all human emotions. As Matte Blanco seldom addressed these issues, character analysis is underemphasized. Perhaps most pronounced of all, psychosexual development is largely missing; being no Darwinian evolutionist, interest in development seems to elude him.

Matte Blanco's clinical examples show consistent use of a classical technique informed also by Klein, but his theory is only rarely mapped onto this in any detail. In his defence it must be said that this neglect was probably necessary in order to concentrate on his first essentials. This chapter now attempts to begin to fill some gaps.

### The sense organs and symmetrization

Let us start at the sensory end of the psychic apparatus. The *distance receptors* must be more highly developed to mediate the discrimination of *asymmetrical* relations than are the interoceptors. Thence secondary process, with its concern for external reality, is more the realm of the exteroceptors and thus of the cerebral cortex. On the other hand, primary process with its preponderance of symmetry perhaps reigns more contentedly with the autonomic and associated nervous systems. It is the eye, the distance receptor *par excellence*, that mediates the discrimination of most delicate differences and is a prime locator of external physical events. Full location is, of course, dependent upon an integration of vision, sound, touch and movement senses, and each one is a highly articulated difference discriminator. The auditory sense, less refined in locating things in space than vision, is none the less highly sensitive in the time dimension and is man's great means of locating the feelings and ideas of others.

The proximal exteroceptive senses – surface pain, touch, taste and smell – and even more so the interoceptors, appear by introspection to be generally less sensitive to complex and subtle difference discriminations. They might thus be more prone to symmetrization. But this must not be carried too far; for instance, location by smell is very acute in some species, such as dogs and fish. Human thought itself, though largely derived from sight, sound and movement, is still highly symmetrizable, so that it is wrong to put the senses along a simple and absolute scale of 'symmetrizability'.

Even so, taste and smell, though crude, are still important early 'abstractors' of noxious and dangerous stimuli for humans. This is obviously expressed by the infant's vomiting noises of 'ugh' or 'yuck'. Olfactory and gustatory senses must play a role in the vital primitive binary distinction between 'good' and 'bad' objects, and hence in the process of splitting. This, as emphasized already, is a differentiating and polarizing activity which is primitively asymmetrical in nature. We have suggested in previous chapters that Matte Blanco neglected this aspect of polarization in his description of the unconscious. As Melanie Klein showed, splitting leads to extreme judgements of pure goodness and badness, which are infinite abstract notions. These appear to be the fruits of infinitized asymmetrization; but we have seen already that this in turn uses symmetrization.

## Motive, drive, instinct and bi-logic

### Drives and mismatch reduction

The omnipresence of motive terms in our everyday language emphasizes the importance of Freud's introduction, following Herbart, of psychodynamic ideas into psychology. Intrinsic to the meaning of motive is its homeostatic nature.

Here the concept of *negative feedback* is fundamental. When there is a *mismatch* between the organism's present state and a criterion, then there is activity until *mismatch reduction* has taken place. This propensity to find equilibrium is a feature of dynamic systems which are, of course, omnipresent in all biological processes. The psychoanalytic model, being dynamic, is naturally based on feedback ideas and thus ultimately belongs in the family of systems theories (Taylor 1987) which are now explicitly and widely used in the biological and social sciences. Notice that the general systems approach should not be confused with family systems theory in particular.

Freud's Principle of Constancy was a type of expression of a feedback-based systemic theory, as was his definition of the source, aim and object of an instinct. But his concept of discharge of psychic energy was not, as it lacked the element of feedback. Having had other fish to fry, Matte Blanco says nothing of his relation to either systems theories or the European structuralist models (see Chapter 9). It can readily be said that he is basically a structuralist in the broadest sense, but perhaps he lacks the evolutionary-biological interest to turn him towards a full-blooded holistic, complex systems approach.

In summary, a systems approach concerns itself with mismatch reduction to attain matching, and this is needed in all recognition. Bi-logic basically focuses upon asymmetry, which is synonymous with mismatch, and symmetry, which is matching. There is thus much in common; however, the systems approach includes interest specifically in mismatch reduction whereas bi-logic is not yet concerned with 'asymmetry reduction'.

### Drives, symmetrical and asymmetrical relations

On logical grounds Matte Blanco queries the usefulness, at the present time at least, of the concept of *discharge of psychic energy* in motivation.

More central for his own formulations is that instinct and drive entail *asymmetrical* relations. In effect, the arousal of any motive occurs when a criterion or 'target' state is *not* happening; this is *mismatch* – and this is an asymmetrical relation.

Put in another way, since a drive is homeostatic it involves a control system and this always involves *limitation*; limits entail *negation* of some sort, which is again an essentially asymmetrical process.

The culmination of a drive, however, is when the organism's state matches a criterion; this is a state of symmetry. Thus, in instincts and drives, symmetry and asymmetry 'lean upon each other'. This is emphasized by Matte Blanco's note (1975) that sexual *orgasm* is obviously an instinctual culmination; furthermore, the two sexual partners often feel that their boundaries fuse. This is an interpersonal or *intersubjective symmetrization*. We have already emphasized that Matte Blanco did not investigate this intersubjective region thoroughly in a bi-logical light. Not in an intersubjective region but still orgasmic, and hence imbued with symmetrizations, are, of course, genital, anal, oral masturbation and other sensual ecstasies.

### Aggression from the bi-logical point of view

Matte Blanco does not say much here, but it is unequivocal. Aggression always involves representations, albeit often fantastical, of muscular movements in space and time. Tearing to pieces, for instance, a most primitive aggressive urge, certainly involves muscular movement. This must entail discrimination of an object to be torn – asymmetry. Hence aggression, like any drive, is fundamentally rooted in asymmetry and is similarly riddled with negation.

Aggressive activity is also intrinsic to the ability to carry out a *separation*, which is a spatial, asymmetric and negating process. Matte Blanco comments:

It is as though the child said to the mother:
'I don't want to be you any more, I want to be myself.' *Such an affirmation amounts to the birth of space (separation, instead of the previous*

*indivisible unity) and hence of time.* . . . (Perhaps the great sin of Adam and Eve, and of Lucifer, was to have affirmed their independence of God.)

(Matte Blanco 1975: 105)

He also sees aggression as a reaction to threats to the self. It is thus viewed more in its *self-preservative* aspects than as a force which is innately formed and arises independently without antecedents. He is here akin to Winnicott (1950) and Kohut (1971).

Matte Blanco was not very concerned with the death instinct: he is more interested in speculating about whether there may be a propensity or drive to find a state of 'just being' (like Freud's nirvana, Zen Buddhism's sartori, or Winnicott's female element) which is in a dialectic, or even an antinomy, with 'happening' – indivisibility versus divisibility.

### *Instincts, their vicissitudes and bi-logic*

It is notable that Matte Blanco appears to make almost no mention of *polymorphous perversity*. This is remarkable, since one glance makes plain that the very *displacements* between one sexual organ and another, and between organs and objects inherent in any perversion, entail symmetrization of judgement. Thus a tongue, nipple, nose, leg or whip will substitute for a penis; or an anus, shoe or mouth will equate with a vagina, and so on. Perversion's *denial* of differences is a symmetrization. It could be said that symmetrization is the great epistemological instrument of perversion's trade.

It is not easy to account for Matte Blanco's omission. He was no prude and had no serious difficulty with patients about sexual matters. Perhaps he felt that classical analytic theory was good enough.

## Libidinal development

The omission of any mention of Freud's *Three Essays* (1905) epitomizes Matte Blanco's lack of interest in developmental questions. However, let us look quickly at the libidinal zones in a developmental and bi-logical light (Tyson and Tyson 1990; Rayner 1986).

### *Orality*

The importance of the 'snout' region in the infant's early relations to objects still remains central to recent infant research (Stern 1985).

Hand–eye–mouth coordination is still crucial in the location of physical objects. Equally, the acts of splitting into good and bad, also paramount, entail very early difference recognition; all are asymmetrical activities. But the tendency after splitting, to go to simple and polarized extreme badnesses and wonderful goodnesses, are gross symmetrizations giving rise to infinities. Thus, in primitive orality both symmetrical and asymmetrical activities must develop *together*. This overall picture endorses Klein's view of the early paranoid–schizoid position.

Infant research would probably give precedence to neither symmetry nor asymmetry in developmental timing. But Matte Blanco (1975), seeing the uterine state as mostly 'just being', seems to think that there are some ways in which symmetry can be paramount before divisive asymmetry. This would agree with Mahler *et al.*'s (1975) symbiosis as primary in development. He would thus disagree more with Daniel Stern (1985) who strongly disagrees with Mahler. But Matte Blanco is not definitive and it is not a crucial issue.

Both orality and symmetrization are clear in the manic processes. For instance, mania often presents a fantasy of incorporation of everything. It is an 'I can eat the universe' using a fantasy of an infinite digestive capacity. Not quite infinite, but getting that way, is this old English nursery rhyme:

> This is a tale of big bellied Ben
> Who made a feast of ten thousand men
> He ate a church
> He ate a steeple
> He ate the priest
> And all the people.

This is said to be about King Henry VIII who dissolved the monasteries of England and took over their lands. He is also well known for being fat, having six wives and cutting off the heads of two of them. He could 'think big', but was also a brutally manic character.

### Anality

At about the age of one year the infant's growing motility brings in the importance of *social control*. This must be mediated extensively through words and intonations. Such auditory sense demands asymmetrical time discrimination, but the use of words with precision needs primitive *abstraction* – symmetry, but without gross symmetrization.

Differential *limit-setting* and asymmetrical *controlling* and being controlled become critical activities for the toddler. Revolt against control brings perversity, and its triumph ensures manic feelings and their opposite.

Hence, power and powerlessness, omnipotence and impotence, with their splitting, symmetrizations and infinities, come in simple extremes. Such swings in self-esteem occur with urethral and anal success and failure. The multiplicity of symbolic equations about excretion in ordinary language shows the prevalence of symmetrization. A few swear words emphasize this, such as: 'piss-off'; 'you're just wind and piss'; 'you little shit'; 'arse licker'; 'you tight-arsed fart'; shit-head'; 'you'll wet yourself when you hear this' and so on. Body functions are here equated with a whole self: part = whole symmetrizations.

With anality and social control, we approach ideas akin to director–directed, dictator–dictated, master–servant, tyrant–slave, king–subject. This is not just about any particular and limited dictator or king, but about the principle of omnipotence in general, and of magical kingship tyrannizing impotent and fearful subjects. From here it is but a short journey to powers that are higher still, to the early precursors of ideas of the gods and devils, so onward to a God immanent in all things, whose human subjects are but dust before him. Infinity is now omnipresent.

Bi-logic helps to open out the question of anal primacy in toddlerhood. Interpersonal *control* is what matters most generally at this time. The abstract notion or propositional function of 'controllingness' appears to be paramount to the toddler and a crucial part of this is anal control. However, with symmetrization the part (anal control) can be indistinguishable in experience from the whole (the general notion of controlledness–controllingness), hence anality can stand for any control be it by self, mother, father, boss, police, queen, king or God. So, too, can they stand for anal control.

### Phallic activity and the Oedipus complex

The propensity for *omnipotent* fantasy in phallic ideas is well known. Another symmetrizing aspect lies in the demand for and conviction of *being* admired at the same time as desiring passionately to admire and *idolize* others. Here subject–object interchangeability is a symmetrizing activity; similarly, idolization is a symmetrized infinity.

Phallic preoccupation in both male and female acutely spots asymmetrical differences, as in: 'I am bigger than you', or 'Pooh, she's a wet wimpy cry-baby'. Likewise, a little boy can be heard saying to his father, 'When I'm a daddy, you'll be a little boy daddy.' At a more theoretical level, Freud (with disagreement from many analysts since) suggested that *both* the young boy and the girl believe to begin with that there is *no* genital difference between them, which is a symmetrized state of *innocence*. Then the first rumblings of the culmination of the *Oedipus* complex come with the *recognition of sexual differences*. Both girl and boy in their different ways recognize the idea of castration which is an asymmetrical discrimination about anatomy. This labile Oedipal anxiety state is resolved, partially at least, by the *affirmation of identification* with the parent of the same sex, a symmetrizing action. All psychological development appears to involve asymmetrizing processes; things known crudely become differentiated. However, integration into new structures involves the symmetries of identification. Development entails a bi-logical dialectic.

### Further Oedipal-level functioning

Essential for a true onset of latency is that the child has begun to *think* at the *three person level* and then goes on to a multi-person comprehension. He or she is beginning to conceive at the same time of self in relation to at least two other people, mother and father, who are exclusively together, while each, and both at other times, maintains a relation with the self. Here is the germ of a very complex *combination* of the following forms of relationship: self in a relation to mother, mother in a relation *to* self, mother in a relation *with* self; self to father, father to self, self with father; mother to father, father to mother, father with mother; self-with-mother to father, self-with-father to mother, and last but not least, mother-with-father to self. Tolerance of the self *being excluded* and of self as observer is an essential element (see also Britton 1989).

This is a remarkable symmetrical feat, but especially also an asymmetrical one, entailing the *renunciation* of many self-gratifying omnipotent and narcissistic dreams. Renunciation of powerful primitive bi-logical structures with the coming of more articulate asymmetries is occurring. Three (and more) person thinking is now visible in the *dignity* that emerges in a child of 4 or 5 who is 'school ready' and self-contained enough to take on tasks by himself all day long away from home.

When the child is able only to think emotionally at the two-person level, *splitting* into simple extremes is facilitated. Mother can be all-wonderful and idealized – or totally denigrated. There is no third neutral mediator. Here raw bi-logical structures reign with crude good–bad polarization and few means yet of combining them.

However, when mother and father can be known as together with each other and excluding the child, yet at other times fully including him or her, they have become combined and yet at the same time separate objects. When this paradoxical combination has stabilized there can emerge for the child the possibility of knowing a whole array of other relationships. We conclude that, when there is a stable, mutually considerate, three-and-more-person level of functioning, *splitting is not facilitated.* The extremes entailed in the two-person relationship are now *also* viewed through a third person's eyes. Previously unintegrated elements of symmetrical and asymmetrical knowledge can now come together by the use of a third, intermediate or *transitional* position. This facility is essentially one of the aspects that Winnicott was working out in his theory of transitional objects, transitional phenomena and the third area (Winnicott 1951, 1971). A newly articulated, highly asymmetrical network has then been introduced. Grandiose and frightening bi-logical fantasies are now located, contained or comprehended in a *context*, which makes them more realistic and 'ordinary'. Wright (1991) and Britton (1989) give a similar picture; so also does Bion (1962) when introducing 'binocular thinking'.

### The mechanisms of defence

Matte Blanco did not address classical defences in detail, but he defined some different *patterns of an array of bi-logical structures* which have defensive functions. These were intended to be a possible replacement for the disparate classical list of defence mechanisms.

We shall not go into detail describing Matte Blanco's list of structures; they are fully described in his *Thinking, Feeling and Being* (1988). His principle is simple. It is to examine the sequence of a thinking process, attempting to locate where symmetrizations have occurred. In practice, this becomes difficult for the non-specialist and needs great patience.

Two of his main bi-logical structures are called 'Simassi' and 'Alassi'. When one knows the code these are self-explanatory. They are: '*Simultaneous* asymmetrical–symmetrical structure', and '*Alternating* asymmetrical– symmetrical structure'. Simassis occur when symmetrization can be detected as pervading a thought sequence *concurrently* with ordinary logical thought. But it would be an Alassi if ordinary logical sequences, without evident symmetrization, *alternated* with sectors of obvious symmetrization. Matte Blanco (1988), for instance, describes in great detail how *projective-identification* is based upon a Simassi structure. In his view many psychotic mechanisms involve this structure. Alassi structures can also be found, particularly in obsessional mechanisms like undoing.

Finding the actual location of these structures is often difficult; so, rather shamefully, they are excluded here as it is a task for a patient and clear-headed researcher. Instead, let us look at some classically used *defence mechanisms* to see whether symmetrizations can readily be detected.

We shall use Anna Freud's classic list in *The Ego and the Mechanisms of Defence* (1937), and then look at one or two emphasized by Melanie Klein (1935, 1940). We shall lean upon Laplanche and Pontalis (1973).

It is a good idea for the reader to imagine carrying out the defensive act. If you spot yourself having a 'sweeping', 'dismissive', 'don't care about the detail', 'gay abandoned' feeling, then you are probably symmetrizing. If you are 'too discriminating', 'picky', 'precise' or 'pedantic' then you are likely to be over-asymmetrizing.

Now let us start with Anna Freud's list.

### Repression

This is an operation where the subject attempts to repel, or confine to the unconscious, thoughts which would risk evoking displeasure.

Matte Blanco never laid aside his reliance on the concept of repression and never associated it with symmetrization but contrasted their effects. However, it might conceivably be that the very process of keeping a representation away from consciousness is effected simply by a gross and instantaneous symmetrization. Then, the process of making an unwanted thought, together with everything closely associated with it, nothing but the same, would homogenize the unpleasant thought itself with its context; thus it becomes indistinguishable to the self and thus unconscious. Matte Blanco describes something like this when a 'symmetrical frenzy' occurs. He gives an instance (1988: 233).

> Many years ago I was submitted to surgical anaesthesia by gas. After a few seconds I saw some things which seemed bright lines. . . . These began to move, something like rotating. The movement became more and more rapid . . . frantically whirling. Everything was losing its identity and fusing into everything else. . . . I became more and more confused until I completely lost consciousness.

Something like this does seem to happen in any falling asleep, though without the frenzy. Incidentally, Piaget (1953) has a rather similar model for repression.

### Regression

This is a reversion to past phases of development. It means the transition to modes of expression that are on a lower level as regards *complexity, structure and differentiation*. This points to symmetrizations. Laplanche and Pontalis say there is a reversion from thought–identity to perceptual identity. This is a primary process and, likewise, points to a symmetrization at a perceptual level.

### *Reaction-formation*

Here a psychological attitude diametrically opposes a repressed wish and is a reaction against it. This may be highly localized or be generalized into character traits. Thus a person will show pity towards living beings *in general* although his or her unconscious aggression is directed against *particular* people.

The emphasis here is upon the *generalization* that occurs in character formation; this is symmetrization again. Laplanche and Pontalis give examples of the equation of opposites in anal-obsessive character attitudes.

> Does not the housewife who is obsessed with cleanliness end up by concentrating her whole existence on dust and dirt? Similarly, the lawyer who pushes his concern with equity to the extreme point of fastidiousness may in this way show his systematic lack of concern for the real problems presented to him by . . . those who depend on him: he is thus satisfying his sadistic tendencies under the cloak of virtue.
>
> (Laplanche and Pontalis 1973: 378)

Here bi-logical structures are working *par excellence*. The defence is started by asymmetrical discriminations but soon generalizes into many different things being treated as the same, and the symptoms tend to go to extremes – infinitization occurs.

### *Isolation*

This consists in separating thoughts or behaviour so that links with other thoughts are broken.

Here, if, as seems true, a *link* between thoughts entails a *commonality* between them, then, when links are broken, awareness of a commonality is obliterated. This brings in that aspect of a bi-logical structure which, we have emphasized, has not been mentioned enough by Matte Blanco. A commonality, an awareness of a *symmetry, is obliterated* in the service of defence. This has been pointed out several times in earlier chapters and it is related to the polarization entailed in splitting, which itself can be seen as infinitization of an asymmetrical relation.

### *Undoing*

Here the person attempts to cause past thoughts or actions *not* to have occurred; to this end he or she makes use of thought or behaviour having the opposite meaning. This is magic, and thus uses an omnipotence with its intrinsic symmetrization.

### Projection

This is an operation where personal qualities, feelings, wishes or even objects, which the person refuses to recognise, are located in another person or thing.

This mental operation starts with asymmetrical discrimination – something in the *self stands out* as *objectionable* and unwanted. It is then *apparently* projected *outwards* on to another object. However, the *choice of the object* of the projection seems to rest on some quality that is the *same* between it and the unwanted aspect of the projector's self. At this level of functioning, subject = object; they are interchangeable. Matte Blanco (1988) calls this the level of the '*basic matrix for all projection and introjection*'. This basic matrix occurs at an unconscious level (strata 3 and 4 of the stratified structure) where any idea is known as *only the same* as any other idea that *has that same quality*. Here a class is identified with all its members and with the abstracted attribute of the class (a conception, notion or propositional function) as well. Having utilized this basic matrix to 'home-in' on similar objects, the projector then simply *denies* that *he or she is the owner of the objectionable quality*. However, he or she still perceives it residing in the outside person or thing.

### Introjection

Here, in fantasy, the objects and their inherent qualities are transposed from the 'outside' to the 'inside' of the subject; it can often, but not always, lead to *identification*.

Something like projection occurs here, but in the opposite direction. Clearly the symmetrized level of the 'basic matrix' of projection and introjection is being utilized again, and, since differentiation is also present, we have a true bi-logical structure.

We shall not attempt to discuss other defences – such as *sublimation* – mentioned by Anna Freud. Suffice it to say that this depends naturally upon a *displacement* which has been shown to involve symmetrization. Let us now move on to one or two defences especially emphasized by Melanie Klein. Here I shall be drawing upon Hinshelwood (1989) as well as Laplanche and Pontalis.

## Splitting

This has been mentioned already. *Splitting of the ego* was used by Freud to denote a special phenomenon at work, above all in fetishism and the psychoses. This is the coexistence at the heart of the ego of two psychical attitudes towards external reality. The first takes a truth about reality into consideration, while the second disavows it and replaces it by a product of desire. The two attitudes persist side by side without influencing each other. There is an *absence of mutual contradiction* which can be the symmetrical aspect of a bi-logical structure.

Now with regard to *splitting of the object*, Klein thought of this at its most basic as the most primitive mode of defence. It is distinctly different from Freud's splitting of the ego which was a dichotomization between awareness of internal and external. Klein, however, thought that it is not possible to have one without the other. With the second form of splitting, the object is dichotomized. This starts with an asymmetrical operation in which one side is endowed with all goodness while the other is created all bad. The badness is thus idealized into an extremity of badness, while the goodness is purified into utter perfection. We have already seen that this purification of goodness and badness involves, first, an infinitization of an asymmetry, then symmetrization towards extremes and infinities. We noted another important consequence of splitting in Chapter 4. This was that *part-objects* are created by it and that they are in fact *abstractions*. We shall discuss this again later.

## Denial

Denial or disavowal of perceptions, either about external or psychic reality, plays an important part in the splitting of the object just as described in the splitting of the ego. Freud originally introduced the term with regard to the *obliteration*, by fetishists in particular, of awareness of the difference between the male and female genitals – a symmetrization. Denial, too, is a *magical* operation based on omnipotence of thought. It is often accompanied by *manic* feelings which, as we have seen, are infinite experiences.

## Part-objects

These are not themselves defences, but often the result of defensive operations. With splitting we are naturally concerned with part-objects, ego-splits and with Klein's paranoid–schizoid position. As noted many times before, part-objects can usefully be viewed as abstractions, notions or propositional functions. The result of the *unconscious* mental operation here is *not* a *particular tangible* thing, a particular person's actual genitals for instance, but the *general idea* of *the* female or male genitals, *the* breast or *the* anus, or rather, 'breastness' or 'anusness'. Seen in this light a part-object is of quite a different order from a three-dimensional physical thing, which could be a particular fragment scattered about with the other bits of a broken object. A part-object is an abstract idea. When theorists mix up the two they are likely to have naïvely been committing a fundamental category error.

### Projective identification

This profoundly important concept was introduced by Melanie Klein in 1946, and is now in the widest use throughout the world. Maybe it has often been used too promiscuously and can become a glib explanation for every mental phenomenon, but it has helped us to leap forward in our understanding, not only of psychotic processes but also of some aspects of normal interpersonal emotional communication. Even today, after half a century, very few non-analysts have begun to grasp its social as well as its personal importance. Matte Blanco, in contrast, valued and studied Klein's insights from the beginning.

Freud's use of the term 'projection' involves wishes or objects being projected from the self. Projective identification, on the other hand, specifically involves projection of the idea of part or whole of the self. In fact it has been pointed out (Spillius 1988) that it is probably impossible to make an agreed and useful distinction between projection and projective identification. However, there is a vital aspect of the Kleinian contribution which was not noted by Freud: this is that part or whole of the subject's self is, after the projection, felt to lodge, reside in, or be *identified* with the object projected into. Here we find the 'identification aspect' of projective identification. A confusion is felt to exist between self and the object, for after all it is still unconsciously part of the self, even though projection has taken place. This may be felt as a weirdness, exquisite intimacy or an extra-special relation.

The motive behind a part of the self being made to reside in another object can be malignant. It can aim to control, punish, torture or insidiously destroy the object. But projective identification can, rather less satisfactorily, describe more benign purposes such as mutual intimacy, empathy and as a means of communicating affect. It was Bion (1962) who pointed to this line of thought.

We have already noted that Matte Blanco (1988), with his appreciation of Kleinian ideas, spent a lot of effort in thinking about projective identification. His contribution to the matter is important. This lies with his conception of the 'basic matrix of projection and introjection' already mentioned. This points towards an unconscious level of highly undifferentiated knowing.

Let us take a very simple example. In the first step of a projective identification the subject feels bad; shall we say that he or she is disgusting in some way. The mind then searches for fellow disgusting creatures (using disgustingness, an abstract attribute or propositional function, for this purpose), and finds the idea of rats, perhaps. The subject has here 'scanned' a basic matrix of projection and identification – the class of disgusting things which includes the subject and rats. At that level there is *no difference* (symmetry) between the subject, rats, all other disgusting things and disgustingness. With this in train, the subject begins to asymmetrize (infinitely perhaps) again, to differentiate the self from rats. This is most crucial for *denial* or disavowal quickly to take place. By this means, the self expunges the idea of being at all disgusting or objectionable. However, it is still in the other object. So the thought would be: 'There is nothing nasty about me', 'How disgusting these rats are', 'I am nothing like them'. The objectionable part of the self is residing only in the object. The effect of the denial within the self gives the impression of a projection into the other object.

However, there is still an unholy affinity between the subject and rats, for something of the self really still resides, now unconsciously, in the rats. Disgustingness identifies them both. Though a projection has apparently taken place when viewed from outside at a conscious level, identification is still as strong as ever at the unconscious level of the basic matrix.

The fundamental act in this is the splitting-off and denial of the badness in the self. This is not itself spatial in nature, but it gives the *appearance to an observer* of an act in space, badness being 'thrown into' the rats – projection.

The benign forms of projective identification do not seem crucially to involve this denial of an attribute from the self. Thus with this, when you see a friend catch his finger in a door, you go 'ouch'. Here, it can be said that you project your imagined pain into him for he may not have actually hurt himself at all, but you are *not denying* the presence of a pain in the self. This lack of denial seems to cast into doubt even the appearance of the spatial, *projectile* nature of this more normal process (Sandler 1993). Thus, it could just as well be said that the friend's imagined finger pain goes into yourself, as that your finger pain goes out into him. The 'direction' of the process can be quite equivocal. Concentration upon the spatial aspect of the process can be misleading, especially when it is often no more than a metaphor. Maybe a term other than 'projection' ought then to be found, particularly when denial about the self is not taking place. A neologism like 'denial free' projective identification is descriptive but the words resonance, attunement, empathy or sympathy are simpler, commonly understood and more precise in the description of the phenomena in question.

The particular contribution of bi-logic here is in saying that there is an unconscious level of mental functioning, the basic matrix, where self, object and attribute are experienced as *only the same*. From this clarifications follow. We see that the basic matrix is frequently a 'pool' which is drawn upon in various mental tricks for many defensive purposes.

The use of this level of the basic matrix means that the bi-logically minded do not start out from a chain of thinking about a psychological process with the assumption that, in such a process, subject and object are known as separate things from the beginning. This separation is good two-valued logic but clearly too simplistic for psychoanalytic use. Rather the 'bi-logician' is geared to be alert for symmetrized undifferentiation at any stage of a thought process under examination.

Matte Blanco is saying that the original Kleinian formulations have made enormous strides in our thinking, but seem to use essentially only three-dimensional spatial, 'mind is a bag' conceptions to create their concepts around projective identification. This means, as we have pointed out previously, that the human mind is then confined to a rather crude three-dimensional spatial entity. Matte Blanco introduces a new sophistication in his multi-dimensionality which makes plain how unlikely it is that the mind functions only three dimensionally as many psychoanalysts have implied so far.

## Love, hate and fantasy

Let us just glance at one or two other major analytic concepts. *Love* obviously aims to be close, to mingle with, thus be the same as, the loved one – or partly so at least; a symmetry between selves is wanted. *Hate*, on the other hand, involves the desire to *exclude* the other from the self – a vehemently, even infinitized, asymmetrical activity. However, *destructiveness*, arising immediately out of it, aims to destroy the structure of the object; it demolishes its relationships. This is a violently symmetrizing activity upon the object.

Turn for a moment to *fantasy*. Insofar as it refers to elements akin to day-dreaming and *unrealistic* processes, it employs the symmetrical 'basic matrix' to find make-belief objects that have similarity with aspects of the self. The symmetrical activity, however, is not itself make-belief: it is a searching out of sameness and is as vital to realistic activity as to fantasy. The basic matrix belongs to neither fantasy nor reality, but lies behind both and may be used by either.

Now let us return to Matte Blanco for his direct views on some classical psychoanalytic concepts. His wording may sound a little too graciously formal for modern ears but his spirit is clear and stirring.

## Emotion and unconscious

Matte Blanco (1988: 88) says: 'In the end nothing is found which leads to a clear and neat distinction between emotion and the unconscious. . . . The conclusion . . . is that differences between emotion and the unconscious, if any, are yet to be defined.'

His opinion here is clear. He is saying that we often use the word 'unconscious' in general conversation when we could just as well say 'emotional' and vice versa. He is *not* saying that there is no conceptual difference between the two. Matte Blanco (1988: 85–7) continues:

> *Why is the Freudian unconscious unconscious?* The answer to this question . . . is relatively easy if it refers to the repressed unconscious: . . . the possibility of entering consciousness may be barred to a given unconscious content. Once the prohibition is cancelled the content may become conscious. . . . The unrepressed unconscious, on the other hand, cannot enter consciousness owing to its own nature.

In Matte Blanco's view conscious thinking cannot manage too many symmetrized ideas (abstract attributes, notions, propositional functions) at any one time. Also, the multi-dimensional aspect of the unconscious cannot be contained by three-dimensional consciousness.

## Freud's id, ego and super-ego

Matte Blanco (1975: 121–4) says:

> Although . . . not intended in [Freud's] theoretical conception, there is a certain natural tendency to identify the person, some call it the self, with the ego. The id and super-ego appear, in a certain way, to be external to *us*, or anyway psycho-analytical thinking tends to look at them as external to the central core of the person or self. This is contrary . . . to the warnings of Freud. . . . All the same, it seems fair to consider the tendency to exclude the id and the super-ego from the most central aspect of ourselves, as an inevitable consequence of the formulation of the theory. . . . In Freud's diagrams of the mind . . . there are zones where there is only ego, others where there is only super-ego and others where there is only id. Psycho-analytical

thinking parallels this exactly, because it continually speaks of the three parts of the mind in a way which reflects this conception. . . .

Clinical reality . . . frequently conveys an entirely different impression from that suggested by the threefold conception. When I am hungry, when I am in love or I am angry with somebody, it is *I* who am hungry, in love or angry and not my id. *My id and my ego coincide on a great number of occasions.* . . . The theory does not account for this. . . .

I do not feel that my id tells my ego to do something and that my super-ego tells me not to do it. I feel, instead, that *I* feel the desire to do it and that *I* feel I should not do it. . . . [The] three agencies [separated like this] are . . . not a true reflection of psychic reality. . . .

[Rather] I would say that I split this desire. . . . The id . . . or the super-ego might be considered a split-off part of the self. . . . The threefold conception would then be an extreme expression of a splitting when things have become intolerable. It is interesting to note that this view is actually the theory underlying much clinical work today, especially, though not exclusively, among the Kleinians, only it is not formulated as such. . . .

It seems truer to the facts to say that what is split off is a 'desiring ego' who cares nothing about what may happen to others if his desires are satisfied . . . and an 'angry ego' who cares nothing of the sufferings of the 'central ego'. . . .

In other words, what we always find is a split-off part exercising id-, ego-, and super-ego-functions which are . . . in contrast to the corresponding functions exercised by the 'central' or main aspect of the self. . . .

In short, instead of provinces which separate three entities, which become like three persons, we would have to conceive the mind or the person as *a self or a person with . . . different functions that can never exist independently from the self.*

Matte Blanco is writing very directly here about the welfare of the sense of self having a dynamic of its own; this then is a motive or drive system in its own right – alongside other drives, of course. It is here that Matte Blanco is close to Kohut (1971) and other self-psychologists. Matte Blanco always acknowledges his debt to Klein. However, interestingly, he does not mention Fairbairn who made these very points fifty years ago. Matte Blanco even uses his actual terminology (e.g. the 'central' ego or self). This plagiarism was certainly not intentional; he is not that sort of person. However, it is one of those instances where Matte Blanco recognized Freud, then Klein, but tended to ignore other contributors.

### The self

In the previous paragraphs Matte Blanco referred repeatedly to the self, but I do not think he devotes much time to its logical status. It deserves more scrutiny than we can give, but here are one or two ideas with which Matte Blanco would probably agree.

The notion of self is quintessentially a finely articulated *asymmetrical* structure. From one aspect it includes an organizing system, the ego, but it also experiences *location* in the world. The self with its body is thus a centre around which motility through the external world takes place; survival depends upon its fine articulation in space and time.

However, the self readily takes on symmetrized qualities, particularly in pathology; but also in the normal and basic intersubjective experiences of empathy. In projective and introjective identification symmetrizations can occur so that, for instance, in psychosis the whole self can even disappear from location in the body into the external world. In less severe states, at least aspects of the self can likewise disappear. Similarly, in many other ways the self can become more or less spaceless or timeless – in omnipotence and omniscience and immortality, for instance. Infinities can reign in the self.

Thus, though essentially asymmetrical, the self is undoubtedly a bi-logical structure. It is different from purely intellectually conceived physical objects, like the self's own somatic body. These are essentially bi-modal structures.

### Objects and object relations

Just as Matte Blanco is dissatisfied with the Tripartite model, so also he criticizes object-relations theory. He quotes Balint:

> In this phrase 'object' does not refer to objects in the everyday sense but to people, and in the same way object relationship means relationship with people not with objects. This curious usage, which invariably puzzles the uninitiated, is well established among analysts.
>
> (Balint 1959: 11)

Then Matte Blanco himself goes on:

> The term [object] is so much in vogue nowadays that, in my view, it has become worn out. . . . [However] it is not only the name that is inappropriate but the handling of the object, and the 'relations' aspect of the theory. . . . Most of the theory could be regarded as a uni-directional object-relations theory because it deals with what the

116

individual feels or does with the object and not sufficiently with the *interaction* between individual and object. The essential and basic unity of both seems not to be sufficiently considered. But that applies, perhaps, to the whole of psycho-analytical theory . . . .

We hear of the object being inside, outside, in bits, bizarre bits, of the relation to the internal breast, of containers, etc. In all these expressions the object is treated as a material object. . . . This [is] making it spatial (three-dimensional). This seems to be the consequence of a purely asymmetrical point of view. Symmetrical being . . . [has been] completely left out of the notion of object. . . . [As a class, objects in the theory are] submitted to vicissitudes which only individuals – or rather only material individuals – can undergo. . . . The result is most unsatisfactory.

(Matte Blanco 1975: 121–31)

### What is an object?

Here Matte Blanco focuses on intersubjective activity. In doing so he comes close to the positions of Winnicott and Kohut.

An object is simply an aspect of the individual. It may represent an external person only if the individual has 'internalized' and made this person part of himself. . . . [However, we can see that] an [internal] object is an aspect of the self exercising id, ego and super-ego-functions, in various respective degrees according to the case. . . .

The notion of object stems basically from asymmetrical thinking. . . . An important danger of this notion is precisely its extreme asymmetry. Because . . . [of this] it leaves out important aspects of psychic reality, which for this reason pass unnoticed by psycho-analysts who look at this reality with 'object-tinted glasses' . . .

[Object theory has tried to avoid the impersonalness of the threefold conception, with its associated concept of energy]. . . . But object-relations theory, in its turn, depersonalised man by transforming him, through its objects (breast, penis, etc.) into a vast collection of footballs [or any other physical objects] which are thrown from one place to another; but this time by angry players who reduce them to bits.

I am proposing . . . another way of looking at things, . . . which does not intend to replace either the 'energy model' or the 'object model' but proposes, instead, a more rigorous meditation upon our use of concepts. Perhaps both our models can remain as parts of our

117

thinking . . . provided we are constantly ready to develop . . . the bases of the theory itself.

(Matte Blanco 1975: 121–31)

Well, there we are. Matte Blanco makes no bones about his view of the poverty of the basic structure of at least some psychoanalytic theory. This is predominantly because it is shrunken by being tied to simple three-dimensional, pseudo-physical models which are inadequate to cover the facts. However, he makes it plain that, though not fully sufficient for future purposes, these analytic theories are still necessary as starting points.

Matte Blanco's way of looking at things enhances our present theory with an awesome richness of possibilities; but it obviously cannot act as a self-contained theory on its own; he never pretended otherwise.

He only points indirectly to the positive values in the conception of an *internal object*. There is no doubt that such objects have aspects which are of quite a different order from conceptions of physical objects. The experience of an internal object is *not* simply in three-dimensional space. It has the often many-sided qualities of abstracted conceptions, notions or propositional functions. Note the plurality here. An internal object gleams with a myriad of qualities. It is full of infinities of portents; it is divine good and evil. But for all this mystic presence it still has some aspects that are particular images from the actual and physical three-dimensional world. Like the top of an iceberg, one's internal mother, for instance, is still accompanied by vital memories of her actual face, smile and way of walking and talking. So an internal object is not *just* an abstract conception or propositional function even though it may carry a million of such essences in it.

At the same time as internal objects, there are many abstract conceptions which infuse our thoughts and feelings and inhabit the unconscious yet are definitely not truly to be conceived of as objects. Examples of such notions are *intuitions* of infinity, stability, fairness, malice, trust, faith, hope, charity, justice, meanness, spite, evil, cruelty, greed, shiftiness and many others. These conceptions, notions or propositional functions can all be symbolized into dream images, so they do not fade to nothing when consciousness falls away into sleep. The unconscious must be inhabited by many internal objects but they are not the only presences in that strange region.

# 8

# The therapeutic process

Matte Blanco has been accused of being short on clinical case studies to lend weight to theory. This is true of his earlier work (1975) but he certainly made up for it later (1988). However, even if the criticism were wholly justified, he still points the way in several new therapeutic directions. We shall look at some of these now, but, more generally, it must be mentioned that bi-logically minded analysts have said that they sit behind the couch in a slightly different basic mood than before. Some have said it helps them with borderline phenomena; others see it as evoking a greater openness to the omnipresence of paradoxes in mental life; and others still suggest that it has helped them use their own emotionality in a more free-ranging but rigorously neutral way (Casaula *et al.* 1994). Let us now look at a few lines of therapeutic enquiry using bi-logic.

## The unfolding function in psychoanalytic therapy

Here is a description of Matte Blanco's most direct and explicit contribution to analytic technique.

### Repressed and unrepressed unconscious

Matte Blanco starts by emphasizing that there is a crucial difference between *lifting* the repression from that which it has made unconscious and *unfolding* that which is unconscious because it does not have the *appropriate structure* to be handled by consciousness.

Freud said, 'the essence of repression lies simply in turning something away, and keeping it at a distance from the conscious' (1915: 147). Matte Blanco argues that for this to happen the *repressed memory* must be *structured entirely in terms of conscious or asymmetrical thinking*. If an unconscious memory

119

is not structured with integrated asymmetricality it cannot have been conscious, so it could not have been repressed. Furthermore, Freud also proposed, of course, that there must be a repressing force to keep these contents repressed. Matte Blanco is quite explicit in agreeing with this (1975: 80–4). He then goes on, like Freud, to emphasize that much unconscious content has never been conscious; it must thus be un-repressed. Becoming more specific than Freud, he investigates what might be the particular *structure* of such unrepressed unconscious ideas. We shall follow his words fairly closely here.

### Translating-unfolding

Consciousness is by its nature spatio-temporal. Symmetrical content, on the other hand, is alien to space and time. Consciousness cannot contain much symmetry; nor can it wholly handle the infinity which is intrinsic in an abstract notion or propositional function (Chapters 4 and 5) which is an abstracted idea of a class but without its discrete elements. Here ideas are unconscious – or also perhaps preconscious – not because they are emo-tionally objectionable and thus repressed, but simply because of the nature of their structure. For instance, the experience of emotion is the nearest we get consciously to imagining a particular infinite set.

What happens if consciousness cannot contain much symmetrical being? All sorts of devices, particularly those seen in dreams, are needed to give some representation of multi-dimensional symmetrizations to conscious awareness. It seems that consciousness selects bits here and there from the amorphous mass of symmetricality and gives them some, even fantastical, order in time and space. It behaves as though it were transforming symmetrical being into something that conveys the appearance of asymmetry. The most that human consciousness (which is by nature analytical) can achieve is, says Matte Blanco, to let the infinite dimensions of symmetrical being enter it *successively*. Consciousness can handle only a few dimensions at one time (possibly three, or at most four). 'It is like when a mass of people have to go through a narrow door – it can only be done one at a time' (Matte Blanco 1975: 106–9).

In summary so far: Ideas that cannot be fully comprehended by con-sciousness, either because they are multi-dimensional or because they are infinite, nevertheless can give successive hints of their presence. Hence, conscious thought can widen itself in some measure to include, find a meaning in, and take account of these hints. This *unfolding* is one of the major features of analytic therapy.

Matte Blanco then suggests that if a symmetry–asymmetry hybrid which is heavily loaded with symmetrizations is felt to be too near consciousness, it is extremely disturbing. It seems to shake the foundations of our being. What a normal person then does amounts to an unfolding function. To comprehend such an experience he or she introduces further asymmetrical relations in the heavily loaded and biased symmetrical–asymmetrical 'compound'.

Analytical work involves unfolding unrepressed unconscious (or maybe preconscious) meanings by letting them appear alongside things of the same class which are still easily and consciously available. These unconscious ideas are *not* repressed and a skilful analyst may unfold such meanings without resistance on the part of the patient. A patient denying, objecting and rejecting indicates resistance, often involving anger, disgust or stubbornness, and hence repression to be overcome in various ways. With unfolding, however, the difficulty lies in comprehending aspects of reality. Here the patient is usually cooperative and even eagerly interested when new views are discovered. Matte Blanco compares unfolding to inflating a balloon that has many pictures on its skin. When symmetrical being is predominant it is as if the balloon were empty, in this case the pictures will hardly be visible; but if it is inflated the drawings become visible and details obvious (*ibid*.: 110–14).

He ponders Freud's insistence that for something to become conscious it must establish contact with memory traces of *words*. He says that he never quite understood the importance of this until he realized that words, which are *abstract* things that rely on symmetry and can apply to many circumstances, none the less act to *differentiate* asymmetrically between concepts and also between other things. '*Words (i.e. their meanings) are the asymmetrical tools of the translating-unfolding function*' (*ibid*.: 115).

### A clinical example by Matte Blanco of the unfolding function

A rather arrogant young man got married during his analysis. A collection for a wedding present was made among his colleagues, who decided to give him money so that he could choose what to get. However, some people had not yet given their contribution and asked if he would please wait a little longer. Some weeks passed and nothing had happened. He began to brood and decided that if the wedding present were not given soon he would refuse it; this would show them how he felt.

Free association in the analysis brought more details. He felt that the whole attitude of his colleagues was one of rejection. This must be because he had often shown off and been ambitious. Their apparent dislike aroused intense feelings of abandonment and guilt. His loneliness was simply the loss of all rights to existence. His companions were trying to make him feel he was the summum of badness and aggression.

121

Matte Blanco sees that the patient, being prey to such violent emotions, was unable to see other alternatives which could explain their behaviour to him. There were many possible reasons for the delay which were just as plausible as his explanation. Matte Blanco then commented to the patient that his decision to refuse the gift *brought him back from total non-existence* in their eyes to having a powerful impact upon his colleagues' feelings. The decision also asserted that his aggressiveness was a not bad thing. The patient, it is important to note, had no difficulty in accepting this interpretation and felt immediate relief. He eventually saw the whole incident as less important and smiled at himself.

Note that Matte Blanco here makes no reference to defence. This is not because it does not apply, but the real issue at that moment was that the patient felt that he was in danger of falling into *non-existence*. The event was centrally felt as an *infinite set*. Hence, therapeutically, reference had to be made to an infinite danger.

Matte Blanco's interpretation about total non-existence was in terms of infinity, but what entered the patient's consciousness was not itself an infinite set. His awareness was a finite one, an intuition of the existence of a hidden infinite set; it was an intuitive notion of such a set. '*Human consciousness cannot contain an infinite set. . . . What we can do instead, is to become (asymmetrically) conscious (aware) of some aspects of symmetrical being.* Just as we cannot make our liver conscious but only become conscious of our liver' (*ibid.*: 294–9).

## The quantum intellect–emotion

Matte Blanco then tries to elucidate the intimate nature of the meaning of the relation between infinite and finite, for he thinks this is very important in the analytic process. A representative of an intensive or extensive infinite set comes to consciousness, as we have seen, through *words*. Matte Blanco says words are like an ambassador of a powerful country. Such an emissary does not have the power of the set itself; it is but a reminder of the power behind it. Previously the patient had seen the ambassador as having the power, but an interpretation momentarily divests the emissary of this threatening presence and brings relief. There is a link between the particular explicit meaning of an emotion and the infinity of possible meanings that are implicit in that very same emotion. Matte Blanco calls this the '*quantum of intellect-emotion*'. Here there is a *union of the finite and the infinite which meet for an instant in consciousness* in spite of the fact that infinity can never fully enter consciousness. He says it is as though they meet at the limit, the border between conscious and unconscious. Such an event is instantaneous, so that it can never be fully dwelt upon.

It only takes place when there is *emotion in consciousness*, for it is this element that is the 'carrier of infinity'. One is reminded of this when thinking of any deep emotion like: 'I love you so very, very, very much', or 'I am utterly, utterly devastated'. Note that repetition suggests going on to infinity (Bomford 1990a). With no emotion there can be no infinite experience; there can then be no unfolding therapeutic function. The moral of this is not that therapists must become acquainted with the logical aspects of infinite sets, rather it suggests that they engage with their patients at a *level of optimal emotionality* that will allow finite and infinite to meet for those mysterious fruitful moments of a quantum leap. The clinical illustrations that follow show instances of the unfolding function at work, though with repressions also embedded in the material. A session usually manifests work on both defence and unfolding at the same time.

Matte Blanco (1975: 300) gives his opinion:

> The consideration of the translating function brings the realisation that much, probably the majority, of present-day analytic work deals with this function rather than the lifting of repression. . . . This is inevitably so because, after all, the repressed is only a small portion of the unconscious, which is a collection of infinite sets. In actual practice we often have to work simultaneously on lifting repression and translation.

This is a useful statement. On the positive side it summarizes the proposal that there are hitherto unknown mental functions which are subject to the action of analytic therapy. An important new region has been opened up. On the other hand, Matte Blanco's choice of words is somewhat unfortunate, for he might be seen to imply that unfolding is more important than the analysis of defence. He never intended this, but unfolding could be used as an excuse to avoid tackling defence analysis which can only too readily be skirted round.

## Further suggestions about therapy arising out of bi-logic

In what must have been one of his last papers, Matte Blanco (1989) advocates several interesting technical devices. They seem to work well but some might think them too enjoyable for the analyst and no more than a self-indulgence. However, Matte Blanco gives good theoretical reasons why he thinks they work. Here are some of the devices.

(a) A very thorough and precise attention to all aspects of the patient's discourse, seen in terms of *classical two-valued logic*, can, by *contrast*, emphasize bi-logical and infinite aspects both for the analyst and patient.

(b) He next draws attention to the fact that a patient's unconscious can 'employ classical logic with as much precision and subtlety as the best Aristotelian logician. But it uses it in the service of its own symmetrical satisfaction. The unconscious is not interested in philosophy but in its own way of satisfying instinctual demands' (*ibid.*: 18).

(c) It is important, Matte Blanco thinks, to *speak to the patient using the language of the unconscious*, particularly the idiosyncratic unconscious language of the patients themselves. One way of doing this is to use *jokes and humour* which are *in tune* with, or have a *form* that is similar to, an essence of the patient. This is a *mapping* which is essential in any true explanation.

He gives an example of this where a patient telephoned one day to say he had 'flu; someone had infected him, the patient insisted, and he did not want to pass it on to Matte Blanco. He did, however, come the next day but still insisted that he did not want to infect his analyst. This insistence struck Matte Blanco and reminded him of a joke from years before in a psychiatric hospital, which he then told the patient. It was that a man suffering from delirium tremens was being interviewed by a psychiatrist. He complained of the itches 'of bugs' and kept brushing them away towards the psychiatrist who said, 'For God's sake don't brush those things on to me'. The patient laughed and Matte Blanco caught him in the middle of this by jokingly saying that it looked as if he, the patient, wanted to get him, Matte Blanco, frightened also of being infected and who might then tell him not to come to the session. This humorous mood appeared to add emotional zest and thence acuity to the search for what was actually being resisted.

(d) Other ways of speaking in the language of the unconscious are to use poetry, to imitate dreams, and sometimes to refer to popular wisdom expressed in venerable maxims.

The point of departure here is Matte Blanco's emphasis upon the importance of the analyst himself quite consciously getting as closely identified as possible in speaking to the 'grammar' or idiom of the patient's unconscious, while at the same time maintaining (asymmetrical) objectivity. By this means a mapping or one-to-one correspondence of the patient's unconscious is carried out by the analyst. And, since mapping is at the heart of any explanation, interpretations in the form of jokes, etc., can be the closest and most appropriate mapping of the unconscious at a particular moment. This line of argument by Matte Blanco is almost identical to one made by the present author in a paper on attunement and technique (Rayner 1992). It is also close to Skelton's (1990b) observation that rhetoric is an essential mode of discourse for analytic therapy.

## Some case illustrations

The descriptions that follow are all about the use of bi-logic; they do not come from Matte Blanco but from the present author or his colleagues.

### *Case A: The use of the 'basic matrix' of projection and introjection*

Chapters 3 and 4 showed how things that are known consciously as similar, and thus as belonging to the same class, are known only as nothing but the same at a less conscious level (strata 3 and 4). Here *subjects* and *objects* of thought seem to *disappear*, and only predicates, notions or propositional functions hold sway. This is the area of the basic matrix. As we have already seen, it is probably from this level that acts of disavowal or denial emerge to start the processes of projection.

This aspect of bi-logic seems to be particularly useful when a patient attends a session feeling distinctly persecuted, guarded and stubborn. This is often explosive and chronic. One has the hunch that insidious projective identifications are running wild. Here is an example.

A patient, who at his best was actually highly intelligent and competent, often got into confused and agonized states where both bitter grudges and self-condemnation seemed incomprehensibly muddled so that neither he nor others could fully appreciate his usefulness. He started a Monday session with a long silence, and when he did speak his voice was hardly more than a mutter, so that he seemed more to be talking to himself than to anyone else. The analyst, struggling to catch the patient's mutterings, found himself feeling angry that the patient hardly seemed to be bothering to notice that he, the analyst, was there as a separate person who needed to hear what was said. However, he said nothing and listened to the patient's rather whining, bitter story of his wife's weekend preoccupation with work worries, her engrossment in her children, and her musical commitments. The patient recalled his dutiful shopping, cleaning and painting of the house. He was not upset about the duties but hurt that she had no time for him except an irritable very busy dismissal. The hurt mood continued in the session and droned on when he recounted how his boss at work clingingly leant upon him, taking up hours of his time, and then importantly whizzed off without a second thought. The patient then shifted gear and made his own transference interpretation. This was that his proneness to be exploited, and his anger when it happened reminiscent of how life was with his mother. She very often expected him not only to do the chores, but even as a child to be also an emotional support for her when busy in social activities outside the home. All this time the patient was talking but seemed to have no interest in whether he was actually being heard or understood.

The analyst, still frankly feeling cross with being subtly ignored by the patient himself, thought of starting out with an interpretation about the patient's denial of his own neglect of the needs of the dutiful listening other person. He also thought of pointing out the projection of this neglectful part of the patient into others – partner, boss, mother and analyst – so that it then resided only in these people about whom he felt an obsessive fury. This sort of rather crude projective-identification interpretation had been tried many times. But they had only ended in a sort of 'verbal tennis', where interpretations of guilt were banged to and fro. They became a quiet form of chronic sadomasochistic stalemate; here the patient was convinced that the analyst was only interested in avoiding any guilt himself and in punishing him into submissive acceptance of his, the analyst's, authoritative point of view.

Knowledge of bi-logic brought the analyst to think about the 'basic matrix of projective identification'. He decided to appeal to the possibility of the patient being emotionally aware of this level of experience. He listened to the patient until the story was completed and, holding his own counter-transference anger in check, said: 'Well, one thing is clear in what you have been saying, and that is that an irritable rather arrogant dismissal is happening pervasively. It perhaps doesn't matter to begin with who is the dismisser and who is dismissed, who is the perpetrator and who is the victim, we can decide that later. But I think we can agree easily enough that this dismissal is our business today.'

The patient readily saw this, was, remarkably, not antagonized into starting up a 'tennis match', and did not feel that the analyst was automatically blaming him. He began to talk less defensively with the analyst in a mood nearer to that of a cooperative venture. Something of a glimmer of recognition that his own dismissiveness might play a part seemed at last to be emerging by the end of the session.

Getting stuck in what amounts to chronic sadomasochistic episodes of blame through glib and very direct interpretations of projective identi-fication is probably common. It is certainly not the case that the concept of projective identification is wrong, but its crude and automatic use during periods of high vulnerablity accentuates mutual intolerance. Such inter-pretations can be experienced as expulsions or disowning of the patient. They then become a polarization, a verbal splitting or infinitized asym-metrization, where the communality or symmetry between analyst and patient is reduced to zero.

The bi-logically inspired appeal by the analyst suggested in the above example is to the patient's awareness of a symmetrized level. No per-petrator of 'guilt-riddance', disavowal or denial, is yet allocated. There is only a general proposition that directs the patient to his and the analyst's 'basic matrix' level – that some underlying threat or persecution is happening.

The subject and object are not yet specified, so no actual guilt allocation has taken place, thus it does not need to be avoided by means of the well-known malignant whining of bitter projective identifications.

Though useful, addressing the basic matrix is no magic panacea. A person who is ingrained with the often borderline propensity to avoid the experience of guilt or shame by use of instant projective identification will readily try to avoid the pain of accusation which is offered by the 'basic matrix' method. The patient will often remain as stubborn as ever in refusing to contemplate any awareness of responsibility for his or her effect on others. In the end the projective identifications do have to be faced and worked through by whatever means.

### Case B: Therapeutic 'argument'; triangulation and unfolding

Interpretive psychoanalytic therapy involves a movement of ideas between different frames of reference and aims to integrate them. It can also be seen as involving a *movement between levels* of higher proportions of symmetry to levels of more asymmetrical thought. This is where the use of words is vital; they are abstract and thus have wide applicability, but their meanings apply specifically and asymmetrically to particulars. It can thus be a movement between the more emotional and the more intellectual levels of thought. This could be viewed as a movement from the deeper unconscious to the more articulated conscious asymmetrical levels of Matte Blanco's 'stratified structure' (Chapter 6). *Movement* of thoughts is essential for thinking to take place.

The therapeutic process can also be seen as a movement of viewpoint or *position of identification*. The analyst, for instance, attunes or transiently identifies with the patient.

From here every utterance, tone and mood by the patient or by the analyst can lead to a new, slightly different interpretation of what is happening by one or other of the protagonists, albeit in simple, primitive, unconscious or preconscious ways. The thoughtful analyst will then often go further than this and move away in his or her imagination to look at the patient from a more distant outsider's eyes. The analyst may then move to and fro between distance and closeness of empathy before composing an explicit overview interpretation for the patient. From his side, optimally the patient listens to the analyst's meanings and compares them with fantasy-laden ideas from his hitherto solitary position. Here psychoanalysis becomes an *inductive* process, akin to a small-scale scientific study (Ahumada 1994). The patient's reply to an interpretation gives the analyst cause to think further, and so on. It has been likened by several authors (Abelin 1981; Britton 1989; Wooster *et al.* 1990) to *triangulation*, like that of a mapmaker. This is a good metaphor but has limitations for it is only spatial and many of the mental events referred to will naturally be non-spatial as well as often having an infinite quality.

For psychic change it is likely that highly asymmetrical thought (spatial or otherwise) must occur at the same time as structures that are deeply emotional, infinite and symmetrized; they can then combine or inter-penetrate. Disparate aspects of the self integrate. This is unfolding. Rather than being just triangulation, it is a *combinatorial movement* of ideas close to Winnicott's transitionality. Pathology often appears to arise from emotional-symmetrized-infinite structures being disintegrated, split-off or disowned from other emotional structures through rejective-asymmetrized-infinite processes. Hence a therapeutic process would be one which reintegrates the disintegrated, discordant and contradictory emotional structures.

In this light the therapeutic process can be seen as a dialogue between patient and analyst – and between different aspects of the patient himself – not to mention those within the analyst. In these dialogues, movement of thought takes place whereby 'propositions' from each point of view are made with the purpose of affecting those from another point of view. This is a *dialectic* and combinatorial process where different protagonists, either within an individual or between persons, are trying by conceptual means to affect each other.

The appropriate word is thus again likely to be 'argument'. As noted earlier, this can have an aggressive, 'point-scoring' connotation; but thoughtful and emotional argument of a mutually sympathetic kind is vital in any working out of an issue. It is synonymous with serious reasoning about a problem. It has been used for centuries in an intellectual-logical sense, and we are simply extending it to the emotional realm. Argument in therapy must not be confused with nit-picking where each side is trying to score self-esteem points. Nor is it concerned only with conscious level, logically two-valued ideas, for we are in the bi-logical region of profound emotions. Argument at its best is the kindly combat of deep-feeling civilized people in pursuit of truths. No lives are lost nor characters assassinated; there are no losers. It is discussion rather than debate.

Here is a brief description of a phase of analysis after about three years. It is condensed, covering about a week of five sessions.

The patient is a married man in his thirties. At work he is obviously very competent and well appreciated; he has the gift, by all accounts, of being able to be administratively tough but kind. At home with his wife he sounds prone to be either soft and innocent or rather piously kind and condescending. This condescension never appeared towards his analyst but the innocent naïvety often did and this was repeatedly pointed out.

He returned from a summer holiday with two pieces of news which he said worried him a lot. The first was that his old father, to whom he was profoundly loyal, had confided in him that he often had horrible thoughts. They were so horrible, said his father, that he just could not say what the thoughts were; he had not even mentioned them to his wife, the patient's mother; he could not think of confiding in her about this.

The analyst had heard quite a lot about the patient's father. Though emotionally unexpressive, he was in fact a kind, tough man who had survived many things. In his work life he had little difficulty in being aggressive. However, at home with his wife it appeared that he could never show assertiveness, let alone aggressive temper, even of a quiet verbal kind. In the patient's memory, at least, father never argued with mother.

The analyst's feeling when he heard this story about the father's confession was a sort of relief on behalf of the family that father was moving at last to acknowledge to his son that he actually could have hateful feelings about people. It was in fact the first time that the patient had spoken about his father's saying anything at all about his own feelings.

However, though the analyst felt quietly pleased, the patient said he was 'very concerned' at his father's confession. As we have said, father and son were alike in having no trouble with being tough and aggressive at work, but seemed appalled by the abstract idea of aggressiveness in general, and particularly any expression of it at home. So here the analyst was pleased at some progress in the family while the patient said he was appalled at it.

By way of interpretation, the analyst gave another point of view, saying that perhaps the patient's father was feeling safer and surer of himself to be able to speak about his bad feelings to his son. His father was, after all, confiding in him for the first time. The patient said that was certainly true. The analyst added, almost as an afterthought, that the patient was probably glad that he, the analyst, had survived the holiday. The patient could thus confide again in the analyst, just as the patient's father had begun to do with him.

The patient went on to say how upset he was that one of his closest friends, an older man who had helped him a lot earlier in life, had told him that 'his marriage was dead'. The analyst noted that here was the patient conceiving of two distinct and troubled marital relationships by parent-aged people. You will notice that these events were experienced as quite distinct from each other; they were clearly asymmetrical, 'out there' and spatially appropriate perceptions. However, his fussy worrying about his father's confession shows an omnipotent, infinitized desire to take over some control of his father's life. The analyst mentioned this.

The patient then said he had had a weird dream. He was wearing a wooden mask which only had two eye-holes in it, so he could see but not speak – and, of course, his face could not be seen. It was somehow a powerfully magical mask, full of import, for it was a 'time-mask' and had something to do with giving immortality.

In the days after this session the dream kept returning, both in the patient's mind and the analyst's. It was noted that the mask in the dream prevented others from knowing the wearer's facial, emotional expressions. It constantly reminded the analyst of the patient's innocent façade behind which any expression of vicious hostility could be hidden; it was also like his father's hiding of feeling, and these were pointed out.

The sense of its being a 'time-mask' and to do with immortality also reminded the analyst of a period in the patient's early latency years that had often been mentioned with amused embarrassment. This was that for some time he believed that: 'Just as cats were cats, dogs were dogs, so too children were children and adults were adults. One never became or grew into the other.' Obliteration of getting older, of development, and thus avoiding rivalry and ideas of replacement, could remain safe with his theory of the timeless class of all children. This had often been discussed in analysis but never quite so pungently as now.

It then emerged that while all this was going on in the analysis, things were happening at work. Several of the staff under him had been making it plain to him that their overall boss ought to be 'given the chop'. They were suggesting that he, the patient, should confront their boss with this estimate of him. He himself gloated a bit at the news, but was also appalled at his hostile and contemptuous thought, and more appalled still at the thought of actually saying so to his boss. The analyst said, with a chuckle, something to the effect that, what with his father, his old friend and mentor, and now his boss, father-men were in trouble this week. Patricide was in the air.

The patient laughed too and said: 'I was just remembering yesterday that I must have been about four when I realized about age and death and I said to my father, "You are an *old* man daddy" – implying that he was going down hill to die. In fact he was only about forty.' To which the analyst asked him: 'And was it *after* this realization that you had the idea that cats are cats, children are children, adults are adults?' He replied that yes it was certainly so. It was when he was about 6 years old that he had had that theory.

The analyst could not help laughing and said, 'There you are, a really clever patricidal 4-year-old Oedipus! Nasty fellow you were! Then you find your "children are children" theory which simply obliterates time and conveniently avoids any idea of nasty patricidal triumph. That was many years ago but that patricidal killer appears to be still alive.' The patient himself laughed about his Oedipal desires and the clever avoidant tricks that his mind could bring into use. All this coming out of the 'time-mask' dream.

You will notice that both analyst and patient are triangulating or being combinatorial, moving their 'positions of the self's observation'. They are comparing and bringing them together. Analyst and patient move levels from 4 years old to latency age to adulthood. They see things from the patient's point of view and his effect on others from their point of view, and so on. While enjoying movement between asymmetrical relations, they stand back, still asymmetrically, and see the patient's mind conveniently symmetrizing into timelessness in his 'children are children' theory.

The analyst's equation of the patient's old friend, his boss, the analyst himself, and his father as all 'father people', together with his Oedipal-patricidal feelings about them, all refer to symmetrizations. A complex of bi-logical structures is being illuminated. These interpretations showing equivalences aim at recognition of the underlying sameness between things in the patient's mind. Such verbalizations weaken his splitting and isolation by which his consciousness sees objects as only different and with essentially no similarities.

In summary, the combinatorial movement in this example was aimed first to look again at difference relations (asymmetries), such as that time goes by and people get old and die, which had been defensively obliterated by the patient. Second, the 'vertical' *movement between emotional levels* aims to evoke, at a conscious asymmetrical level, a recognition of the emotions which are in common between his feelings about different people – symmetrization. These will originally have been at a basic matrix level. They are the commonality of feeling about his father, friend, boss and analyst as objects of Oedipal death wishes. The very crudeness of his feelings seemed to be constricting his ability to feel subtly and think appropriately towards these people in his adult life.

The patient's amusement at many of the analyst's comments, together with his enjoyment of his own contributions, suggests that unfolding is playing an important part here. However, obviously the main work in this phase is concerned with undoing the defensive structures against murderous Oedipal desires which, being timeless, utilize unconscious symmetrization. Unfolding and defence analysis are taking place at the same time. This is probably what usually happens in any fruitful session.

The analyst is trying to help the patient alter his emotional conceptions by conceptual means – the analyst is 'arguing' with him at an emotional level.

## Examples from psychoanalytic psychotherapy

The most systematic exponent of the clinical use of bi-logic, from Britain at least, has been Klaus Fink (1989, 1991, 1992a, b, 1993). He has described cases of both full analysis and psychotherapy.

## Case A

Here is a summary of a psychotherapy session (taken from Fink 1992b). He describes how parapraxes, 'Freudian slips', not only happen to patients but to the analyst also. However, though they are embarrassing, they can be used. He tells us of a mother who had come to therapy because of uncontrollable furies with her neighbours followed by depression about the incidents. She attends a session with her baby, who rests happily enough with a dummy (comforter) in her mouth. Meanwhile the patient begins to describe an argument with neighbours. Fink continues:

> . . . she got wound-up reliving the episode, becoming more and more angry and disturbed, ending up having a great tantrum. She shouted, stamped her feet, cried and ranted and raved. . . . The baby lay sucking its dummy and falling half asleep, woke up with the commotion and began to cry. [The patient] in the midst of her anger noticed it and picked up her child. She sat it on her knee and bounced it trying to calm it down, while she herself continued to shout in anger. . . . The baby eventually dropped the dummy out from its mouth onto the floor. . . . I noticed the dummy on the floor in front of me . . . rinsed it . . . and stuck it back in the baby's mouth. The baby kept the dummy for a couple of minutes while his mother continued her tantrum then spat it out once more. Again I bent down . . . cleaned it . . . and proceeded to stick the dummy into the mother's mouth. . . . I took it out immediately and gave it to the baby; [the mother] and I instantly burst into laughter and [she] . . . said she fully understood the meaning of what had happened.

[Fink continues by explaining some of the facets of this incident, where the mother begins to give an account of the episode with the neighbours.]

> . . . she gets carried away and relives the whole affair in my office. . . . Time gets distorted or ceases to exist . . . she is no longer totally aware of being in my room . . . the argument with the neighbours is happening in the here and now . . . the concept of space is also partly missing, [so that she] can find herself simultaneously in two different places, the estate [where she lives] and my office. . . .
>
> Internal and external images and objects become confused and perhaps exchangeable. [She] is a mother, her baby is also . . . in the office, but at the same time she is a baby herself, having a tantrum. She needs a mother and I seem to pick up this wish. In my unconscious I become this mother . . . I first mother the [real] baby and then decide to mother [the patient] herself making at the same time clear to her my wish for her to shut up and stop her tantrum. . . .

Only when I enact this unconscious wish . . . does it become conscious to me [and to the mother, for I and she laugh together]. . . .
We both simultaneously recover our faculty to judge.

This small instance crystallizes time and space disappearance. It is an
illustration of interpersonal *symmetrization* in *transference enactment*. For a
moment the analyst became the mother of both the patient and her baby.
This in itself can be seen as a spatial confusion – a loss of an asymmetrical
aspect.

Fink made good use of his mistake by examining it openly with his
patient and wondering with her about her part in it. She responded with
humorous cooperation, and one more step in mastering her rages was
achieved.


*Case B*


From London, comes another paper (Wooster *et al.* 1990) describing
weekly psychotherapies with borderline patients.

Deborah Hutchinson describes the case of May who was 36 and lived
alone. She was referred for therapy because of three annually repeated
requests for termination of pregnancy.

Fate produced a sibship of 4 [for May]: first 2 boys then 2 girls. Their
mother gave both boys the same initials. The first girl was stillborn;
initially May was to have been given her maternal aunt's name, but it
was changed to the name given to her stillborn sister. In her mind
May had made symmetry where others might notice opposites, or
even asymmetry. Her mother was black haired, her father blond. Her
stillborn sister had been described as half-black (presumably due to
the pooling of blood in part of her body post-partum). However,
May believed that her sister's father had been a black American
Serviceman. She described herself as half-black on account of the
difference in colouring of her parents, and chose a black man as the
father of her various pregnancies, in order to reproduce a half-black
child. The need for the termination of pregnancy was based on her
feelings that in order to give life to the half-black baby she would
have to die, thus repeating the fantasy situation of her sister.

(Wooster *et al.* 1990: 447)

The symmetrizations, with near-delusional force, are here obvious.
Hutchinson also noticed the symmetrization of the relation with her. She
had the feeling that she was closely marked. 'May was sitting facing me and
I felt scrutinized visually and emotionally, so that May could follow any

lead and all feelings of difference were obliterated' (*ibid*.: 447). It was also noted that when the therapist took a two-week break, this was automatically followed by the patient's taking a two-week break from work.

This symmetrizing 'copycat' imitation was seen as a defence. It saved May from feeling rejected, a painful asymmetrical experience. What might be done to her, however, was then forestalled by her doing it actively herself. The sense of being half-wanted, half-unwanted, half-wanting, half-unwanting, pervaded her life, her love-life, her friendships, even everyday thought and decisions. 'I'm never the right one, always a replacement.' But success was feared as much as rejection: 'Oh that's quite a responsibility, that's almost too much to take, it makes me feel worse, I can't handle that. To have to be the one that's wanted, it's just too much' (*ibid*.: 447).

After a good many months of therapy, May came half an hour late – half-way through the session. Hutchinson suggested that she was half present and half not. May replied, 'I sometimes wonder why I came at all, but then that's not an equal equation. If you're not being equal to others then you've lost something. I . . . never make the first move. I always let the other make the first move and then I equal it' (*ibid*.: 449).

There is no happy ending given in this story of May; it is just a quiet tragedy of a chronic need to symmetrize away certain aspects of things which have similarities with her very painful maternal and sibling relationships.

## Case C

Christopher Evans's patient, a woman called S, shows similar bitter fixations upon aspects of the maternal relationship.

> During the interviews it emerged that when S was born her mother suffered a severe blood-loss and was unconscious in intensive care for several days. This was recalled with intense anger by the father who felt that the doctors had mis-managed the birth in a seriously negligent manner. Apparently he was told that his wife would not survive.
>
> During the assessment . . . details of physical abuse of S by her mother emerged. This took the form of beatings, kicking, washing with scalding hot and freezing cold water, scrubbing the genital region until she bled, blocking of access to the toilet, being left outside in the cold for hours, refusals to let her wash, change her underwear, bathe or receive tampons or sanitary towels (which the patient used to steal). The abuse started shortly after the birth of the next sister, V. . . . Potentially contributory issues emerged including

the mother's own beatings within her family in her childhood . . . but mother commented [later] 'that does not excuse what I did' and S pointed out: 'I still do not know why me – what was different about me.'

(Wooster *et al.* 1990: 450)

Increasingly [S] talked about her experience of her mother's presence always with her 'like a curse'. . . .

We started to recognize the pervasive symmetry of the processes which followed the near lethal birth. It appears that S and her mother became fused in a mutually abusive experience that is so primitively symmetrical and undifferentiated that it almost precludes any sense of autonomy or responsibility. I think it is this fusion that underlies her need to check every week whether the I/she fusion is well enough to cope with the pain of recollection and rebirth. . . . This symmetrical processing . . . consists of . . . S, her mother and, very often, any important other, all interchangeably and indistinguishably mutilated and mutilating each other. Within this symmetrical logic there is no differentiation of subject and object – none of the asymmetrical distinction of directional operations that we usually take for granted. Here the relationships between all objects are symmetrical, so if S's birth put her mother at risk, her mother putting S's life at risk is an extension of the same process, not a reciprocation, not a process where a sentient and responsible individual initiates something. . . .

The catastrophic bleeding at birth is a focus of such intensity that the birth became a mirror creating a symmetrical relationship between mother and daughter. . . . Although S is convinced that she should not, 'cannot' have children because she would repeat the treatment she received, nevertheless the dynamic is not of the directional transmission from grandmother to mother to daughter, but of reflection.

(*ibid.*: 451–2)

Evans notes that the more he recognizes the importance of symmetry, the easier interpretation becomes. For instance, when he phrased something to S that implied that she is being hurt while there are 'others' who actively hurt her, he was met with blank incomprehension. He then came to the mode of 'dropping even the active verb, commenting only on so many experiences being hurtful or full of pain'. This is very similar to my description of the analyst's use of the basic matrix of projection and introjection. Evans finds that the *intransitive* form of his interpretations seems to have enabled him to point out the chronic use of symbolic equations that can be accepted and understood by S.

Wooster ends the paper with a summary noting that here fathers seem to be conspicuously absent psychodynamically. An inadequate differentiation of mother and child may hold up the registration and acceptance of a third person, usually father, in the creation of 'triads of ideas' (Abelin 1981). It is often the father, says Wooster, who is the vital agent in *playful* time/space sequences which provide freedom to explore and learn. Jordan (1990) makes the same point (Chapter 6). Wooster then thinks of envy. When it is too intense this play is not possible. Envy is here "the self's experience of the unattainability of symmetrization or identity with an object' (Wooster *et al.* 1990: 453). Freedom to play requires an assumption that such symmetrization with an object is possible. This is a sort of optimism.

## Conclusion

Quite apart from the specific uses we have been discussing, it is, perhaps strangely, the very abstract generality of bi-logic, its being a meta-level theory or a metapsychology, which can give it an elusive but omnipresent therapeutic usefulness. Perhaps it is also the combination of emphasis upon emotionality and on a wide-ranging intellectual rigour of inquisitiveness together with meticulous specificity that has value. Bi-logic's intellectual argumentation balances or detects equally both differences and identities. This appears not only to loosen the grip of proneness to awestruck disciple-ship, but also checks the analyst's grandiose self-indulgences. Emotionality on behalf of neutrality could be its watchword.

# 9

# Bi-logic, a crossroads between disciplines?

The remarkable thing about bi-logic is that people from different intellectual backgrounds can easily gather together and use it as a common ground.

The London-based bi-logic group has about twenty members with ten disciplines represented. The number of subjects presented by members illustrates the breadth of its ideas. For instance, there have been Arden (1984), a psychoanalyst, on Bateson and bi-logic; Ahumada (1994), a psychoanalyst, on the inductive process in psychoanalysis; Bettcher (1991), a philosopher, on the logic of bi-logic; Bomford (1989a and b, 1990a and b, 1992), an Anglican priest, on the characteristics of the unconscious compared with those of God, on the logical foundations of bi-logic, on the use of metaphor, and on myth and meaning; Duran (1989), a philosopher, on ideology; and Carmen Fink (1991), a lawyer, on bi-logic and the concept of criminality. Klaus Fink (1989, 1991, 1992a and b, 1993), a psychoanalyst, has been the group's most prolific clinical contributor. Elkan (1989, 1992), a child psychotherapist, has spoken on the book of Genesis and psychic development; Evans (1990, 1993), a forensic psychiatrist, on paradox; Jiménez (1990), a psychoanalyst, on dreams and bi-logic; Jordan (1990), a psychoanalyst, on a clinical study about inner space; Mordant (1990, 1992, 1994; Mordant and Rayner 1990), a mathematician, on bi-logic and logical analysis; Maw (1990), a linguistician, on bi-logic and language; Rayner (1991, 1992), a psychoanalyst, on abstraction and on attunement in psychoanalysis; Reyes and Lucey (1990), a child psychiatrist, on bi-logic, families, money and symmetrization; Skelton (1984, 1989, 1990a and b, 1992), a logician and psychotherapist, on logic, infinity, rhetoric and psychoanalytic therapy; Sporrong (1992, 1993), a psychiatrist and philosopher, on logical analysis and bi-logic; Wilson (1989), a psychiatrist and group therapist, on bi-logic and group phenomena; Wohlmuth and Goldberg (1990), a lawyer, on bi-logic and justice; and lastly Wooster (Wooster et al. 1990, 1992), a psychoanalyst, has written about the book of Genesis and on Shakespeare.

137

Visitors have been struck by the group's combination of direct intellectual criticism with open-minded friendliness. This will have been due not least to the lead given by Matte Blanco's personal intellectual curiosity and searching argumentativeness, together with his warmth and total absence of cruelty or contempt. The group's unity could not have come from the piety of discipleship, for this has been noticeably absent.

The group's fruitfulness appears to have come also from something in the nature of bi-logic itself. Perhaps it is because its concepts are of such an abstract and general nature, and yet applicable to real situations. They can certainly be shared and used by many different sorts of people as long as they enjoy open-mindedness and abstract ideas at the same time.

One obvious intellectual thread that runs throughout Matte Blanco is the sheer definitory precision of his concepts of logical analysis combined with a sensitive introspection that few psychoanalysts attempt. We have already noted that bi-logical argumentation contains at least two dialectical pairs: that between classical rationalism and romanticism (Strenger 1989) and that between detecting differences and identities. These together appear to assure a blessed stringent tolerance.

Let us look, very briefly indeed, at a few other authorities in different fields, chosen almost at random, who have also emphasized the use of logical analysis and see if they point in any similar directions. These will be Piaget, Lévi-Strauss, Bateson, Edelman and Bion. There are many other psychoanalysts, such as Money-Kyrle and Rapaport and, more recently, Schafer and Strenger, not to mention Lacan, who have been interested in formal logic. But this will have to be a selective and cursory flight over complex intellectual territory.

Remember that the present author is an amateur in virtually all the disciplines mentioned. He cannot even pretend to portray in an overall way or do justice to the great contributions which the authorities referred to have made to the world. This bird's-eye view must be superficial and unsatisfying; it aims only to whet the appetite.

All the authors mentioned, especially Piaget, Matte Blanco and Bion, are concerned with understanding more about the *thinking* process, and this has also been the main theme of this book. Thinking has been seen as a structured path in time of different patterns of knowing which envisage a particular aim. Since thought is about knowing, it must also be about some sort of truthfulness. This concerns the correspondence and coherence of thoughts with at least some facts. Not that all thinking aims at truthfulness: much cunning thought can be directed towards concealing a truth. But some aspect of truthfulness, either about inductively perceived facts or those of a deductive nature, must be taken into account if proper thinking is to emerge from mere disparate thoughts. Note also that there is no presumption by the authors we mention to know 'the' truth as an absolute, but simply to search for truthful ideas.

## Piaget

What is the common ground between Jean Piaget, who was a biologist before turning to child psychology, and Matte Blanco? Piaget's life's work was to distinguish crucial developmental stages in thought (1950, 1951, 1953) by using a combination of observation and questioning children of various ages as they were carrying out intellectual tasks.

His philosophy is basically *structuralist* (1971). This, he says, starts in mathematical logic. It is 'gestalt' oriented, and *counteracts atomism* of ideas by finding *isomorphisms* (samenesses, symmetries, mappings, one-to-one correspondences, matchings, resonances, harmonics, etc.) in phenomena. These reveal *underlying unities* of form in what might appear to be disparate data.

Piaget thinks that, in its most general essence, an intellectual structure is a *system of transformations*. Furthermore, the *operations* necessary to transform from one state to another can be specified. Next, any system, including intellectual thought, is not just a collection of disparate elements; there must be *laws* or *regulations* describing the transformations. The general notion of any living structure thus, for Piaget, comprises three key elements. These are the ideas of *wholeness, transformation* and *self-regulation*.

A *formally logical operation* is a piece of *'perfect' regulation*. In such an ideal model errors are excluded. A fully logical group of perfectly deductive operations, whether they be ideal or carried out by computer, must have certain definable characteristics. One of Piaget's great tasks was to specify these, but we will not attempt to describe them here. He had to carry out this specification of logic because he needed to use it as a criterion to compare the actual thought of growing children with it.

The very heart of Piaget's work has been his empirically based developmental psychology. He sees that an individual's capacity to reach full logicality in any mental function must *first* involve exercise of incompletely logical elements of thought. These must then be developmentally integrated by experience over time into meaningful wholes or systematic thoughts which he calls 'psychological groups', and he takes great pains to define them.

With detailed illustrative evidence he describes phases of development from birth onwards whereby logically mature intellectual structures appear to be achieved. For instance:

1  *Infancy* is epitomized by sensori–motor *trial and error*.
2  *Preconcepts* from *toddlerhood* onwards mark the beginning of coherent imagination and thence of *symbolic thought*. Here is the flowering of *make-belief*.
3  From about *4 years old onwards* Piaget sees the time of *intuitive thought* where make-believe is honed down to restrict omnipotence.
4  From *7 onwards* he sees the stage of *concrete operations*. Here logicality is possible as long as the child can see, hear or touch the elements being thought about.
5  Finally from 11 onwards, with luck, comes the ability to think in terms of fully *abstract operations*. This involves the ability to think logically about ideas which have *no tangible instances*. The capacity to think consistently is, according to Piaget, the fruit of years of integrative activity.

There have been many criticisms of Piaget's dating and stages, but he remains one of the great intellectual forces of the twentieth century. Educational theory and policy would not be the same without his contributions.

Do Piaget and Matte Blanco fit at all? They were temperamentally dissimilar and their centres of interest were very different. Piaget is evolutionary and developmental; he is classically rationalistic and also largely concerned with preconscious and conscious levels of thought. He is a master of secondary process. Matte Blanco is no evolutionist and little interested in development. He is most concerned with unconcious structures; he is a master of primary process. Do the two men have anything in common?

Here is one line of similarity. Piaget's work on the earliest stages of development points repeatedly to the importance of matching, mimicry and resonance. These are symmetrical processes, of course, and Piaget sees, without explaining why, that they can give rise to infinitization. For instance:

> Thought alone breaks away from these short distances and physical pathways [of sensori–motor levels], so that it may seek to embrace the whole universe including what is invisible . . . this infinite expansion of spacio-temporal distances between subject and objects comprises the principal innovation of conceptual intelligence.
>
> (Piaget 1950: 121)

The beginning of mental operations naturally proceeds through the formation of *symbols* which Piaget sees as arriving through *imitation*. This starts first with the *mimicry* of *actions* by others, to be followed, after repetition of the sequence, by mental representations (symbols) of these imitations of

140

actions being laid down. Intellectual symbols are derived from the imitations of actions by skeletal muscles; whereas symbols of affects are representations of smooth muscle and hormonal activity. Symbolic play 'always involves an element of imitation functioning as a significant' (*ibid*: 126). Imitation, being mimicry or matching, is a symmetrizing activity. Note here that Piaget was, through the idea of imitation, in effect more alerted to *interpersonal* symmetrization than was Matte Blanco himself.

The very process of a specific symmetrization is well described by Piaget (1950: 127):

> The child aged 2–3 will be just as likely to say 'slug' as 'slugs' and 'the moon' as 'the moons', without deciding whether the slugs encountered in the course of a single walk or the discs seen at different times in the sky are one individual, a single slug or moon, or a class of distinct individuals. On the other hand, he cannot yet cope with general classes, being unable to distinguish between 'all' and 'some'.

Piaget (1951: 199) sees unconscious symbolism in a similarly symmetrical light when he says:

> In a state of radical ego-centrism [as can be approximated to at times in the utterances of any small child] there is complete lack of differentiation between the ego and the external world. . . . The origin of the unconscious symbol is to be found in the suppression of consciousness of the ego by complete absorption in, and identification with, the external world, it therefore constitutes merely a limiting case of assimilation of reality to the ego, i.e. of ludic symbolism.

Here unconscious symbolism occurs through an overall non-differentiation, a state of symmetrization, between ego and external object. Piaget also sees the very condition of unconsciousness as an extreme instance of non-differentiation. He seems to go further than Matte Blanco here, for he is surely proposing that repression itself is an instance of symmetrization.

Note again that Piaget sees that imitation (itself a useful symmetrization) is the key to symbolization and play. This view is close to the central place that recent infant researchers (Stern 1985) allot to sympathy, resonance and attunement.

It seems plain that Piaget and Matte Blanco have chosen different levels of mental functioning to be the focus of their lives. Piaget chose conscious and preconscious intellectual structures; Matte Blanco chose unconscious and emotional knowing. However, their chosen regions overlap and here they both recognize the central importance of symmetry. The two men together provide an enthralling overall view which no one has yet properly explored.

## Lévi-Strauss

Perhaps the most influential theoretical anthropologist of the past half century, Claude Lévi-Strauss (1966) has, like Piaget in psychology, carried forward the structuralist point of view. Analytic structuralism in the social field sets out to explain different forms of cultural practice, often ritualistic in nature, that exist in many communities.

Lévi-Strauss thinks that it is possible to describe 'deep structures' from which manifest social phenomena can be derived. These can, according to him, best be based upon logico-mathematical models. The models are not themselves tangible facts and so individual members in the communities under study would be unaware of the deep structures. They are models, and, at root, creations of the anthropologist. As in any structural approach, Lévi-Strauss's models are the means by which *laws of transformation* can be illuminated. For instance, in many societies there are definite and important rituals of gift exchange. Lévi-Strauss shows how one gift can be made into the *equal of another*.

We shall not go into this further other than to point out how Lévi-Strauss (1966) systematically searches out what he calls the '*logic of the categories*' in cultural practices – for instance, those seen in totem and caste groups. Here members of the same caste or totemic clan have some characteristics in common which make them different from other people. He thus shows how there is a multiplicity of cultural ways of making *binary distinctions*. Similarities and differences are universally detected in both nature and culture by all mankind.

For example, it is common in many societies for certain animals or objects of nature to be conceived of as clan totems. They symbolize and embody the clan; hence they have a similarity with the idea of the clan and its human members. Artefacts can likewise be symbols for a whole ritual practice. Binary distinction is also exhibited in rules of *inclusion* and *exclusion* in kinship systems and other habitual groupings.

Many binary distinctions can be seen as forms of dichotomization. This bears comparison with the polarization and splitting occurring in the individual unconscious (as described in Chapters 3 and 5) when infinitized asymmetrization occurs. It is in contrast to what Lévi-Strauss (1966) calls the 'synchrony' in cultural practices, which can be seen as akin to unconscious symmetries.

Just as insistently as Piaget, Lévi-Strauss's model is about dynamic, equilibrating and conserving structures which may be logically analysed. He sees the whole of culture as a mode of *mapping* or creating homologues. Leach (1976), discussing Lévi-Strauss, says that our whole social environment is map-like. We need order in our surroundings. Visible wild nature is 'a jumble of random curves'; but we construct dwellings and lay out settlements in straight lines, rectangles, squares, triangles, circles and so on.

Culture is full of such 'mathematical' ordering, and it can be shown to rest on 'binary coding', which itself rests on acts of binary distinction into 'is' or 'is not'. With such dichotomization, *abstraction* becomes possible. By this means the wild, complex asymmetries of the visually perceived external natural world can be forgotten and the simplicities of cultural practices can emerge. In this way culture is laden with dichotomizations, asymmetries and symmetrizations.

Naturally we must not forget that Lévy-Strauss's discipline about social processes is quite different from that of Matte Blanco on the individual unconscious, so it may be that the similarities detected are due simply to the limitations of the human mind's ways of knowing. Even so, the basic likenesses in Piaget, Lévi-Strauss and Matte Blanco are striking.

## Bateson

Margaret Arden (1984) first drew attention to Matte Blanco's and Bateson's common interest in logical *category errors*. Bateson was first an anthropologist; then, aroused by cybernetics and systems theory in the 1940s, he turned to communication questions. This alerted him to the need to understand the structures of formal logic.

His first approach to the logic of communication was zoological (Bateson 1973), leading to work on primates and then on humans. Thence he came to the communication problems of schizophrenics. It was here that his logical knowledge came fully to the fore. Like Matte Blanco he saw that schizophrenic patients were chronically in the grip of making logical category errors. For example:

> I somehow, from the way he [a schizophrenic patient] spoke 'space', got the idea that a space was his mother and said so. He said 'No, space is *the* mother'. I suggested that in some way his mother might be the cause of his troubles. He said 'I never condemned her'. At a certain point he got angry, and he said – this verbatim – 'If we say she had movement in her because of what she caused, we are only condemning ourselves.'
>
> (Bateson 1973: 168)

Bateson naturally sees this as a category error; it could well be a quotation from Matte Blanco. Their similarity of approach is obvious; but Bateson then went in a different direction. Unlike Matte Blanco, he looked for the causes of schizophrenic mentation and firmly pointed towards the family environment. He particularly saw the illogicality of the mother's thought as a prime causal factor. It was he and Jay Haley who developed the

143

concept of double-bind, which is naturally about antilogical activity which perhaps can be schizophrenogenic.

Etchegoyen and Ahumada (1990) have drawn out some further valuable but different parallels between Bateson and Matte Blanco. They describe how Bateson saw that Russell and Whitehead's theory of logical types deals strictly only with *digital*, two-valued, binary, yes–no types of communication. Here symbols are essentially *conventional* and *verbal* – they need have little similarity with the things symbolized.

However, much communication is of an *analogue* form – it is iconic (like an icon). The symbol then has *similarity of form* or is actually more directly bound to the thing symbolized. Here there are few signals for 'no', nor any sense of paradox. It is reminiscent of Freud's absence of negation and Matte Blanco's symmetrical logic.

Thus, say Etchegoyen and Ahumada, there is a correspondence between digital communication and asymmetrical logic, and analogic communication and symmetrical logic. Also, digital communication corresponds to Langer's 'discursive symbolism' whereas analogic communication is akin to her 'presentational symbolism' (see Chapter 2 and Langer 1942).

In the realm of emotions, Bateson thinks communications are largely analogic, or presentational as Langer stressed. It is the analogic or emotional mode that animals use to communicate in, and naturally humans too. Digital language, involving naming by convention, is a newcomer in evolution. Inappropriate as it is for emotional communication, the digital mode is nevertheless uniquely powerful; with its possibility of precision, it makes the communication of *deductive* steps possible. It is almost totally a human preserve. Lower animals can probably make simple preverbal deductions about tangible operations, but they cannot communicate such steps to others.

Etchegoyen and Ahumada then make an interesting suggestion. Bateson says that any new explanation must start with some *new* information, but this will be meaningless until it is *mapped on to*, matched or made to correspond with an *old*, familiar description; this is *recognition*. Although this act of *redescription* adds no new information whatsoever, it is what formal logic is concerned with. There is no new information from the outside but connections between propositions through similarities are found.

Assimilation of new information involves not only this recognition and redescription but also *trial and error* activity where a *selective process* operates upon *populations* of events. Trial and error systems often require a representative sample of the information, but this must be done randomly. Hence there must be a *random* element in such mental selectivity. It begins here to become apparent that the question of randomness in mental activity is probably fundamental. This will bring us to yet another theory. But before we move on, note that Bateson lies midway between Matte Blanco's and Piaget's focus upon the individual and Lévi-Strauss's concern with social processes.

We now move to a more microscopic level.

## Edelman

A physiologist, Gerald Edelman first became well known in 1972 when he was awarded a Nobel Prize for work on the immune system. Since then he and his co-workers have moved primarily to neuro-science with studies of the brain. His orientation is that of a neo-Darwinian and biological evolutionist.

Edelman (1987, 1992) emphasizes that cells in the nervous system organize themselves into *neural groups*. For him it is the particular *patterning* of cell groupings that enables the brain, and hence the organism as a whole, to respond effectively to the environment. Neurons must 'club together' to perform essential *recognition* tasks. A basic task of living cells, particularly in the brain, is recognition. This takes place, Edelman thinks, when the *pattern* of an incoming signal *happens to match*, resonate, attune or correspond with the firing pattern of a particular neural group. Once a match has occurred the firing of that group will be strengthened. It is pattern-matching that matters.

When input signals can be differentiated one from another by the brain through selective matching and non-matching, recognition occurs. Edelman then observes that a certain number of neurons interacting together in a group are essential to a specific recognition. For example, recognition of a *location* necessitates the registration of input from *two* or more different groups of sensors, depending on the number of *dimensions* involved in the location.

A non-neuronal example explains this simply. A radar station locating a ship at sea (two dimensions) needs enough sensors to measure distance and angular direction in the horizontal plane. But a radar station locating an aircraft in the sky needs more sensors in order to take measurements in three dimensions (distance and horizontal and vertical angles). This sort of requirement applies equally to brain mechanisms. Recognition takes place through *populations* of neurons working together.

If a neuronal group fails to resonate with (and so recognize) anything then it does not survive as a neuronal group, and cells may even die. Edelman calls his major recent work *Neural Darwinism* (1987) and we can begin to see why. He sees that *memory* is not a matter of passive imprinting like photography. Rather, memory comes about by neural groupings of certain patterns *surviving* by continued use through resonating with other groups which have similar patterns, while others with fewer to resonate with fall away. Memory is not static but essentially dynamic in nature.

Edelman considers that the *integration* of complex recognition tasks into higher thought processes ultimately achieves the high degree of complexity necessary for levels of consciousness, which has *intentionality* as a salient characteristic. This is achieved by hierarchies of neural groups, and groups of groups, forming themselves and *interacting in feedback arcs* with *each other*. These may span widely different areas of the brain. Thus, groups react by matching each other across different regions of the brain, just as, with exteroceptive sensations, groups match incoming stimulus patterns. The internal matching between groups is called *re-entry* by Edelman.

This group-centred view is evolutionary. The human brain has evolved racially over millions of years by survival of the fittest species. But each individual member of a species, animal or human with a particular inherited brain, also adapts and survives (or not) to carry on the species by an evolution on a shorter time base. This occurs in an individual's lifetime of personal development which rests on neural recognition and memory. Here populations of neural groups are generated, some of which survive by pattern-matching well with, and thus recognizing, input signals from the environment and being strengthened thereby. Others which do not fit die out. Thus Edelman's theoretical model, like Darwin's, is essentially *both developmental and statistical*.

Edelman is convinced that the brain does not function like a present-day computer which learns from its software. The brain has no software to use. It only has itself, its own body and its environment, and, unlike software, these are not conveniently precisely precoded into logical categories. Furthermore, computer elements have to be perfectly homogeneous and quite specifically 'hard wired' together in order to be logical. Brains are not like this; they vary greatly in random ways yet often end up with identical recognitions. Logicality must be found in other ways. Edelman thinks that the brain must work statistically; single specific connections cannot function like computers do. The brain with minimal genetic prestructuring must learn its programs; it has to develop advantageous, dynamically structured, memory systems for itself.

Edelman (1992) shows that, since ordering of information by the brain does not occur by preset means but can be achieved by statistical combinations, recognition and categorization can only take place with vast numbers and differently structured neurones. However, it looks as if there are enough. There are about 10,000 million ($10^{10}$) cells in a human cortex and these give the possibility of up to about 1,000 million million ($10^{15}$) connections. Hence, if we counted the connections at one per second we would be finished in about 32 million years! However, this is only counting the actual connections; the number of possible ways these can be combined is of the order of 10 followed by millions of zeros. There is room in the brain for neural groupings and hierarchies of groups which can be enormously complex structures.

Edelman wonders about many things; for instance, how *consciousness* has arisen and how it differs in neural patterning from unconscious processes, but we cannot dwell on these here. His prime interest is discrimination and recognition which occurs even at basic cellular levels; the immune system, for instance, recognizes at the molecular level. He thinks a special *recognition science* is called for:

> What is perhaps not appreciated outside the community of physics . . . is a key mathematical principle: symmetry. . . . Symmetry is a stunning example of how a rationally derived mathematical argument can be applied to descriptions of nature and lead to insights of the greatest generality. I want to discuss symmetry a bit because I plan to contrast it with another principle I believe underlies the mind, and indeed of all biology, the principle of memory. Later I will argue that an understanding of these two principles, interacting in a tense harmony, will allow us to see more clearly the place of our minds in nature.
>
> (Edelman 1992: 199)

Edelman then points out that there are many forms of symmetry. Bi-lateral or mirror symmetry is well known; but there are, for instance, symmetries of rotation and of displacement in time and space. Many symmetries are only detectable after complex mathematical operations are carried out to reveal them.

We noted earlier that Matte Blanco's symmetry in the unconscious seems to be centrally about recognition and memory, even though he does not say this very definitively or clearly. We shall soon note that Bion was more explicit than Matte Blanco about the importance of memory. So, incidentally, was Freud (1911).

What must be discriminated by any higher animal's recognition system are, Edelman thinks, first, *wide categories* of things (for example, dangerousness or digestibility) and, second, *high specificity* (such as the location of an individual's one and only mate or offspring in a herd). As a biological requirement these two kinds of recognition must be integrated to happen at the same time. For this, Edelman says, a nervous system needs at one extreme some neural groups to match and be responsive to one and only *one particular* input pattern. At another extreme there also needs to be neuronal groups which are *very non-specific* in their matching. The two types of grouping must interact for efficient recognitions to occur.

Edelman contends that there is a tense dialectic between wide-category and highly specific neural groups in adaptive life. It was Paul Wohlmuth who first suggested a fascinating parallel with Matte Blanco here. Wide-category but crude generality bears a striking resemblance to the principle of symmetry; while the concept of high specificity neural groupings bears kinship with asymmetrical functioning.

In summary, because of their clear vision of the fundamental importance of symmetry in common, it is perhaps Edelman, of all the authors mentioned here, who is closest in reasoned meta-theory to Matte Blanco.

However, in this region it is Matte Blanco who has gone further than Edelman into the question of symmetry because he has seen how essential is the contrast with asymmetry and its qualities. Though Edelman is biologically more important, it may be that Matte Blanco will be judged to be epistemologically to the fore.

Meanwhile, let us not forget that Matte Blanco contents himself with introspective data and inferences from it. He is a phenomenologist at heart, not a neuroscientist, and it is upon that level of data that he stands or falls.

## Bion

We turn now to a comparison with another psychoanalyst who was using mathematical intuitions and formal logic concurrently with Matte Blanco, but actually published his main work in book form some time before him. Our discussion will be brief. Both Bion and Matte Blanco were focally interested in that systematic aim-oriented process of intentional knowing which is thinking. Here conceptions of knowledge and anti-knowledge rest upon truthful and anti-truthful ideas.

Bion's writing in the 1940s and early 1950s conceptualized some basic phenomena of human groups. At this stage crucial ideas from logic, like the conception of *basic assumption*, are just beginning to emerge. Then during the 1950s and 1960s came his seminal contributions about psychotic patients, processes and their therapy. His consideration of splitting, denial, projective identification, and of obstructive and bizarre objects, are cornerstones in psychoanalytic knowledge. His understanding of violent projective identification as an act specifically to rid the self of knowledge is of special note.

In the early 1960s, perhaps stimulated by earlier work of Bowlby and Winnicott, came his more controversial notion of normal projective identification and of mother–infant empathy. Thence came the conceptions of maternal reverie and the container–contained.

In the 1960s Bion also began to formalize his ideas about thought in abstract terms. First was *Learning from Experience* (1962). Logic is now explicitly to the fore. By now of first importance was the theory of beta-elements and bizarre objects. But it is the concept of *alpha-function* that beckons to us most. Bion follows Freud (1911) in realizing that something which is *already familiar* needs to be stored ready to be used by later conscious thinking when need arises. Bion conceives alpha-function as transforming emotional experience into alpha-elements which make dreaming and thence long-term memorization, ready for future recognition, possible. This obviously has affinities with what has been referred to in this book as 'same again' matching, recognition and memorization. Both Freud and Bion, not to mention Edelman, saw the vital importance of this recognition; Matte Blanco was less explicit about memory but was the most systematic of all psychoanalysts about the importance of the symmetry upon which recognition rests.

Bion (1962) also introduced the concepts of 'K' and '–K'. It is '–K' that seems most valuable; through it Bion is emphasizing the importance not only of evasion but of active anti-knowledge, and thus the anti-truth functions in psychopathology. Matte Blanco is not as clear as Bion about this anti-knowing. For instance, Bion shows how there is a peculiar lack of 'resonance' (*ibid*: 15) between a psychotic person's ideas and those of other people. This points towards what we now think of as the need for normal resonances and attunements – which entail symmetrization (Sandler 1993; Stern 1985; Emde *et al.* 1991; Rayner 1992). Bion also enquires about abstraction in thought along lines that point close to the later concept of cross-sensory perception; this has already been associated in Chapter 3 with symmetry (Stern 1985).

Soon after 'K' and '–K' came Bion's *Grid* (1963); this, among other things, formulates his view of the emergence of the elements necessary for thinking – from alpha-elements, through dream thoughts, preconceptions, conceptions and concepts to scientific deductive systems and thought in the algebraic calculus. This bears comparison with Piaget's schema of the development of thought culminating likewise in the algebraic calculus. Skelton (1992) has emphasized that Bion's logical inspiration came, no doubt originally, from his study of the Greeks, but more immediately from *Model Theory*, coming first from Alfred Tarski in the 1950s. Matte Blanco stuck with the classical Russell and Whitehead of the 1900s.

Throughout the 1960s and 1970s, Bion's work consistently used logical ideas centred on his grid. As time went on he seems to have become dissatisfied with explanation by the usual method of discursive argument. Instead he felt it best to communicate by something closer to dream imagery and poetry. In Langer's (1942) terms, this is nearer to a pre-sentational symbolic mode with its greater content of symmetrization. However, Bion appeared to use enigma and often mystical modes of expression. It is an open question whether this was mistaken. For some it was inspiring; for others, confusing.

Matte Blanco and Bion knew and respected each other. Bion's daughter, Parthenope Bion-Talamo, now a psychoanalyst, wrote a doctoral thesis (1973) comparing the uses of logic by Bion and Matte Blanco. She told us that her father recommended that students interested in his (Bion's) theories should use Matte Blanco as basic reading. There is a contribution by Matte Blanco in the memorial edition to Bion (Grotstein 1981). He is here genuinely enthusiastic while holding to some criticisms.

Venturing a comparison between the two men, perhaps Bion was the more deeply reconciled into disillusion about human life, with its base motives and pleasures in violent splitting, than was Matte Blanco. Bion reflected this in his laconic humour. This had no doubt been achieved the hard way, by his open-eyed courage in the blood-bath of the First World War, close to it in the Second, and facing the tragedy of his first wife's death soon after childbirth. Matte Blanco has been more romantic and optimistic in character, maybe sometimes too far. Perhaps he could be accused of being slightly naïve sometimes. Bion had the disillusionment necessary to be an impressive portrayer of individual character, and its therapeutic analysis.

Because he started earlier in life, Matte Blanco actually spent more years than Bion engrossed in psychoanalysis as therapy, and was by all accounts profoundly effective at it. However, we have already noted that he does not put a particular person's whole self and character centre stage; thus his clinical descriptions lack dramatic form. Psychoanalysts, rightly using this kind of story-telling as their basic evidence, see this as a weakness. Matte Blanco could perhaps argue that stringent attention to the minutiae of thought is just as centrally important to psychoanalysis.

Apart from this, how do the logics of Bion and Matte Blanco compare? Matte Blanco seems the more thoroughgoing in his use of formal and mathematical logic, probably because of his long connections with university mathematics departments. Bion is less obsessive about it than Matte Blanco; he dips into mathematical concepts for use as illustrative metaphors. He does not define concepts and argue from them step by step so that they can be examined. It is this intention to be consistent that is the essence of the logical method and, later in his life at least, Bion felt this was inappropriate for his purpose.

It has been said that Bion moved more and more to mysticism as a way of knowing towards the end of his life. It has even been commented that perhaps he was returning to the ways of thought of the land of his birth, to India and Hinduism. Whether he was right to move to mysticism remains an open question.

Matte Blanco's idiom is rather different. Like Bion he introduces many subtle mathematical-logical conceptions or intuitions for psychoanalytic use; and then, rather unlike Bion, he meticulously endeavours to define them. In the crucial first hundred pages of *The Unconscious as Infinite Sets* (1975) he argues his psychoanalytic theory from these conceptions in a brilliantly clear step-by-step way. Inconsistencies can then be shown up (Skelton 1990a). Matte Blanco, like Bion, also sometimes felt that much experience could only be communicated by metaphysical if not mystical means. However, he remained firmly in the western rationalist tradition. To the end he tried to argue and explain what he meant. Which of the two men was the more right remains to be seen.

## Conclusion

We shall leave our final summing up on this subject to our last chapter, just noting here how omnipresent among the writers mentioned are under-lying ideas that amount to symmetry and asymmetry. However, it is certainly Matte Blanco who stands alone as having centrally and consist-ently explored and explained these two contrasting but complementary functions.

All these authors, being interested in logic, often directed their thought to general and abstract meta-levels of theory and, because of this, in varying ways lighted upon symmetry and asymmetry. The authors were perhaps reaching basic levels of the mind's functioning, and it is in these regions that recognition, as Edelman says, has to reign supreme. With the problem of recognition, symmetry and asymmetry emerge with greatest clarity.

# 10

# Complex systems, mathematical chaos and bi-logic

This chapter must be viewed as no more than fancifully speculative as yet. It is a line of thought worked out over the last few years by the present author and Ian Mordant, a mathematician. We think its argument might bear directly upon psychoanalytic metapsychology. It may thus have value as a framework for practical psychoanalytic workers in the future.

## Complex systems

We shall begin with a well-known non-psychoanalytic theoretical point of view, mathematical chaos theory, which is proving to be of interest to biological sciences. We shall constantly be moving across to bi-logic, using this as a link back into psychoanalysis.

Throughout this book a point of view of looking at *systems* as a whole and the important consequences of their *complexity* has crept in even though Matte Blanco himself was not explicitly concerned with them. Let us look at General Systems thinking to see whether bi-logic links with it. Freud naturally used the concept of a system but did not dwell upon its characteristics or upon the consequences of small systems con- joining into a larger organized entity. We have just noted in the previous chapter that the structuralist approach by Piaget and Lévi-Strauss is very close to a systems approach; even more explicitly so are Bateson and Edelman.

For our purposes, let us start with *structure* which is a familiar enough idea. A structure is any set of interrelationships that have a continuity in time. Basically its emphasis is upon that which is *static*. However, structures can change while still maintaining their basic form; they are then often called *dynamic* structures. Strictly speaking, the term 'system' refers simply to *complex* structures; however, they frequently change, transform or evolve and are thus dynamic systems, but are just called systems for short.

152

The specifications of changes in a system are usually referred to as *transformation* rules or laws; for instance, the laws of planetary motion are rules of dynamics about the movements or transformations that can occur within a system of heavenly bodies. The sequence in time of the evolving states of such a dynamic system are called its *trajectories* or *paths*.

Living systems have, among other things, the characteristic of being dynamic in a *negative feedback* way. Here *criteria* are an essential aspect such that, when a part or whole of the system diverges from a criterion, there is activity until a return to the criterion occurs. This is *mismatch-reduction*. Physiology, including neuroscience, often sees the living body as largely composed of very complex systems of feedbacking which may evolve and decay over time. In living things, *regulation*, control and hence *limit-setting predominantly occurs by processes involving this negative feedback*.

We have noted that, as it stands, Matte Blanco's bi-logic fails to address fully dynamic systems because it does not specify feedback or mismatch-reduction processes. However, it is very easy to introduce this into bi-logic for, since asymmetry is a mismatch and symmetry a matching, negative feedback is a process of a limited 'asymmetry reduction'. Positive feedback, on the other hand, is a *multiplication* of an asymmetrical relation so that an infinitizing process occurs.

Next, since any living dynamic system is regulated by complex negative feedbacks, then, specifically, psychodynamics must also be about this. As this is psychology, we are thus concerned with feedback systems of *knowing*. Are there any links with bi-logic? One in the realm of *limits* is important. We have just said that, in living systems, limits are often set by feedback mechanisms. The notion of limit is central to Matte Blanco even though he does not speak about it much explicitly. From the *experiential* point of view, a limit or border is where an *affirmation* changes into a *negation*, or conversely. Apprehension of limits rests upon *consistent* registration of *both* asymmetrical and symmetrical relations. Symmetrization involves a loss of negative feedbacking limitation.

This becomes most evident with experiences of *infinity*. This, by definition, is where there is an *absence* of finiteness or limit. When a limit is lifted, a feedback regulation is loosened, and a symmetrization occurs which is experienced as an infinity. This can be seen in the *elation* of freedom; or, when destructive triumph is paramount, in *mania*.

Incidentally, in this light we can see that Winnicott's conception of maternal holding and Bion's of containment, both of which imply limits, really entail feedback processes between mother and infant. In this light, perhaps both holding and containment have too simple a physical connotation to be optimally descriptive. They do not evoke the idea of a psychological feedback occurring. Perhaps the term '*maternal comprehension*' is better for it implies knowing, holding and containing together.

153

Summarizing so far. We are arguing that psychoanalysis generally, including bi-logic, can usefully be viewed in the light of the theory of *complex* systems. It is becoming evident that the behaviour of individual processes depends upon the *overall* form of the complex system's patterning. This is the *context* in which the individual processes exist.

We now come to the next vital step: the very *degree of complexity* of a system makes its elements prone to behave in most peculiar ways that had not even been conceived of a few years ago. To understand this we move on to the next section.


## Mathematical chaos theory

We must begin with a set of definitions. (As an amateur I am particularly indebted here to Professor Jim Meiss of the University of Colorado; any errors must be mine not his. See also Gleick 1987; Stewart 1989.)

A system that is *deterministic* is one where, *given an initial state*, there is *precisely* one state that follows it at any one point in time. The classical fundamental laws of physics are about such phenomena. However, there are many natural systems that are indeterminate, especially living ones, where absolute precision of *prediction* is not possible; yet some limited or *probabilistic* prediction or *expectation* can be achieved. We must now move across to a mathematical–*statistical* or probabilistic way of thinking, for this is necessary when there is insufficient knowledge about the states of, and influences upon, a system to have precise expectations. In nature there are innumerable such indeterminate systems where future states cannot be precisely predicted, but a set of possible states can be envisaged; probabilities of events can even be calculated and hence probabilistic theories may be developed.

With such uncertainties we move into the realm of mathematical chaos theory. Here, the term 'chaos', though suitably dramatic, is rather ill-chosen for it is not about total disorder; 'complex factors theory' is perhaps better.

It will be necessary here to start by introducing some new notation. We have so far used several terms to indicate modes of control, such as regulation, homeostasis and feedback. Chaos theory does not use these but instead sees them as forms of *attractor*.

For instance, the path or trajectory of a simple physical system may be influenced by a *fixed point* attractor; in this case the system will ultimately become *stationary* unless there is a countervailing source of energy. An example is that of gravity acting so that a ball rolls downhill until it comes to rest at the bottom. Another is an ordinary pendulum when it is under the influence of air resistance and friction of the fulcrum; these act as fixed point attractors so that the pendulum will slow down and come to a halt.

A *limit-cycle* attractor is one where the system's trajectory becomes *periodic*. This occurs, for instance, with the action of gravity between the sun and its planets so that the earth goes round it cyclically within a period of about a year. Another example is an 'ideal' or perfect pendulum where there is no resistance to its swing. In this case gravity and the inertia of the pendulum resolve to combine into a periodic attractor, the pendulum swings back and forth within a fixed period without impediment *ad infinitum*. Turning to quite a different medium, there are innumerable approximations to such periodic systems in the human body: the sleep, hunger and breathing cycles are the most obvious; so is the heart beat.

Lastly there are *strange attractors*; these are influences that make for non-periodic movements. They produce apparently *random*, or 'strange', elements in the trajectories of the system. It is in strange attractors that mathematical chaos theory is especially interested.

We shall now move on to the occurrence of so-called chaos. With a perfect pendulum, as we have seen, the swing is determined and periodic. Given its initial state its next state can be *perfectly predicted* by the use of a mathematical calculation. A mathematical *equation* can be used to do the predicting; in this case the swing can be represented by the well-known sine curve, so calculation and prediction can be precise. However, if we make the system even only a little *more complex*, very strange things are found to happen.

When a function expressed by a *non-linear equation* (which is one, like a sine curve, that is not represented by a straight line) is *combined* with a similar non-linear function, so that a 'function of a function' is created, then prediction becomes very problematic.

This will become clear with an example. If *one* perfect pendulum is made to swing on the end of *another* perfect pendulum, then exact prediction becomes almost impossible. What happens to the second pendulum from instant to instant depends with near *infinite* sensitivity upon the *initial conditions* of *both* pendulums. What, to the observer, were two perfectly predictable determined elements (the pendulums) have apparently suddenly become *unstable* and probabilistic. This happens with even the simplest of mathematical functions as long as they are, like a sine curve, non-linear. It is most peculiar and unexpected.

This possible outcome was in fact first pointed out by the mathematician Poincaré at the beginning of the century, but it had never previously been conceived and was not really worked upon until a few years ago. We now know that two perfectly undampened pendulums *interacting* is a simple example of a chaotic system. The full and wide importance of this phenomenon only became apparent with the coming of computers, when calculation could be carried out with extreme speed. It then became plain that this unpredictability occurs both theoretically and in nature itself.

The computer graphics that have been generated by combinations of quite simple equations are now well known. They contain highly unpredictable elements but are statistically lawful, behaving in ordered and periodic ways. The curves of probability are often of great complexity with a strange beauty. Perhaps the most well-known and vivid of these are the eerie graphics of fractal geometry and Mandelbrot sets, known to any TV watcher of science programmes. Incidentally, *these sets are infinite* and so we naturally look for a link with bi-logic. (We shall discuss this shortly.) Such sets also have the remarkable quality of *repeating* their pattern irrespective of the scale on which they are being manifest. They are thus startling examples of the part = whole characteristic of infinite sets, giving us another link to bi-logic.

In summary, when elements of a system, which behave towards others in determinate but non-linear ways, are combined with other non-linear functions, the overall system may become infinitely sensitive and the behaviour of its elements can still be known, but only probabilistically.

## Unpredictability in living beings

Having generated such complex probabilistic systems on computers it began to be apparent that the mathematical models used were approximating to many things in nature. Water flow, air turbulence and the weather were some of the phenomena to be tackled first, followed soon by economic models of markets and now, most interestingly for us, by biological systems. For instance, many of the computer graphics of chaotic systems bear a striking resemblance to *living* vegetation like trees, leaves and plants and also to animal tissue.

It was also found that in order to simulate *animal movement* on a TV screen it is essential to incorporate a more or less unpredictable element into the program. For instance, a moving dot on a TV screen, however complicated its movement, does not appear to the human eye to be *alive* unless a degree of uncertainty is incorporated into its program.

It was soon discovered that many physiological processes involve apparently unpredictable elements; for instance, the heart beat, which is basically periodic, of course, must involve such elements. Once the uncertainty begins to disappear so that a more perfect periodicity begins to emerge, as shown on an EEG, *death* is now known to be imminent. It is now also known that many other physiological systems, such as the brain, have similar uncertainties and it begins to be evident that *life necessarily involves unpredictable elements*. It can be said poetically that death brings an end to the necessary chaos in life's instincts.

156

Two other features of chaotic systems need to be mentioned. The first, already described above, is called *scaling*. This means that a system's chaotic behaviour often shows a remarkable *repetition of form* on different scales. For instance, it can be shown on a computer that the statistical pattern of the position of a second pendulum measured over a time of a few minutes may have a similarity of shape to when it is measured over a few thousand years. These repetitions are very remarkable when such 'magnification' is simulated instantaneously on a computer screen. The same is manifest in nature when, say, the air turbulence in a back garden has a similarity of pattern to turbulent air flow over a vast ocean.

Another feature of the behaviour of chaotic systems is that they behave in recognizably special ways when changing from one state to another. An example of this is when the steady flow of a river turns into white water foam or turbulence; here the water molecules move more sluggishly than usual. These are called *transitional states*. When the transition has passed the white water moves fast and more randomly in a typically chaotic way. White water is now a common phrase for a chaotic state. Incidently, Winnicott's (1951, 1971) transitional states and phenomena are probably quite unrelated to this.

## Chaos theory and psychoanalysis

Moran (1991) has, almost alone, pioneered the applicability of chaos concepts to psychoanalysis. He lists the main features of chaotic systems which have just been described here. He then sees whether the psycho-analytic processes display similar features to chaotic systems.

Moran says that chaos models can only apply to complex systems with *interactive* elements. He then looks at psychoanalysis and sees that it is most certainly concerned with interactivity. An obvious example is *conflict*, which can take place between a multiplicity of relatively simple instinctual urges and countervailing forces interacting together to produce a highly complex variety of outcomes. These, being instinctual drives, will involve combinations of feedback arcs, and each of these will involve oscillations around a criterion state, and thus may have *cyclical*, that is non-linear, elements. These, combining with other cyclical elements from other drive systems with which they may be in conflict, will then induce the instability characteristic of a mathematically chaotic system. In summary, the forms of interrelationship in a drive system fulfil the fundamental chaos feature that interactions within a system must be non-linear.

Other clear examples of cyclical, repetitive interactive systems are, of course, also seen in internal object relations, for they are in continuous interplay with each other. Even clearer examples of such complex cyclical systems appear in intersubjective and interpersonal activities.

Next, Moran mentions the feature of special *sensitivity to initial conditions*, which has been mentioned previously. This is most evident in the crucial importance of *early child development* to the course of later events.

*Periodicity* is evident, of course, in many physiological processes, including the brain. The sleep cycle is perhaps one that is particularly central to psychoanalysis; so is hunger, breathing, female periodicity and many other basic bodily functions. But more focal for psychopathology, Moran thinks, is the phenomenon of repetition compulsion. Here a repetition is not precisely predictable, as random or chaotic elements are always present. However, repetition of a certain form can be expected as a strong probability.

*Scaling*, mentioned above, where the same form appears at both the macroscopic and microscopic levels, is manifest in such phenomena as that which allows a clinician to say, 'all the main features of a long analysis are visible in the first interview'. Likewise, the features of a whole life situation can be condensed into one dream image. Here, Moran sees that well-known phenomemon – the part = whole equation, which is so common a characteristic of unconscious process. It makes a bridge to Matte Blanco's understanding of infinity. You will remember that the equation of part and whole occurs only when sets are infinite.

*Transitional states* are certainly features of the analytic process, especially in the abrupt changes of state followed by turbulence when *insight* is occurring. The chaos feature of the probability of *numerous solutions* is also a feature of transition in psychoanalytic change. Moran also sees an unconscious fantasy as a *strange attractor*. This seems right; Mordant and I in similar vein have seen internal objects as possible strange attractors.

It will be argued that chaos theory is not applicable to psychoanalysis which is an experiential and introspective, phenomenological discipline. Moran argues that psychoanalysis has, from Freud onwards, used physical models and must do so, just as physical science has borrowed ideas from introspective experience. Use of a model from another discipline does not imply overall identity between the disciplines. A model's use depends not upon its origins but its correspondence to the phenomena being mapped by the model.

Following a line of thinking close to Moran, it had also occurred to us that unpredictable elements are actually omnipresent phenomena to the everyday psychoanalyst. *Play*, for example, must, it seems, have both an undertow of predictability *and* of uncertainty; this is mathematical chaos. Without a certain unpredictability playfulness disappears and becomes a compulsion which is boring at best, or it may even have autistic features which are even more disturbing. Certainly a psychoanalytic therapist, as well as anyone else, who is forever predictable is maddening and undoubtedly useless to the recipient.

*Spontaneity*, essential not only for happy playfulness but also for authenticity, necessitates an element of unpredictability. Furthermore, it appears that spontaneity within the setting of reliability is essential for the psychoanalytic therapist to be effective. This must mean that unpredictability within the context of a steady predictability is necessary for such therapy.

On the other hand, when predictability disappears a game turns into trauma. Obsessional frenzy often appears to be a desperate attempt to maintain predictability in the face of randomization. Psychosis itself often appears to involve the catastrophic chaos of utter unpredictability. It may, for instance, be a valuable task for the future to distinguish the forms of uncertainty or apparent randomness in manic-depressive psychosis as distinct from those in schizophrenia.

Useful thoughtfulness, on the other hand, must have play in it and needs some unpredictability; but it must also incorporate consistent, central, comprehensible and predictable elements. Piaget said somewhere that optimal development of thought needs 'moderate newness'; we could rephrase this and say that thought requires moderate unpredictability. However, we come to a paradox here: no doubt the mind needs unpredictability, but consciousness and hence thinking can only manage small doses of it, just as it can only manage small doses of symmetry and infinite experiences. Simplification is necessary and perhaps this uses *abstraction*. The reader will recall Leach's (1976) observation that nature is a jumble of random curves but humans need to create – by abstraction – straight lines, squares and circles.

It seems that, since the human being has uncertainty built into his or her physiology, the human brain and thence the mind must be capable of recognizing these unpredictable elements of the body. What is more, as humans are group-living creatures, they have to be, and optimally are, very sensitive to others. This is the gift of empathy. The mind must thus be able to recognize the unpredictability patterns of other living things.

Perhaps this is most poignantly visible in mother–infant attachment behaviour, such as in the disturbance that is evoked when a person replaces ordinarily expected lively bodily movements, with unpredictability in them, by an expressionless stillness producing predictability. This happens in several well-known infant research findings (Murray and Trevarthan 1985). Thus, if an infant and mother are playing happily together and the mother then becomes quite still and freezes her expression, her baby is first puzzled and then within seconds becomes distraught. It may be the disappearance of randomness in facial movement that is so disturbing. Absolute predictability is maddening; complete unpredictability is terrifying.

159

Finally, it is worth noting one more paradox: humans from infancy onwards need to attune with each other in order to be social animals. We have also been arguing that they must be able to be sensitive to another body's own unpredictability. However, these will clash with attunements, or any of the matching that is essential to recognition. This is because an unpredictable sequence can be neither attuned to nor matched, at least until the sequence is completed, because by its nature it is unpredictable. We shall have to leave this question as a conundrum for the future.

## Mathematical chaos, unpredictability, infinity and bi-logic

It is now possible to come to our first conclusion. A characteristic of living creatures, which are complex systems using non-linear functions, is that they manifest unpredictable aspects in their physiology. Human beings are no exception. As the mind is first and foremost a monitoring, evaluative and integrating system it must be sensitive and adaptively reactive to the presence of uncertainty. In monitoring its own body it is quite likely that the mind registers the aliveness or deadness of a particular physiological function by whether or not unpredictability is still healthily active. However, we have no direct evidence about this as yet. With regard to awareness of externals we have quoted two lines of evidence: first, that randomness is necessary to simulate livingness to humans watching computer graphics; and, second, there is the distress that is immediate when a mother suddenly stops playful expressions of the face with her infant. It seems most likely that the human mind not only functions with many apparently random aspects but is also sensitive to them in others.

Moran, using a rather different approach, has also gathered many reasons why mental functions of prime interest to psychoanalysts appear to be products of chaotic systems. It appears, therefore, that psychoanalytic therapists must take the unpredictable aspects of mental functioning into account in future theory and therapy.

The presence of such chaos means that the therapist must always be prepared to *doubt*. The practical necessity of having to make decisions requires that every therapist must naturally still act with pragmatic definiteness; but he or she needs to be aware that this certainty in action involves a gamble, however slight. Complete certainty about a theoretical position is a delusion, a sloppy, omniscient self-indulgence at best.

Whether it is the unconscious or preconscious that is sensitive to uncertainty is an open question; it is probably both. On the other hand, from introspection it is plain that although we can clearly be aware of unpredictability, it is not easy to handle the conscious idea of several such functions at once. Just as Matte Blanco observed that consciousness could not handle too much symmetry; nor, it seems, can it manage too much unpredictability.

This finally brings us to the link between chaos theory and bi-logic. The crux, as we see it, lies in the relation between *unpredictability and infinity* and hence to symmetrization. It is best to start here with the ideas of predictability and unpredictability. For an event to be predictable the existence of a relation between *present and future* must be known (note that this is an awareness of an asymmetry). The absence of such a relation obviously must produce unpredictability. Note now that, just as predictability is asymmetrical, so unpredictability creates a symmetrization.

Turning now to introspection, it appears that the experience of uncertainty and unpredictability has a feeling of infinity within it. There is an ineffableness about both ideas. Does this apply on more precise conceptualization? We think it does. While a condition of unpredictability continues, there is *never a time* when a prediction can be certain. Put in another way, there must be an *absence of limit* to that particular uncertainty; it has an unlimited or infinite element. The uncertainty may be quite circumscribed but it is infinite none the less.

For example, if one is tossing a coin, the uncertainty is very circumscribed indeed. It will certainly fall either heads or tails, but which way it will fall at any throw is unknown *ad infinitum* as long as the unpredictability continues. In other words, while this applies no sequence of heads and tails can ever be predicted. We can conclude that *insofar as a set has uncertainty it also has an infinite element.* If we turn for a moment to the converse of this, although an unpredictable set is necessarily infinite, this does not necessarily mean that an infinite set must be unpredictable. However, we must leave this question aside.

We have reached the following crucial point: psychologically, *uncertainty generates both symmetrization and the experience of infinity.* In other words, at the infinite limit unpredictability generates *zero discrimination*, zero order and hence zero asymmetry. The effect in experience is naturally a blur, 'white noise' as it is called, or total blackness. Whether all symmetrization occurs through, presumably neuronal, uncertainty must remain an open question, but it seems possible.

It would seem that we have now pointed out the essential bridge between chaos theory and bi-logic as lying in the relation between unpredictability, infinity and symmetrization. A movement between knowledge of chaos theory and of bi-logic could take place. This means that a new conceptual link between biological thought and psychoanalysis might develop via chaos and bi-logical theories.

Through Matte Blanco has come important understanding of the importance in the unconscious of the dialectic between symmetry and asymmetry, its manifold patterning, the value of recognition, and the omnipresence of infinities. From chaos theory has emerged the importance of the effect of the very complexity of systems including mental ones. Complexity creates an unpredictablity, and it appears that this indeterminacy is intrinsic to our mental lives. Those acquainted with chaos, who will usually be of a mathematical or biological frame of mind, might find their thinking can benefit from Matte Blanco's deep and subtle knowledge of unconscious processes. On the other hand, bi-logicians and most other psychoanalysts can learn much about the biological roots of unconscious processes from those acquainted with chaos theory.

Freud spoke of psychic determinism; and although this is by no means totally overthrown, it does look as if psychoanalysts will now have to conceive also of psychic indeterminacy. It appears that the combination of chaos theory and bi-logic might be a strong addition to metapsychology and could, perhaps, engage fundamental psychoanalytic thinking at some length into the twenty-first century.

# 11

# Final summary

Though attempting to be a faithful portrayal of some of Matte Blanco's basic thoughts, this book has moved towards its end by going into other ideas as well. It is to be hoped that this has not obscured the original Matte Blanco. Here are the main points that we have emphasized.

Why is Matte Blanco so little known? This is primarily because his mathematical logic is unusual and difficult for psychoanalysts and others in the field. It is also because psychoanalysts are prone to ignore theory that is not backed up by clinical narrative, which is the case with Matte Blanco's early work, but not his later. Clinical narrative involves the use of case histories putting the whole self of the patient centre stage with the analyst. Such histories, as well as being vital, have well-known weaknesses as evidence; and there is no good reason why a useful theory must always arise from clinical histories. Nevertheless, their lack must surely be one reason for the general ignorance of Matte Blanco's work; and this neglect has probably meant that progress in psychoanalytic meta-theory and its useful bridging with other disciplines has been seriously impeded.

Matte Blanco's most general potential contribution is his passionate, precise curiosity about the ways we apprehend our knowledge as well as his insistence upon detailed argumentation. His most original gift lies in discovering intuitive conceptions, that are used every day consciously and unconsciously in feeling and thinking as we go about our business, but which have then become formalized throughout history as pure mathematical concepts. Instances of this used by Matte Blanco are set, numeration, symmetry, asymmetry, dimension and infinity. This conceptual analysis is one aspect of logical analysis in its broadest sense. Matte Blanco's writing is, at the same time, full of internal dialogue about the implications of these conceptions and their consistency. This gives necessary substance to his argument but it is in the development of useful concepts for psychoanalysis that his great contribution lies.

Though totally absorbed in his own ideas, he has not demanded that he be thought to be always in the right. His combination of precise argument and tolerance of uncertainty has been a fine recipe for open-mindedness. His bi-logical approach centring upon symmetrical and asymmetrical knowing, combined with tolerance, seems to be a rare meeting ground where members of different disciplines can easily communicate with each other. This communality is largely due to the very wide generality and applicability of Matte Blanco's concepts; his is a meta-theory which is really an aspect of psychoanalytic metapsychology. Thus, to the dynamic, economic, topographic, structural, adaptive and developmental aspects of psychoanlysis should be added the bi-logical point of view.

Because it functions conceptually at a meta-level, and clearly so, it is widely comprehensible and usable to anyone who enjoys abstract thinking. Intellectually minded members of other professions can grasp bi-logic even though they may be unversed in clinical psychoanalysis. It thus assists psychoanalysis in taking its proper place among other sciences.

Above all, Matte Blanco has been a man of profound emotions who really believed in and valued them. He devoted himself to understanding them and their expression. At the same time precise and stringent thought is brought to bear to investigate, almost for the first time in psychoanalysis, the logical and cognitive structures of emotionality.

The prime elements of bi-logic are the concepts of logical symmetry and asymmetry. Though Matte Blanco himself did not emphasize this, it is plain that the function of registering symmetries is in the service of everyday recognition; bi-logic must thus take its place in the recognition sciences. Asymmetry, on the other hand, is essential to locating the self in the world. In addition, symmetry and asymmetry have mental acts of negation and affirmation behind them, so that it might be these that are primary, irreducible, epistemological constituents of psychoanalysis. Matte Blanco's final intellectual love has certainly been epistemology.

Ideas of symmetry and asymmetry can often be seen to form together combinatorially into either bi-modal or bi-logical mental structures. Bi-modal structures are those that maintain the logical consistency of their elements. Bi-logical structures, on the other hand, give up some aspect of consistency in the act of symmetrization. This occurs when there is a restriction of awareness of a particular asymmetrical relation so that only symmetricality or sameness is known, when full consciousness would also detect asymmetrical relations. This is recognized as being pervasive in emotional states and also in the unconscious. It has great value in everyday life, as in the quick appraisal of the immediate circumstances of the external and internal world simultaneously. It is also essential in communication of emotion as in the arts and in rhetoric. Likewise it is paramount in psychopathology. Seeing the psychological importance of asymmetry, symmetry and symmetrization are Matte Blanco's first great steps.

Defence mechanisms and other psychic structures and states can also be described in terms of the different patterning of bi-logical structures. The Simassi and Alassi structures are the most notable of these. Matte Blanco saw that not only emotion but also other preconscious and conscious structures – including interpersonal ones such as empathy, intuition and projective identification – could contain certain symmetrized elements.

Through bi-logic the unconscious can be seen as being populated, not so much by specific subjects, objects and predicates as by propositional functions where subjects and objects are interchangeable. This being so, it appears that the unconscious deals largely in abstractions – attributes, conceptions, intuitions or notions. It becomes apparent that part-objects are abstractions.

It also becomes plain that there are many mental structures as well as objects, part-objects and object relations. There are, for instance, a vast array of generalized sentiments or intuitions, like charity, justice, dignity and faith, which are abstractions and bi-logical structures but not specific object relations.

The next leap of Matte Blanco's thought was the step from noting the frequent presence of part = whole identities in unconscious processes to the part = whole property of a mathematically infinite set. This brings out the conception of the unconscious mind operating with infinite sets. It illuminates the omnipresence of infinite experiences in human mental life, especially in emotions.

From here Matte Blanco proceeded to think about mental space. He noted that consciousness can only think in three spatial and one time dimension. The unconscious, on the other hand, appears to be able to contain many more dimensions than this, but it cannot consistently combine them together. Remarkable consequences of the process of dimensional transformation have been noted mathematically. When a form in several dimensions is represented in fewer dimensions there is a repetition of points, lines and spaces, and, conversely in some circumstances, with dimensional increase.

Such dimensional transformations can produce consequences that are equivalent to symmetrization. Whether it is best to view symmetrization as being the more fundamental, or whether this itself is best seen as resting upon dimensional transformation, remains to be seen. At all events Matte Blanco's analysis makes it plain that psychoanalysis has tended to consider mental space to be three dimensional, as if it is like physical or geographical space. He has shown how misleading and inadequate such a simplistic model is. One thing is certain: as he puts it, 'the mind is not a bag'. If his work on psychic space is properly heeded, psychoanalytic theory will never again be quite so naïve.

A steady grasp of bi-logical thinking appears to make therapeutic thinking more comprehensive. Its general underlying concepts, revealing similarities and the gross differences arising from splitting, may often make for quicker and deeper linking by the psychoanalytic therapist.

One particular therapeutic use arises out of a clear differentiation of the repressed and unrepressed unconscious. Unrepressed unconscious content, Matte Blanco asserts, is highly loaded with symmetrized thought structures, and consciousness cannot cope with so much symmetry. The bringing of symmetrized content into close proximity with conscious asymmetrical ideas is the task of what he calls therapeutic *unfolding*. It can best be carried out by sequential glimpses and is a process that is quite distinct from the *lifting of repression*. The unfolding is usually enjoyed by the patient as enriching and does not evoke the resistances typical of raising repression. Though Matte Blanco did not emphasize it, we have raised the question of how this unrepressed unconscious may be related to that which is preconscious.

Matte Blanco also observes that psychoanalytic interpretations are, like any explanation, a mapping of unconscious processes. As in any mapping, interpretations must have at least some one-to-one correspondence with their object, and in this case it is the unconscious. As the unconscious is replete with primary process, so also then should interpretation contain some quite direct reference to primary process. The conclusion to be drawn from this is unusual and will be unpopular at first sight. It is that interpretations will be most usable if done using explanatory ideas imbued with bi-logical structures, such as emotionally loaded language, metaphor, other figures of speech, jokes and poetry. Thus, in this light the therapeutic process can be seen as being essentially rhetorical at certain stages. Less controversially the verbal spelling out of symmetrizations by both analyst and patient very often appears to be beneficial, especially to patients in borderline states.

Towards the end of the book we noted that, more generally, authors from a range of other scholarly disciplines can often be seen to imply the importance of symmetry and symmetrization in knowledge and its distortions. This often occurs without the authors quite noticing the importance of these concepts. It is plain that it is only Matte Blanco who has centrally observed and argued for the importance of the interplay together of both symmetry and asymmetry in knowledge.

There is a strong suggestion from neuroscience of the need for a general recognition science which will rest upon the conception of symmetry. Although Matte Blanco was not himself centrally interested in memory or recognition, it appears that, among other things, bi-logic is eminently suited to act as a link between psychoanalysis and recognition sciences.

Matte Blanco saw things in terms of a fundamental form of mental interaction. This was concerned with the dialectic and even antinomy between pairs of intentions, and it deserves careful thought. However, the viewpoint of the latter part of this book turned in a somewhat different direction towards seeing mental events as occurring in complex systems. We noted that remarkably strange events can happen simply as a consequence of the complexity of a system. For instance, it is now known that in many circumstances there is a nigh infinite sensitivity to the initial conditions of such a system. The implication from this is that complex systems, which means all living things including human minds, inevitably have unpredictable or mathematically chaotic processes occurring within them.

It thus appears that the human psyche not only has to adapt to uncertainty, but also has unpredictable elements as essences in its functioning. Following from this, one feature of the experience of randomness seems to be a feeling of infinity; and it was Matte Blanco who first noted this imbuing any emotion.

We conclude that, from now on, psychoanalysis might well need to take both unpredictability and infinity into account it its theory and practice.

# References

Abelin, E. L. (1981) 'Triangulation, the role of the father', in R. Lax (ed.) *Rapprochement*, New York: Aranson.

Ahumada, J. (1994) 'What is a clinical fact? Clinical psychoanalysis as inductive method', *International Journal of Psycho-Analysis*.

Arden, M. (1984) 'Infinite sets and double-binds', *International Journal of Psycho-Analysis*, 65: 443–52.

Balint, M. (1959) *Thrills and Regressions*, London: Hogarth.

Bateson. G. (1973) *Steps to an Ecology of Mind*, London: Paladin Books.

Bettcher, T. (1991) 'Understanding the Matte Blanco–Skelton debate' (unpublished).

Bion, W. (1962) *Learning from Experience*, London: Heinemann.

—— (1963) *Elements of Psychoanalysis*, London: Heinemann.

Bion-Talamo, P. (1973) Tesi de Laurea: *Meta psicologia e Metamatematica in Aleune Recenti Teorie Psicoanalitiche*, doctoral thesis, Univérsità degli Studi, Firenze.

Bollas, C. (1989) *Forces of Destiny*, London: Free Association Books.

Bomford, R. (1989a) 'One, two, three' (unpublished).

—— (1989b) 'Foundations' (unpublished).

—— (1990a) 'Basic notions – metaphor' (unpublished).

—— (1990b) 'The Attributes of God and the characteristics of the unconscious', *International Review of Psycho-Analysis*, 17: 485–91.

—— (1992) 'Myth and meaning – metaphor' (unpublished).

Bowlby, J. (1969) *Attachment and Loss, Vol. 1: Attachment*, London: Hogarth.

Britton, R. (ed.) (1989) *The Oedipus Complex Today*, London: Karnac.

Casaula, E., Coloma, J., Colzani, F. and Jordan, J. F. (1994) 'The bi-logic of interpretation', Anglo-Latin-American Conference, Santiago, Chile.

Chomsky, N. (1965) *Aspects of the Theory of Syntax*, Cambridge, MA: Massachusetts Institute of Technology Press.

Courant, R. and Robbins, H. (1941) *What is Mathematics?*, London: Oxford University Press.

Duran, C. (1989) 'A bi-logical approach to the study of ideology' (unpublished).

Durst, M. (1988) *Dialettica e bi-logica*, Milano: Marzorati Editore.

Edelman, G. (1987) *Neural Darwinism*, New York: Basic Books.

—— (1992) *Bright Air, Brilliant Fire*, New York: Basic Books.

Elkan, J. (1989) 'The binding of Isaac', *European Judaism*, 22: 26–35.

—— (1992) 'Dialogue in Genesis: steps in psychic development' (unpublished).

Emde, R., Birigen, Z., Clyman, R. and Oppenheim, D. (1991) 'The moral self of infancy; affective core and procedural knowledge', *Developmental Review*, 11: 251–70.

Etchegoyen, R. H. and Ahumada, J. (1990) 'Bateson and Matte Blanco, bio-logic and bi-logic', *International Review of Psycho-Analysis*, 17: 493–502.

Evans, C. (1990) In Wooster, G., Hutchinson, D. and Evans, C., 'Two examples of supervised weekly psychotherapy illustrating bi-logic in relation to birth', *International Review of Psycho-Analysis*, 17: 445–54.

—— (1993) 'Bi-logic as paradox' (unpublished).

Fairbairn, R. D. (1952) *Psychoanalytic Studies of the Personality*, London: Routledge & Kegan Paul.

Fink, C. (1991) 'Bi-logic: the concept of intentionality in criminal cases' (unpublished).

—— (1993) 'A fairy-tale for grown-ups' (unpublished).

Fink, K.(1989) 'From symmetry to asymmetry', *International Journal of Psycho-Analysis*, 70: 481–8.

—— (1991) 'Parapraxis, counter-transference interpretations and bi-logic', *British Journal of Psychotherapy*, 7: 243–50.

—— (1992a) 'Poor rich man', (unpublished).

—— (1992b) 'Distorted listening and learning' (unpublished).

—— (1993) 'The bi-logical perception of time', *International Journal of Psycho-Analysis*, 74: 1–10.

Freud, A. (1937) *The Ego and the Mechanisms of Defence*, London: Hogarth.

Freud, S. (1900) *The Interpretation of Dreams*, SE 4 and 5, London: Hogarth.

—— (1905) *Three Essays on the Theory of Sexuality*, SE 7, London: Hogarth.

—— (1909) 'Notes upon a case of obsessional neurosis', SE 10, London: Hogarth.

—— (1911) 'Formulations on two principles of mental functioning', SE 12, London: Hogarth.

—— (1915) 'The Unconscious', SE 14, London: Hogarth.

—— (1925) 'Negation', SE 19, London: Hogarth.

—— (1938) 'Findings ideas problems', SE 23, London: Hogarth.

Gleick, J. (1987) *Chaos*, London: Heinemann.

Greenson, R. (1967) *The Technique and Practice of Psychoanalysis*, New York: International Universities Press.

Grotstein, J. (ed.) (1981) *Do I Dare Disturb the Universe?*, London: Karnac.

Hall, C. (1954) *A Primer of Freudian Psychology*, New York: Methuen.

Hartmann, E. (1984) *The Nightmare*, New York: Basic Books.

Hinshelwood, R. (1989) *A Dictionary of Kleinian Thought*, London: Free Association Books.

Hodges, W. (1977) *Logic*, Harmondsworth: Penguin.

Jiménez, J. P. (1990) 'Some technical consequences of Matte Blanco's theory of dreaming', *International Review of Psycho-Analysis*, 17: 455–570.

Jones, E. (1916) 'The theory of symbolism', in E. Jones, *Papers on Psychoanalysis*, London: Maresfield Reprints.

Jordan, J. F. (1990) 'Inner space and the interior of the maternal body', *International Review of Psycho-Analysis*, 17: 433–44.

Joseph, B. (1985) 'Transference: the total situation', in E. Spillius (ed.) *Melanie Klein Today*, London: Routledge.

Khan, M. (1974) *The Privacy of the Self*, London: Hogarth.

Klein, M. (1935) 'A contribution to the psychogenesis of manic-depressive states', in *The Writings of Melanie Klein*, vol. 1, London: Hogarth, pp. 262–89.

—— (1940) 'Mourning and its relation to manic-depressive states', in *The Writings of Melanie Klein*, vol. 1, London: Hogarth, pp. 344–69.

—— (1946) 'Notes on some schizoid mechanisms', in *The Writings of Melanie Klein*, vol. 3, London: Hogarth, pp. 1–24.

—— (1952) *Developments in Psychoanalysis*, London: Hogarth.

Kohut, H. (1971) *The Analysis of the Self*, London: Hogarth.

Laplanche, J. and Pontalis, J. B. (1973) *The Language of Psychoanalysis*, London: Hogarth.

Langer, S. K. (1942) *Philosophy in a New Key*, Cambridge, MA: Harvard University Press.

—— (1953) *An Introduction to Symbolic Logic*, New York: Dover Publications.

—— (1967) *Mind: An Essay in Human Feeling*, vol. I, Baltimore, Johns Hopkins University Press.

—— (1972) *Mind: An Essay in Human Feeling*, vol. II, Baltimore, Johns Hopkins University Press.

—— (1982) *Mind: An Essay in Human Feeling*, vol. III, Baltimore, Johns Hopkins University Press.

Langs, R. (1979) *The Therapeutic Environment*, New York: Aronson.

Leach, E. (1976) *Culture and Communication*, Cambridge: Cambridge University Press.

Lévi-Strauss, C. (1966) *The Savage Mind*, London: Weidenfeld & Nicolson.

Mahler, M., Pine, F. and Bergmann, A. (1975) *The Psychological Birth of the Human Infant*, London: Hutchinson.

Matte Blanco, I. (1940) 'Some reflections on psychodynamics', *International Journal of Psycho-Analysis*, 21: 253–79.

—— (1943) 'An approach to the problems of spatial extension in the mind', *International Journal of Psycho-Analysis*, 25: 180.

—— (1959a) 'Expressions in symbolic logic of the characteristics of the system unconscious or the logic of the system unconscious', *International Journal of Psycho-Analysis*, 40: 1–5.

—— (1959b) 'A study of schizophrenic thinking: its representation in terms of symbolic logic and its representation in multidimensional space', *International Congress of Psychiatry Report*, vol. 10: 254.

—— (1975) *The Unconscious as Infinite Sets*, London: Duckworth.

—— (1976) 'Basic logico-mathematical structures in schizophrenia', in D. Richter (ed.) *Schizophrenia Today*, Oxford: Pergamon.

—— (1981) 'Reflecting with Bion', in L. S. Grotstein (ed.) *Do I Dare Disturb the Universe?*, Beverley Hills: Caesura Press.

—— (1984) 'Reply to Ross Skelton's paper "Understanding Matte Blanco"', *International Journal of Psycho-Analysis*, 65, 4: 445–60.

—— (1988) *Thinking, Feeling, and Being*, London: Routledge.

—— (1989) 'Bi-logical psychoanalytical technique, a proposal' (unpublished).

Maw, J. (1990) 'Symmetry and asymmetry in language', *International Review of Psycho-Analysis*, 17: 481–5.

—— (1991) 'The medium is the message' (unpublished).

Meltzer, D. (1967) *The Psychoanalytic Process*, London: Heinemann.

Meltzoff, A.N. (1981) 'Imitation, intermodal co-ordination and representation in early infancy', in G. Butterworth (ed.) *Infancy and Epistemology*, London: Harvester.

Moran, M. (1991) 'Chaos theory and psychoanalysis', *International Review of Psycho-Analysis*, 18: 211–22.

Mordant, I. (1990) 'Using attribute-memories to resolve a contradiction in the work of Matte Blanco', *International Review of Psycho-Analysis*, 17: 475–80.

—— (1992) 'Who's afraid of Matte Blanco?', *British Journal of Psychotherapy*, 10: 5–14.

—— (1993) 'Psychodynamics and mathematical texts', *For the Learning of Mathematics*, 13: 20–3.

—— (1994) 'Freud and Langs: Zeno theorists of Abstraction' (unpublished).

Mordant, I. and Rayner, E. (1990) 'Abstraction, independence and the unconscious' (unpublished).

Murray, L. and Trevarthan, C. (1985) 'Emotional regulation of interactions between two months' olds and their mothers', in T. Field and N. Fox (eds) *Social Perceptions in Infants*, Norwood, N.J.: Ablex.

Palombo, S. (1978) *Dreaming and Memory*, New York: Basic Books.

Piaget, J. (1950) *The Psychology of Intelligence*, London: Routledge.

—— (1951) *Play, Dreams and Imitation in Childhood*, London: Routledge.

—— (1953) *The Origins of Intelligence in the Child*, London: Routledge.

—— (1956) *The Child's Concept of Space*, London: Routledge.

—— (1971) *Structuralism*, London: Routledge.

Plato (1946) *Complete Works*, Spanish Edition, Buenos Aires: Ediciones Anaconda.

Rayner, E. (1981) 'Infinite experiences, affects and the characteristics of the unconscious', *International Journal of Psycho-Analysis*, 62: 403–12.

—— (1986) *Human Development*, London: Routledge.

—— (1991) *The Independent Mind in British Pychoanalysis*, London: Free Association Books.

—— (1992) 'Matching, attunement and the psychoanalytic dialogue', *International Journal of Psycho-Analysis*, 73: 39–53.

Reyes, A. and Lucey, C. (1991) 'Family dimensions and the child who steals' (unpublished).

Russell, B. (1919) *Introduction to Mathematical Philosophy*, London: Allen & Unwin.

Russell, B. and Whitehead, A. N. (1910) *Principia Mathematica*, Cambridge: Cambridge University Press.

Rycroft, C. (1968) *Imagination and Reality*, New York: International Universities Press.

Sandler, J. (1993) 'On communication from patient to analyst', *International Journal of Psycho-Analysis*, 74: 1097–1108.

Schafer, R. (1976) *A New Language for Psychoanalysis*, New Haven, CT: Yale University Press.

Segal, H. (1957) 'Notes on symbol formation', *International Journal of Psycho-Analysis*, 38: 391–7.

Sharpe, E. F. (1937) *Dream Analysis*, London: Hogarth.

Skelton, R. (1984) 'Understanding Matte Blanco', *International Journal of Psycho-Analysis*, 65: 453–60.

—— (1989) 'Logic and infinity in primitive process', *Free Associations*, 14: 79–89.

—— (1990a) 'Generalizations from Freud to Matte Blanco', *International Review of Psycho-Analysis*, 17: 471–4.

—— (1990b) 'Rhetoric and free association', *The Journal of the Irish Forum for Psychoanalytic Psychotherapy*, 1: 171–5.

—— (1992) 'Six essays on logic, infinity and rhetoric in unconscious phantasy' (unpublished).

Spillius, E. (1988) *Melanie Klein Today. Volume 1, Mainly Theory*, London: Routledge.

Sporrong, T. (1992) 'Binary oppositions, binary distinctions and bi-logic' (unpublished).

—— (1993) 'The unconscious has no sex' (unpublished).

Stern, D. (1985) *The Interpersonal World of the Infant*, New York: Basic Books.

Stewart, H. (1992) *Psychic Experience and Problems of Technique*, London: Routledge.

Stewart, I. (1989) *Does God Play Dice?*, Harmondsworth: Penguin.

Strenger, C. (1989) 'The classic and romantic vision in psychoanalysis', *International Journal of Psycho-Analysis*, 70: 593–610.

Suzuki, D.T. (1949) *Essays in Zen Buddhism*, London: Rider.

Taylor, G. (1987) *Psychosomatic Medicine and Contemporary Psychoanalysis*, Madison, CT: International Universities Press.

Thomä, H. and Kächele, H. (1985) *Psychoanalytic Practice*, Berlin: Springer-Verlag.

Tyson, P. and Tyson, R. (1990) *Psychoanalytic Studies of Development*, New Haven, CT: Yale University Press.

Von Domarus, E. (1944) 'The specific laws of logic in schizophrenia', in J. Kasanin (ed.) *Language and Thought in Schizophrenia*, Berkeley: University of California Press.

Wilson, J. (1989) 'Matte Blanco's theory of bivalent logic and its relevance to group analysis' (unpublished).

—— (1993) 'Matte Blanco and group analysis' (unpublished).

Winnicott, D.W. (1950) 'Aggression in relation to emotional development', in *Collected Papers (1958)*, London: Tavistock.

—— (1951) 'Transitional objects and transitional phenomena', in *Collected Papers*, London: Tavistock.

—— (1956) 'Primary maternal preoccupation', in *Collected Papers (1958)*, London: Tavistock.

—— (1965) *The Maturational Processes and the Facilitating Environment*, London: Hogarth.

—— (1971) *Playing and Reality*, London: Tavistock.

Wohlmuth, P. C. and Goldberg, L. J. (1990) 'Justice and the crisis of human membership', *Proceedings of the International Society for Systems Sciences*.

Wolf, E. (1988) *Treating the Self*, New York: Guildford.

Wooster, G. (1992) 'Abraham and Isaac' (unpublished).

Wooster, G., Hutchinson, D. and Evans, C. (1990) 'Two examples of supervised weekly psychotherapy illustrating bi-logic in relation to birth', *International Review of Psycho-Analysis*, 17: 433–44.

Wright, K. (1991) *Vision and Separation Between Mother and Baby*, London: Free Association Books.

# Name index

# Subject index

abstract: concepts 27, 47–9; notions 12, 33, 47; operations 140–1

abstractions: and conscious 143, 159; sensory 47–8; and unconscious 22, 47–9, 110–11

abuse: child 54

affects: as biological structures 60; communicating 17; and infinity 58–60; as psycho-physical structures 65–8; *see also* emotions

aggression 101–2

alpha-function 148–9

alternating asymmetrical–symmetrical structures (alassi) 106

ambiguity 24

anality 103–4

analogic communication 48, 144

analytic disciplines 12

anthropology 142–3

anti-knowing 149

anti-logicality 54

antinomy of being and world 64, 77–9

appraisal: and emotion 17–18, 50–1, 73

argument 13, 72; therapeutic 127–31

asymmetry: and consciousness 24–5, 27, 70, 74–5; and extremes 62–4; and splitting 63–4, 70, 77, 99–100, 105–6; and symmetry 23–6, 28–31, 164; *see also* bi-logic; symmetrization

atomism 139

attention 67

attractors: fixed point 154; limit-cycle 155; strange 155, 158

basic assumption 148

basic matrix: of projection and introjection 109, 112, 113–14, 125–7

Bateson, G.: compared to Matte Blanco 143–5

beauty 16, 65

bi-logic 1–2, 164–7; and chaos theory 154–62; and characteristics of unconscious 40–54; and complex systems 152–4; and dimensionality 74–94; and infinity 55–73; and psychoanalytic concepts 95–118; and symmetry 23–39; and therapeutic process 119–36; use in different disciplines 137–51

bi-logical modes 34, 35–6

bi-logical structures 1–2, 34–5, 36, 38, 74–7, 164–5

bi-modality 35–6, 78, 164

binary distinctions 99–100, 142–3; logic 13–14

Bion, W.: compared to Matte Blanco 148–51

bivalent logic 13, 25

categories: logic of 142; wide 147–8

category errors 143

chaos theory 154–62, 167

child abuse 54

child development *see* development

classes, whole and part: symmetrization of 33–4, 75–7

classical philosophy 71–2, 138

classification 19–20, 33–5, 47; hierarchical levels of 36–8

clinical narratives 6, 163

collections 20, 33